THE ARAB LEFT

TAREQ Y. ISMAEL

THE ARAB LEFT

SYRACUSE UNIVERSITY PRESS
1976

◄(( ))►

Copyright © 1976 by Syracuse University Press
Syracuse, New York 13210

All Rights Reserved

First Edition

Library of Congress Cataloging in Publication Data

Ismael, Tareq Y
    The Arab left.

    (Contemporary issues in the Middle East series; 4)
    Includes bibliographical references and index.
    1. Socialism in Arab countries—History. 2. Arab countries—Politics and government. 3. Political parties—Arab countries. 4. Nationalism—Arab countries.
I. Title. II. Series.
HX434.A6I77   320.9'17'4927   76-48136
ISBN 0-8156-0124-7
ISBN 0-8156-0125-5 pbk.

Manufactured in the United States of America

To Abu Tareq,
my father and mentor;
to the Hajjiah,
my mother and conscience;
and to Jackie,
my wife.

Tareq Y. Ismael is Professor of Political Science at the University of Calgary, Calgary, Alberta, Canada. He is the author or editor of many books on the Middle East, including *Canada and the Third World* (1976), *The Middle East in World Politics* (1974), *Canada and the Middle East* (1973), *The UAR in Africa* (1971), and *Governments and Politics of the Contemporary Middle East* (1970).

CONTENTS

29658

PREFACE

ARAB NATIONALISM has been termed the principal force shaping the lives of the Arab people in the twentieth century. But Arab nationalism is not a stable, constant influence upon the Arab environment. Rather, it is a multi-dimensional dynamic process that interacts with the Arab environment—local, regional, and international. In the interaction, Arab nationalism has itself been transformed from the relatively conservative, tradition-based impulse to sovereignty and unity of the early twentieth-century Arab nationalists to the complex leftist ideologies of contemporary Arab nationalists. How is one to account for this markedly leftist orientation of contemporary Arab nationalists? In particular, what is the origin of the radical trend in Arab politics, known as the New Left? These are the key questions that this book addresses.

Part of the answer, at least, is found in the impact of the Arab environment on Arab nationalism. Three issues in particular have catalyzed the nationalist orientation to the left: the problem of Arab unity, the Palestinian question, and the issue of social transformation. How these issues have affected Arab nationalism, and how the ideologies discussed here have responded to these issues are examined in this book.

The trends depicted in this study have not been uniform throughout the Arab political spectrum. Not all nationalist organizations are leftist, and vice versa. This book deals only with the nationalist left—its origin, development, and trajectory. The nationalist left is defined as those political organizations and/or movements in the Arab world that are Arab national in orientation, that adopt socialism (in any of its forms or schools) as their creed, that seek a radical change in the existing socio-political and economic structures and processes in Arab society in an engineered or planned manner, and that advocate neutrality in foreign policy. Thus, for example, the communist parties have been excluded because they are supra-national in orientation and not neutral in their foreign policies. Also, the Palestine Liberation Organization (PLO) has been excluded because it does not represent an integrated leftist ideology; rather, it functions as an umbrella organization for several distinct ideologically based movements. Al-Fateh, a major component of the PLO, has similarly been excluded because it has not developed an integrated socialist world view. Although it has borrowed liberally from socialist thought and polemics, al-Fateh remains basically conservative and pragmatic in its definitions of problems and in its formulation of programs. This basic conservativism is most clearly reflected in the kind of government and economy al-Fateh advocates for a liberated Palestine.

Chapter 1 serves as an introduction by examining that transformation of Arab nationalism brought about by the interjection of socialist thought into nationalist ideology following World War II. Chapters 2, 3, 4, and 5 examine the four principal leftist nationalist forces that emerged in the post–World War II era: the Ba'ath, the Progressive Socialists of Lebanon, the Arab Nationalist Movement, and Nasserism (written by Jacqueline Ismael). The Progressive Socialists of Lebanon was chosen because it is similar to a number of parties that have appeared and disappeared in the Arab World, such as al-Hizb al-Watani al-Dimuqrati (the National Democratic Party) in Iraq and the Wafd Party in Egypt. Chapters 6 and 7 examine the second major transformation of Arab nationalism—the interjection of Marxist-Leninist thought into Arab nationalist ideology—that occurred in the aftermath of the June 1967 Arab-Israeli war to give rise to the latest phenomenon in Arab politics—the New Left.

The Appendixes are translations of documents not readily available in English.

As this book is going to press, the sanguine civil war in Lebanon has again focused world attention on the Middle East. North American news media have portrayed the conflict as a purely sectarian civil war between Christians and Muslims. The problem of explaining the political issues in the strife has been easily resolved by dubbing the Muslims as leftists and the Christians as rightists. The prominent Palestinian role in the conflict has similarly been explained by placing them on the left side of the dichotomy. The entire formula reduces to a simple equation: Christians, rightists; Muslims, leftists; good guys, bad guys. The labels are half-truths that reveal the obvious and conceal the significant. This is demonstrated by the characterization of Kemal Jumblat as the sole leader of the Muslim-leftists—only half true and at any rate an incongruous conjugate that would be humorous in a less tragic situation.

While an examination of the Lebanese civil war is not within the framework of this book, the strife in Lebanon does emphasize the radicalization and polarization of ideologies in the Arab world. The Lebanese situation cannot be understood outside the larger context of the transformation of Arab nationalism. Lebanon, indeed, is a tragic manifestation of the transformation that is polarizing the ranks of Arab nationalism.

This book adheres to the Library of Congress system of transliteration. While the titles of books have been given in full transliteration and translation for reference purposes, only the translation has been given for the titles of journal articles in order to reduce the cumbersomeness of footnotes. After the initial transliteration of books, subsequent references present only the English translation.

I wish to express my appreciation to the Canada Council and The University of Calgary Grants Committee for providing funds to facilitate this research. Also, I am grateful to The University of Calgary for granting me a sabbatical leave for the purpose of carrying out the research.

Calgary, Alberta, Canada   TAREQ Y. ISMAEL
July 1976

THE ARAB LEFT

THE TRANSFORMATION OF
ARAB NATIONALISM

GEORGE ANTONIUS brought the phrase "Arab Awakening" to the attention of the world, but the awakening which occurred prior to 1939 was
relatively unstable and incomplete. The form of Arab nationalism
which arose in the early 1900s and swept the area before World War
II led to the attainment of formal superficial political independence by
the Arab states of the East (with the exception of the Arabian littoral
states). But this formal liberation proved unsatisfactory in achieving
the objectives of Arab nationalism—namely, emancipation from foreign
domination, socio-economic development, and political unification[1]—
and new leaders moved to the fore with popular bases and ideological
views formerly of little consequence. New policies were evolved, both
domestic and foreign institutions were challenged, and a disregard
was shown for the niceties of law and custom. This marked the transformation of Arab nationalism to a new, more radical, orientation.

Such changes in acceptable or popular ideologies are of consider-
able significance but difficult to trace. To study the process, we must
have some framework in which to place it for analysis. A starting place
is the list Mary Matossian has constructed of critical decisions which
underlie ideologies in developing nations. Implicitly or explicitly, each
ideology must provide answers to these questions: "(1) What is to be
borrowed from the West? (2) What is to be retained from the nation's
past? (3) What characteristics, habits, and products of the masses are

---

1. Fayez A. Sayegh, *Arab Unity: Hope and Reality* (New York: Devin-Adair,
1958), p. 5.

to be encouraged?"[2] The various nationalist and other ideologies current in the Middle East since 1900 have given radically different answers to these questions.

EARLY VARIANTS OF ARAB NATIONALISM

We will deal only briefly with the earliest variants of Arab nationalism,
which became dominant in the 1920s. There were two types of nationalism current in that era: dynastic and liberal. Dynastic nationalism, as in the Hejaz and Saudi Arabia, was hardly nationalism as the
word is generally understood today, but was based upon primordial
sentiments of personal loyalty and presumed kinship. There was an in-
group feeling and a desire for autonomy, but the primary character
was traditional rather than innovative, indigenous rather than populist.
Little was to be borrowed from the West, much was to be retained
from the past, and little attention was paid to the characteristics of the
masses beyond their piety, loyalty, and military prowess.

Liberal nationalism, which was most fully developed in Egypt, was
quite frankly imitative of the West in its ideas, institutions, technology,
and aims. Imitating Westernized elite groups, separated from the
masses, and disenchanted with the national past, the liberal intellectuals sought to duplicate a West European state. However, though this
was largely true on the explicit level, two qualifications which proved
to be of some importance must be mentioned. The first is that certain
Islamic leaders, in the tradition of Rashid Rida, while not attacking
nationalism, turned to a re-examination of Islam.[3] Also, and perhaps
more important, because they were unconcerned with the masses, the
elite did little about changing the existing conditions and, hence, provided no mass basis for their institutions and no major changes in the
economic system. At the same time, the economic change initiated by
the colonial connection continued. Thus, the attempt to imitate the
West proceeded without (as is often emphasized) a proper understanding of the conditions in Western history which led to liberal nationalism and (what is more often neglected), without a deep understanding of the realities of indigenous society.

2. Mary Matossian, "Ideologies of Delayed Industrialization: Some Tensions
and Ambiguities," in *Political Modernization: A Reader in Comparative Political
Change* edited by Claude E. Welch, Jr. (Belmont, Ca.: Wadsworth, 1967), p. 334.

3. Wilfred Cantwell Smith, *Islam in the Modern World* (Princeton, N.J.: Princeton University Press, 1956).

Constantine Zurayk of Syria and Abdul Rahman al-Bazzaz of Iraq were foremost exponents of what we have termed liberal Arab nationalism, and we shall consider their works as examples of the mainstream of liberal nationalist thought. These intellectuals, educated in the United States and Britain in the late twenties and thirties, respectively, were deeply influenced by classical Western liberal thought in the course of their studies; their political writings are characterized by their attempts to reconcile the past and present social, political, and economic conditions of Arab society with the political norms of the West and the West's evident material and technical development. Broadly speaking, we can identify four sets of common concerns that set the liberal nationalists apart from both the earlier pan-Islamist or regional nationalists in the area and from the later radical Marxist nationalist interpretations: (1) the relationship between Islam and the Arab nation; (2) the relationship of the individual to the state in Arab society; (3) the modernization of the Arab world; and (4) the Palestine defeat and the nature of the Zionist threat.

Constantine Zurayk

Constantine Zurayk may be considered the intellectual father of the liberal nationalist tradition.[4] Inspired by his studies in history at Chicago and Princeton in the late twenties, Zurayk soon distinguished himself in the literary circles of Beirut and Damascus as a promising intellectual. In his first volume of essays on national consciousness (al-Wa'y al-qawmi), which appeared in late 1939, Zurayk discussed the general concept of nationalism, the historical basis of the Arab nation, the function of religion in the state, and a political program for the practical realization of the aims of Arab nationalism (as he conceived it).

In dealing with the fundamental issue of the relationship between Islam and Arab nationalism, Zurayk argued that a basic problem of Arab society as it emerged from the Ottoman era was the lack of a

4. Other works not specifically cited in the following discussion include *Fi ma' rakat al-hadarah* [On the Battle of Civilization] (Beirut: Dar al-'Ilm lil-Malayin, 1964); *Hadha al-'asr al-mutafajjir* [This Explosive Age] (Beirut: Dar al-'Ilm lil-Malayin, 1963); *Nahnu wa-al-ta'rikh* [We and History] (Beirut: Dar al-'Ilm lil-Malayin, 1963); *Ayyu Ghad?* [What a Tomorrow?] (Beirut: Dar al-'Ilm lil-Malayin, 1956).

collective conscience—a sense of solidarity governed by a larger moral order. Lacking a collective conscience, Zurayk argued, the Arabs are unable to subordinate their individual desires and passions to an organization rooted in abstract social goals; therefore, they cannot act successfully as a group. The Arabs need a sense of collective responsibility, a feeling of belonging to a nation, but one of a special sort: a nation which draws its inspiration from a religion. For the Arabs this religion can only be Islam.

This assertion of Islam as the moral core of the Arab nation may seem surprising, for Constantine Zurayk was a Christian. However, he draws a sharp distinction between the "religious spirit" and "sectarian fanaticism." The assumptions underlying this distinction appear to be twofold: first, all religions contain the same core of moral truth, accessible alike to all men; second, the principles of personal morality based upon individual constraint are necessary to build a stable and prosperous society. In this sense, then, "sectarian fanaticism" consists of the dogmatic assumption by adherents of a particular religion that their particular religion has a special claim to moral validity, while "religious spirit" means participation of the individual in the moral truth inherent in all great religions.

The symbols in which these principles are expressed differ from one religion to another, but the difference is of a normative rather than theoretical importance. There is an essential connection between the Arabs and Islam. Muhammad was the creator of Arab culture; the unifier of the Arabs; the man of principle and conviction from whose inspiration the Arabs can draw the strength of conviction and firmness of belief. But there is no suggestion that they should look upon him as anything more than a symbol of cultural unity or that they should be guided by Islamic law or the institutions of the Caliphate. In later writings, Zurayk emphasized that Islam is the Arab past, not the future. The state must preserve the mental and spiritual values of Arab civilization, for progress depends not only on the acquisition and efficient use of material technology, but also on the steadfastness of moral character, depth of belief, patience in adversity, and earnest pursuit of the greater social goals. However, the state must be absolutely separated from religious institutions, for nationalism is inconsistent with literal theocracy. This clear-cut dissociation of religion from social institutions but not from culture was Zurayk's unique contribution to Arab liberal thought of the period.

For Zurayk, the fundamental unit of Arab society is the individual, and the fundamental goal of society is the maximization of individual potential. Social reform, then, Zurayk suggested, should be based on the encouragement of individual initiative, the propagation of knowledge and culture, and the expansion of political, social, and intellectual liberties. In the vanguard of progress, Zurayk envisioned a dedicated intellectual elite working to create an enlightened national opinion and to initiate peaceful social reform. From this elite would emerge true leadership for the task of modern nation-building. It is incumbent upon this elite to organize and unify itself into well-knit political parties and social organizations in order to elaborate the practical meanings of nation, nationalism, state, independence, liberty, and unity. In the economic sphere, this elite must face the problems of industrialization and land reform for the development of a viable economy. In the educational and cultural spheres, this elite must face the problems of the family, the school, the village, and the workshop for the development of a viable social milieu. The rule, indeed duty, of the intellectual elite, then, was to provide leadership for the modernization of Arab society within the Arab cultural context.

For the modernization of the Arab world, Zurayk advocated the adoption of institutions characteristic of the West. In particular, efforts must be directed toward the realization of the greatest possible degree of scientific organization, supported by educational emphasis upon the positive and empirical sciences. To turn Arab life away from the modes of ancient and medieval times to the modes of modern times, Zurayk demanded the adoption of Western technology on the widest possible scale. He considered technology as one of the foremost factors in the development of the West and considered that its introduction into the Arab milieu would lead to the ultimate destruction of the barriers to nationalism, particularly tribalism and feudalism.

The need for fundamental modernization of Arab modes of thought, action, and life was made urgent for Zurayk by the threat of Zionist expansion. Nothing, he asserted, was more dangerous to the Arabs than this threat. The basic danger did not lie in the innate superiority of one people over another. The Zionists, he maintained, live in the present and for the future, while "the Arabs continue to dream the dreams of the past and to stupefy themselves with their fading glory."[5] Zurayk therefore urged the Arabs to meet the Zionist challenge

5. Constantine Zurayk, *The Meaning of Disaster*, translated by R. Bayly Winder (Beirut: Khayyat's College Book Cooperative, 1956), p. 34.

by adopting the technology and rational organization of the West. He saw in the threat of Zionist aggression "one of the most potent forms of . . . imperialism and one that is replete with the most serious dangers to the very existence" of the Arabs.[6] This threat emerged from Israel's superior technological resources and rational social organization. It could be overcome through the acquisition of similar technology and the adoption of rational social organization.

With the wholesale adoption of Western techniques and institutions, would the essential identity of the Arabs not be lost by assimilation in Western civilization? Zurayk answered "no," believing that the moral and spiritual—derived from distinctive historical, linguistic, and cultural factors—could be separated from the political and economic— derived from technical and organizational factors. Rather optimistically, Zurayk believed that the Western model of economic and political development could be assimilated into the Arab cultural milieu without fundamental transformations of either; in this adoption of Western techniques and institutions lay the solutions to the problems of Arab society in general.

Abdul Rahman al-Bazzaz

Abdul Rahman al-Bazzaz, educated in law at the University of London in the late thirties, returned to his home in Baghdad in 1939 imbued with the humanistic conception of classical Western liberalism.[7] In distinguished careers first as a teacher and scholar and later as a diplomat and statesman, al-Bazzaz remained faithful to his fundamental conception of Arab nationalism in terms of a humanistic perspective of individual emancipation within the framework of evolutionary social progress. Summarizing this view in 1964, al-Bazzaz wrote:

> We sincerely believe that our enlightened, civilized nationalism is our ideal way to humanism in every reasonable and acceptable sense of this word. Our concern is for many millions of people in two continents

6. Costi K. Zurayk, "The Essence of Arab Civilization," *The Middle East Journal* 3 (April 1949): 137–38.

7. Another work not specifically referenced in the following discussion is *al-Dawlah al-Ittihadiyah wa dawlah al-Wihdawiyah* [The Unitary State and the Federal State] (Baghdad, 1968).

(Africa and Asia) and our endeavor to participate in the internal and external liberation of these peoples and in the raising of their material, moral and spiritual level through the setting up of a common structure in which the welfare of every individual will be assured—all this is without doubt the most practical way in which we can serve humanity. . . . It is clear that there is nothing in our liberated and free Arab nationalism opposed to the highest human sentiments. The call of Arab nationalism is a call for humanity in the truest sense of the word.[8]

Much of al-Bazzaz's early writing is concerned with defining the relation between Islam and Arab nationalism. In *Min Roh al-Islam* [From the Spirit of Islam] published in Baghdad in 1959, he advanced the thesis that there is no real opposition between Islam and Arab nationalism: the Arab nation is the core of the Islamic community; most Muslims are also Arab; the Koran is in Arabic and embodies the traditional morality of the Arabs; the Prophet was an Arab; Islam is the medium through which the Arabs made their contribution to history.[9] As al-Bazzaz wrote in *From the Spirit of Islam:* "There is no opposition either basic or apparent between Arab nationalism and Islam. The nearest description of relationship between them is that it is the relation of general to particular. And if we wish to describe this relationship geometrically, we would represent Islam and Arabism as two intersecting circles which had the large and more important part in common, while that which remained outside the common part would not conflict in any basic manner with the other part" (p. 184).

This conception of the essential unity of Arab nationalism and Islam runs through al-Bazzaz's early formulation of the four bases of Arab nationalism: language, history, literature, and customs and character. Arab nationalism for al-Bazzaz, like Zurayk and other liberals, is inextricably fused with Islam. However, unlike Zurayk, who viewed Islam as a cultural rather than religious phenomenon, al-Bazzaz did not make this analytic distinction, perhaps because he was a Muslim. In *This Is Our Nationalism* he reduced his four bases of Arab nationalism to one common denominator—language—and attempted to deemphasize the role of religion in the definition of Arab identity. He identified the essential criterion of Arab nationality as the ability to participate in Arabic culture, an ability for which language is an indispensable element. Nevertheless, he considered that non-Muslim Arabs

8. *Hathihi Qawmiyatuna* [This Is Our Nationalism] (Cairo, 1964), p. 70.

9. Albert Hourani, *Arabic Thought in the Liberal Age, 1798–1939* (London: Oxford University Press, 1962), p. 309.

should be intellectually familiar with the traditions of Islam to demonstrate and participate in nationalism. For al-Bazzaz, the role of non-Muslims in what he considered an essentially Muslim context remained problematic. He was unable fundamentally to dissociate the religious from the cultural, a distinction that was perhaps inherently easier for a Christian nationalist like Zurayk to make.

Like Zurayk and other liberal nationalists, al-Bazzaz's primary concern was with individual freedom and dignity. Emancipation from ignorance, poverty, and social discrimination were the goals of an Arab nationalism that identified the barriers to social progress as tribalism, feudalism, and lack of education—barriers to individual initiative. The role of the state, then, is to secure individual freedom while protecting social justice as he wrote in *This Is Our Nationalism*—"a happy mean between the absolute individualism that gave rise to capitalism and Marxist-inspired communism. . . . Our Arab nationalism strives for social justice in every sense of the term, while at the same time it seeks to reinforce the bases of social solidarity between the individuals of the entire community in order to prevent exploitation and class domination" (p. 66).

A principal goal of the state is the maximization of individual initiative which would lead to the raising of the standard of living of the Arab nation as a whole. State intervention would be required to prevent the accumulation of land or capital in a few hands and to insure equal opportunity for all individuals. Al-Bazzaz, however, saw private property as the basis of individual initiative. He considered that its elimination, as in the communist system, "completely destroys individual initiative" and ultimately leads to "the extinction of all public liberties."[10]

Whereas Zurayk considered the essential link between the individual and the state to be an intellectual elite a particularly bourgeois Western concept), al-Bazzaz considered the state to be the mediator of private interests. His modified capitalist conceptions reflect the influence of Islamic political concepts regarding the normative role of the body politic in integrating individual interests within the broader community context. In particular, al-Bazzaz disparaged the concept of an elite, ruling on the pretense that it is alone capable of knowing what is good for the nation. Rather, in the Muslim tradition, al-Bazzaz emphasized community consensus and social solidarity as the basis of social control and political organization. He considered democracy—

10. *Min Wahy al-Urubah* [From the Inspiration of Arabism], 2nd ed. (Cairo, 1963), p. 157.

in terms of a consultative system of government rather than a particular set of institutions—to embody the political goal of Arab nationalism, and he felt the appropriate constitutional structure would somehow naturally evolve out of the historical experience of the Arabs.

Al-Bazzaz strongly advocated the technical and institutional modernization of the Arab world along the lines of the Western model, but was far more concerned than Zurayk about the cultural consequences. In particular, al-Bazzaz believed that the preservation of Arab cultural identity should be facilitated by a state-supervised educational system that strongly emphasizes Arab historic, literary, and scientific achievements. Al-Bazzaz felt, for example, that it was not enough for a teacher of chemistry to teach his pupils the principles of chemistry. The teacher must, in addition to that, tell them about the contribution of the Arabs to this science. In contrast to Zurayk, al-Bazzaz considered the development of Western techniques and institutional forms an inevitable evolutionary trend, and he emphasized the preservation of Arab identity as an essential problem of Arab nationalism.

Like Zurayk, al-Bazzaz viewed the loss of Palestine and the threat of Zionist aggression as the most fundamental threat to Arab existence. For al-Bazzaz, however, the essential struggle was not technological, but cultural—the clash of Western civilization with Arab culture. His primary concern was not with technological development or modern macro-political organization; rather, it was with the cultural unification of the Arab world—a unity that supersedes regional political and economic differences and provides the context for the evolution of real political unity. Al-Bazzaz's nationalism, as he wrote in *This Is Our Nationalism,* was cultural rather than political in its import: "Nationalism is the effective belonging, by feeling and belief, to a group whose individuals think alike, are mutually responsive in feelings, and aim at certain common goals which they seek to attain in their own political ways. . . . Nationalism expresses the belonging to a people in a way that does not depend on the soil inhabited by that people" (p. 138).

Within this context, the threat of Israel was an aggressive expression of the manifest Western confrontation with the Arab nation. The danger of Zionist expansionism lay not only in the physical threat but also in cultural fragmentation of the Arab identity, as al-Bazzaz stressed in *From the Inspiration of Arabism:* "It [Israel] is a centre from which dangerous principles are disseminated that conflict with the basic formative elements of the Arab nation" (p. 156).

Thus, al-Bazzaz's cardinal concern was with the consolidation of Arab identity as the essential humanistic complement of economic and social modernization. While he viewed modernization a universal process of social evolution, he feared the assimilative impact of Westernization. Al-Bazzaz considered the fundamental role of Arab nationalism to be the maintenance of cultural unity against the fragmenting influence of different regional rates and trends of modernization.

Constantine Zurayk and Abdul Rahman al-Bazzaz reflect the essentially evolutionary perspective adopted from conservative Western social philosophies. Fostered by Zurayk's seminal work on Arab nationalism, social evolutionism was the fundamental model of change adopted by the liberal Arab nationalists. They saw Arab society as a social entity evolving from the dynamics of Arab nationalism. While Zurayk emphasized technology as the principal independent variable affecting Arab nationalism, and ultimatively the evolutionary nature of Arab society, al-Bazzaz emphasized culture. All the liberal Arab nationalists, however, were keenly concerned with the relation between Islam and Arab nationalism—a fundamental issue of the post-Ottoman era when the Arab world emerged from the religious fragmentation of the Ottoman millet system of social organization and faced the major issue of reintegration. The problem posed by the close association between the religion of Islam and the heritage of the Arabs was that Islam was neither an exclusive nor a universal attribute of Arab identity. Liberal nationalist thought essentially laid the boundary definition problem to rest by giving a linguistic definition to Arab identity (al-Bazzaz)[11] and a cultural interpretation to the role and place of Islam in Arab society (Zurayk). This is the great and fundamental contribution of liberal nationalist thought to modern Arab nationalism.

Reflecting the influence of conservative Western social philosophy was the liberal Arab nationalist conception of the state as the servant of individual development. The liberal Arab nationalists in general strongly abhorred Marxist interpretations of the dynamics of social life and emphasized instead the maximization of individual freedom as the motive force of political organization. Stemming from this was a

---

11. Sati al-Husri, considered by many the father of Arab nationalism, was actually one of the earliest and for a half-century the consistent proponent of an Arab nationalism based on linguistic and cultural factors. For a thorough study of his work, see William L. Cleveland, *The Making of an Arab Nationalist: Ottomanism and Arabism in the Life and Thought of Sati al-Husri* (Princeton: Princeton University Press, 1971). Also see, Muhammad abd al-Rahman Burj, *Sati' al-Husri* (Cairo: Dar al-Katib al-'Arabi, 1969); L. M. Kenny, "Sati' al-Husri's Views on Arab Nationalism," *The Middle East Journal* 18 (3) (1963): 231–56; Ilyas Murqus, *Naqd al-fikr al-qawmi: Sati' al-Husri* [Criticism of the Nationalist Idea: Sati' al-Husri] (Beirut: Dar al-Tali'ah, 1966).

faith in Western democratic principles in general and Western democratic institutions in particular. The liberal nationalists also had a strong faith that the glories of Arab heritage could be revitalized through the adoption of the West's material technology. This optimistic faith that evolutionary continuity and revolutionary change could be somehow harnessed together within the Arab social milieu was put to the crucial test in the period immediately following World War II.

The Liberal nationalist movement hardly managed to survive World War II, but it paved the way for the emergence of counter social forces.[12] In fact, from its very inception, the tide of liberal nationalism was bound to fall. For neither the social forces that fostered liberal nationalism (the landed aristocracy and the prosperous commercial and industrial bourgeoisie) nor imported Western institutions were compatible with the social milieu and the new rising social forces. In consequence, liberal nationalist regimes collapsed in Syria, Egypt, and Jordan in 1949, 1952, and 1957 respectively.[13] Saudia Arabia, Yemen, Tunisia, Libya, Algeria, and Iraq either never had the chance to experience liberalism at all or, despite all appearances, never indeed practiced it. The Sudan and Morocco vacillated between liberalism and oligarchy until both succumbed to authoritarian regimes, military and civilian, respectively. These developments, whether toward a military hegemony or toward a civilian oligarchy, constituted two different responses to the same challenge: namely, the rise of the new, more radical, social forces of the middle class.[14] While the civilian

12. Among other works on the subject those of Leonard Binder, *The Ideological Revolution in the Middle East* (New York: Wiley, 1964); Hisham B. Sharabi, *Nationalism and Revolution in the Arab World* (Princeton, N.J.: Van Nostrand, 1966); and George Lenczowski, ed., *The Political Awakening in the Middle East* (Englewood Cliffs, N.J.: Prentice-Hall, 1970), provide material and analysis concerning the differences in the two eras.

13. P. J. Vatikiotis, *The Egyptian Army in Politics, Pattern for New Nations?* (Bloomington: Indiana University Press, 1961), pp. 21–43; also ————, *Politics and the Military in Jordan* (London: Frank Cass, 1967), pp. 145–54; also E. Hrair Dekmejian, *Egypt Under Nasser: A Study in Political Dynamics* (Albany: State University of New York Press, 1971), pp. 17–21.

14. For details see, Manfred Halpern, *The Politics of Social Change in the Middle East and North Africa* (Princeton, N.J.: Princeton University Press, 1963), pp. 51–78; also in ————, "Middle Eastern Armies and the New Middle Class," in *The Role of the Military in Underdeveloped Countries*, edited by John J. Johnson, (Princeton, N.J.: Princeton University Press, 1962), pp. 277–315; also in Tareq Y. Ismael, *Government and Politics of the Contemporary Middle East* (Homewood, Ill.: Dorsey, 1970), pp. 116–19.

oligarchies represented a self-defense measure on the part of the old traditional establishments against the new rising social forces, the military regimes, on the whole, were a manifestation of the ascendance to power of some sectors of the middle class with their *radical* nationalism (in contrast to the outdated liberal nationalism).

In a critical reappraisal of the liberal nationalist movement in 1967, Constantine Zurayk identified two main reasons for its failure:

> First, from its infamy it was challenged by another doctrine [socialism] which had more vitality. . . . A main reason for the weakness of [our] nationalist call at its initiation was its primary concern with the achievement of independence and unity without a reform program aimed at unlocking the internal shackles, combating social and economic tyranny, and working to give all citizens equal opportunities. This factor [lack of a reform program] worked to the advantage of socialist thought. In addition to this internal factor, an external factor played its role in that direction, too. That is, the continuation of the West's support of Israel and denial of Arab rights; also, the emergence of the socialist bloc in the Arab sphere—supplying the Arab world with arms and ammunition, international political support, and economic and technical aid.[15]

THE BIRTH OF RADICAL ARAB NATIONALISM

The birth of radical Arab nationalism can be traced to the Palestine War in 1948 and the consequent emergence of Israel. So traumatic to the Arab masses was the loss of Palestine and the alien cleavage of the Arab homeland that it fostered a transformation of Arab nationalism. This transformation shifted the emphasis of Arab nationalism from the glories of the past to the failures—particularly the failure in Palestine—of the present.

Palestine symbolized the failure of Arab nationalism to meet the supreme challenge: the challenge of national survival. Liberal Arab nationalism had fed on the euphoria of Arab heritage; such euphoria appeared bankrupt indeed in the reality of Arab ineptitude in Palestine. Thus a profound reappraisal of Arab society has ensued. Every

---

15. Constantine Zurayk, *Ma'na al-Nakbah mujaddad-an* [The Meaning of Disaster Reconsidered] (Beirut: Dar al-'Ilm lil-Malayin, August 1967), p. 29.

aspect of Arab society has come under fire—social, political, economic, religious. Under the threat of extinction as symbolized by Palestine, Arab nationalism has reasserted itself, not in the glorification of the past but in the reform of the present.

Manif al-Razzaz, an eminent Arab spokesman and ideological leader of the Ba'ath Socialist Party, described this in the following manner:

> A crisis—a total catastrophe—to completely overwhelm us and threaten our very existence was necessary, in order to open our eyes to the reality of our existence. A catastrophe was needed to teach us the true difference between façade and reality and to make us aware that the rottenness and corruption of the past were still with us. Instead of altering our society at its very base, we had tried to cover up the un-healthy core by a thin, attractive but brittle veneer, which, although pleasing to the uncritical eye, did not alter reality. A disaster was necessary to strip off this deceptive veneer and to lay bare our desper-ate need for facts, not illusions, for changes in the very fundamentals of our society, for a revolution in means and techniques—in short, for a total rejection of all those elements which had led to weakness and dissension in the past in order to bring about a true revival.[16]

The struggle for political independence, a struggle spearheaded by the liberal nationalists, had neither unified the Arabs nor made them masters in their own houses. Control of Arab destiny had merely shifted from Istanbul to Western capitals. It appeared then that the liberal Arab nationalists had betrayed the essence of Arab national-ism—the struggle for freedom and unity—for a superficial political in-dependence that protected their power and privilege behind façades of Western democratic institutions. Within a decade of the Palestine defeat, these façades were dismantled by coups in Egypt (1952), Syria (1954), and Iraq (1958), and were severely challenged in every other Arab country where they existed.

The Palestine defeat, then, sounded the death-knell of liberal na-tionalism in the Arab world, and with it has come the growing rejec-tion of Western models of government. The Palestine defeat sparked the re-evaluation of Arab society; and from this has arisen what may be called radical Arab nationalism—a nationalism dedicated to funda-mental social change to achieve the objectives of freedom and unity. In

16. Manif al-Razzaz, *The Evolution of the Meaning of Nationalism: A Study*, translated by Ibrahim Abu-Lughad (New York: Doubleday, 1963), p. 3.

terms of Matossian's categories, the radical Arab nationalist regimes
have been fairly consistently anti-Western and have returned in many
ways to the policies of the Ottoman reformers by restricted borrowing
from the West, except in the areas of military and some economic technology. This same restriction generally applies to their relations with
the Soviet Union. Although Marxist and some Leninist terms and ideas
have been adopted, the interpretations placed upon them do not ac-
cord with accepted Marxist doctrine. The past, in terms of social organization and doctrine, has been decisively broken with; indeed, after
the beginnings made in the 1920s and 1930s, it would have been almost
impossible, as well as unthinkable, to attempt a return to tradition.[17]
On the other hand, although some attempt to use tradition to justify
present action has been made, tradition, rather than being retained,
has been reinterpreted so that new content is pressed into old language forms.

In effect, then, we have explained political behavior as far as we
can by Matossian's criteria because we have already established that
the transformation in Arab ideology over the period 1900–60 displays a
growing anti-Westernism and a non- (if not anti-) traditionalism.[18]
This distinction seems of little explanatory value in itself, and we must
pursue the causes of this condition a bit further before we can explain
its consequences.

It seems to be agreed among analysts of the subject that the major
trend in Arab nationalism has been away from the individualistic rational model of Mill and Locke, toward the more emotionally based,
romantic model of Herder, which stems from the confusion of state and
community in Rousseau. The identification of the state with the people
as a necessary connection, rather than a conventional alliance, allows
the doctrine of the general will, embodied in the leader, to supplant
the expression of will in an elective process. This personification of the
general will gives romanticism a tendency to lead to dictatorship, due
to the belief in the illegitimacy of dissent. But it is also more compatible with traditional Arab political modes wherein the leader embodied,
in pre-Islamic times, the general will, and in the Islamic period, God's
will.

17. Edward Shils, "The Military in the Political Development of the New
States," in *The Role of the Military in Underdeveloped Countries*, edited by J.
Johnson (Princeton, N.J.: Princeton University Press, 1962), p. 61.

18. Hisham Sharabi, "The Transformation of Ideology in the Arab World," *The
Middle East Journal* 19 (Autumn 1965): 471–86, provides an excellent description
of this transition.

Another major factor was the occurrence of nationalism before statehood. When a working, well-established government becomes the object of national feeling, the constitutional basis of its working is likely to become sanctified. When, on the other hand, a national movement is seeking to establish a government capable of realizing its ideals, the products and not the form of government are likely to be the sacred objects. This is pernicious to stability, because formal justice (i.e., the right procedures) is easier to establish than substantive justice (i.e., the right outcomes). On the other hand, concern with collectivity is again more compatible with the traditional Arab political milieu. Whereas in liberal Western philosophy the individual has been the basic unit of organization, in the traditional Arab world, the collectivity has been the basic unit—whether it be family, tribe, or community (religious, ethnic). Thus, Sharabi says that for the new revolutionaries: "True democracy is impossible to achieve without social and economic liberation. It is defined not in terms of individual freedom and traditional parliamentary structures, but in terms of social and economic justice."[19] The Algerian FLN puts it this way: "Since the lot of the individual is indissolubly linked with that of society, democracy cannot be restricted to individual freedom, but should be the collective expression of the people's responsibility."[20]

This last phrase is the indicator of another line of thought characteristic of the revolutionaries of the 1960s: the priority of the state, or, perhaps more precisely, the nation, over the individual. This is implied by Rousseau's famous comment about forcing men to be free, although Rousseau had in mind, insofar as it is possible to tell, a political community rather than a nascent national community. As Gregor has pointed out, all movements which place collectivity before the individual as the source of the human personality become totalitarian in principle, if not in practice.[21]

A serious examination of the various and sometimes contradictory currents of thought that have characterized Arab ideologies in the twentieth century reveals the following features: First, the basic traditional values of the society have been displaced, but not replaced.[22]

19. Ibid., p. 483.

20. *Barnamaj Jabhat al-tahrir al-jaza'iriyah*, May 27, 1962, *Watha'iq wa dirasat* 3 (Nov. 1962), translated by Sharabi, in ibid., p. 485.

21. A. James Gregor, *Contemporary Radical Ideologies: Totalitarian Thought in the Twentieth Century* (New York: Random House, 1968), pp. 14–21.

22. Halpern, *Politics of Social Change*, pp. 114–18. Also in Ismael, *Government of Middle East*, p. 120.

Second, because the West offered a vast and complex range of alternatives and because of the great influx of ideas into the area, Arab thought tended to be both eclectic and rapid in adopting, as well as rejecting, a multitude of ideas and formuli both political and social. Consequently it found itself tempted to accept "ready-made" notions that satisfied and enforced the inherent tendency for simplifying issues, problems, and solutions.

The simplification of issues on the ideological plane is at once a response to the unmanageable complexity of the issues of Middle East politics and the result of the unconscious acceptance of certain common ideas and definitions of reality. Actually, the latter are far more important as determinants of behavior. As has been pointed out, the laissez-faire and liberal individualism which provided the motivation for the democratic state, and for its policies, was never well suited to the Arab political culture. Despite the wide range of European opinions adopted by Arab thinkers, individualism seems to have been swamped by the more romantic images of collective cooperativism.

We cannot here examine the roots of individualism in Western society, but two concepts are basic. The first is privacy: It is held that there are areas of private rather than public concern and that the state may not interfere with these. Even in Europe a long struggle with religious factions was necessary to establish this view, and at the time that Arab nationalism was in its infancy, the progressive (as well as socialist) movements were attempting to widen the concept of legitimate areas of government concern. The Prohibition movement, laws concerning public decency, the security laws occasioned by the world wars, as well as social welfare legislation, reduced the area of individual autonomy in the West, but at every step the supporters of such legislation had to justify their actions. It can be seen that this was not the case in the Arab world, where the government was traditionally responsible for public morality and where few, if any, actions were in principle out of the purview of the state.

The second principle is individual liberty. Consequent upon the limited state, but also upon the position that, as Hobbes makes clear in *Leviathan*, no man should be governed without his consent, and upon a tradition reaching back to Luther that every man may judge for himself the will of God, each individual is at liberty to do what he will so long as he does not harm others. This is the basis of the principle of private concerns, as between individual and state, but also a defense of individuals against the community.

Lacking a thoroughgoing individualistic philosophy, Arab society, faced with the demands of nationalism and of interpreting equity and justice in substantive terms, became enamoured of the concept of integral nationalism, as has been pointed out above. The point we would make is this: once on the path of socialism and nationalism, both of which confer upon the state as the representative of the society or nation certain rights as against the individual, and without the resistant force of a well-developed belief (for here we are at the non-rational level) in individual autonomy, there is little to prevent the state from becoming totalitarian in fact and in principle. However, there is a certain amount of effort involved in extending the authority of the state, as there are groups who resist on the ground of self-interest, if not of doctrine. Therefore, justification is required; but given justification, the development is almost inevitable.

Then two problems remain: the objective events which provided justification and the reactions which, determined by states of mind, interpreted them as justificatory. The first is hardly a problem. War and defeat, injustice and failure to reform, hunger and a failure of development, disappointment with the consequences of independence, reaction to and fear of imperialism—the list goes on. The point is that the institutions in the Middle East did not produce the results expected of them by people with the power to overthrow them. As the eminent student of Arab nationalism, Fayez A. Sayegh, wrote in *Arab Unity:* "If the good society had not been created immediately after the attainment of independence—the young Arabs argued—it was because the leaders of Arab society represented the institutions which were the main barrier to a better life. The removal of foreign domination, therefore, was not enough; it had to be followed by the emancipation of Arab society from the tyranny of domestic forces perpetuating backwardness and hindering progress" (p. 159).

Summarizing these points, we may note that the concept of individual autonomy inherent in liberal Western models of government had no corollary in the Arab milieu. The institutions thus established were quickly corrupted to the protection of power and privilege and subverted to the control of external powers. In seeking social reform, the radical Arab nationalists have been evolving a position that rejects the fundamental concept of individual autonomy in favor of a vision of a unitary organic community. The view of the unitary organic community is clear in the Arab conception of freedom, which does not so much connote individual liberty as societal freedom from exploitation, poverty, ignorance. The conception of society as a unitary organic community is not only more compatible with traditional Arab values, but also in its development in socialist thought provides the conceptual framework for analyzing the ills of society and for achieving a more equitable society. Indeed, as we shall witness in the following chapters, concepts of social justice became integral to the radical Arab concept of nationalism and in New Left ideologies (Chapters 6 and 7) have evolved as strategies for social transformation.

As a pivotal point in Arab history, Palestine occupies a central place in Arab nationalism. To Arab nationalists, it symbolizes such a degree of degeneration of Arab life as to render the Arabs not only incapable of controlling their own destiny, but, even more fundamentally, incapable of protecting their own integrity. The liberal nationalist hope for socio-economic progress, emancipation from foreign domination, and unification through the adoption of Western social and political models appeared pale in light of the Palestine debacle. The loss of Palestine had, in effect, catapulted the issue of social transformation into the principal focus of Arab nationalism. In the eloquent words of Fayez A. Sayegh in *Arab Unity:*

> To millions of Arabs, the loss of Palestine was the indictment of a whole generation. The import of that harsh verdict of history, as envisioned by the Arabs of the day, went beyond Palestine, beyond military power or impotence; it was a judgement on values cherished for thirty years, on premises of thought considered axiomatic since the end of the First World War, on age-old traditions and systems of social organization; in short, on an entire mode of existence. . . . The dark crisis of Palestine . . . lent urgency and imperativeness to the desire already expressed for drastic change and far-reaching transformation in Arab life. (pp. 160–61).

Impatient of slow developmental progress, and embittered with the West for its role in the Palestine affair, Arab nationalists have rejected liberal Western social and political philosophies as inadequate in the Arab context, with socialist models of change and development moving to the forefront of Arab nationalist ideologies. The 1950s and 1960s witnessed the evolution of socialist doctrines in the popular movements and parties in the Arab world, as discussed in Chapters 2–5. These doctrines emerged as the principal challenge to the status quo in Arab politics, have gained broad acceptance, and have popularized the issue of social transformation at all levels of Arab society.

Socio-economic development, then, has been transformed from an aspiration of Arab nationalism to one of its principal issues. The concept of Arab unity has undergone a similar transformation. Whereas under liberal nationalism unity was conceptualized as the cultural unity of the Arab peoples, radical nationalists consider the usurpation of Palestine a consequence of the political fragmentation of the Arab homeland following the First World War. Politically divided, the rationale runs, the Arabs have been easy to control, exploit, and even displace. Politically divided, the Arab states comprise seventeen disparate, weak nations—some overpopulated, others underpopulated; some oil-rich but dirt poor, others agriculturally endowed but lacking developmental funds; some governed by conservative monarchies, others by radical regimes; all politically unstable. The demographic, economic, and political tensions generated by national fragmentation are not only sapping the tremendous developmental potential that exists in the Arab world, maintain the nationalists, but also leave each individual Arab state prey to foreign intervention. And Palestine portends of the worst fate of such weakness: extinction. Strength, the nationalists maintain, lies in unity—the strength to release the economic potential of the Arab world; the strength to resist foreign domination; the strength to defend the Arab homeland. The loss of Palestine thus transformed the nationalist aspirations for development and unity into urgent issues of national survival.

The convergence of nationalist leftist ideologies around three issues—Palestine, social transformation, and Arab unity—has been a central phenomenon of Arab political development in the last quarter-century. But this convergence has been obscured by the proliferation of parties, doctrines, and personalities. What appears on the surface to be a fragmentation of nationalist politics in actuality has been a coalescence of doctrines around three key issues. The role of these issues in fostering the growth of the Arab nationalist left and the role these issues play in each major nationalist left ideology are the subjects of the following chapters.

HIZB AL-BA'ATH AL-'ARABI AL-ISHTIRAKI
(The Socialist Arab Ba'ath Party)

IN HISTORIC sequence, the Socialist Arab Ba'ath Party emerged after the Arab Communist parties. Thus, it represents the first non-Communist political movement in the Arab world. Its early activities took place at Syrian University, particularly in 1940–41. At this time it represented a collection of informal, fragmented groups galvanized into action by immediate Syrian and Lebanese issues. The concern with the broader political issues of Arab liberation and unity, however, is reflected in the main activities of these groups, which were to mobilize interest in issues of liberation and unity via the preparation and distribution of political leaflets and the organization of demonstrations.

These groups began to shape their basic ideas into a doctrine in July 1943, when Michel Aflaq ran for a parliamentary seat. His political platform, in essence, outlined the basic political principles of the yet-unborn party, and may be summarized as follows:[1]

1. Emphasis on the dynamic nationalist idea which represents the aspirations of the Arab people.
2. Emphasis on protecting the integrity and unity of Arab culture from the fragmenting influences of Western culture.
3. Rejection of religious factionalism and localism.

1. Shibli al-Aysami, *Hizb al-Ba'th Al-Arabi al-Ishtiraki: 1—Marhalat al-Arab'inat al-Ta'sisyah, 1940–1949* [The Arab Ba'ath Socialist Party: 1—The Formative Forties Stage] (Beirut: Dar al-Tali'ah, 1974), pp. 27–28.

4. Condemnation of communism which represents an artificial materialistic progress.
5. Emphasis on the freedom and unity of the Arab world.

It should be noted that at this early period no mention was made of socialism. In fact, there appears to have been little consideration of the fundamental issues of social justice or social transformation. In this early period, Ba'athist doctrine perhaps more accurately, pre-Ba'athist ideas) was akin to, indeed not distinguishable from, liberal nationalist thought. These seedbearers of Ba'athist ideas held the optimistic belief, like the liberal nationalists, that freedom and unity represented the necessary and sufficient conditions for justice and progress. Since the founding conference, however, there has been internal conflict within the party between essentially conservative liberal nationalist ideas and the more or less comparatively radical ideas of social transformation. The slow and often erratic process of (synthesis between these two factions within the party is what sets the Ba'athist party apart from the liberal nationalists. *Al-Thawra* (Baghdad), reported on December 11, 1975, that in a public lecture at the College of Law and Politics in Baghdad, the Assistant General Secretary of the Ba'ath National Command, Shibli al-'Aysami, noted that the early "period distinguished itself by its concentration on freedom first [i.e., liberation from foreign domination], then unity. Little attention was at first given to socialism until the end of the forties. . . . The slogan 'freedom, unity and socialism,' representing the integrated relationship between these ideas, was not created until 1949."

The first constituent conference of the party, attended by two hundred delegates representing Syrian and some Lebanese and Jordanian intelligentsia (university graduates, government employees, professionals, and teachers in particular), convened in al-Rashid Coffee Shop in Damascus on April 4, 1947. The main business of the three-day meeting comprised discussion of the party's constitution, election of the head (Dean) of the party and his executive committee of three, and discussion of political and ideological reports. At its completion, the conference issued its first official declaration announcing the birth of the party.[2]

The conflict between liberal nationalist and scientific socialist ideas was manifested in the first conference. A fundamental difference that

2. *Nidal al-Ba'th* [The Struggle of the Ba'ath], vol. 1, 3rd ed. (Beirut: Dar al-Tali'ah, 1972), p. 20.

arose in this conference centered around the meaning of the concept of socialism. The debate was resolved in favor of the liberal nationalist proponents, as reflected in the conference's adoption of the assertion that "socialism shouldn't limit the freedom of individuals. The owner of a private factory is not necessarily and always a beast [who] exploits the work of laborers. He might be a creative inventor in industry whose genius results in progress for the country."[3]

The First National Congress elected by acclamation Michel Aflaq as a "Dean of the Party." (Aflaq was later called the "general secretary" and finally, the "founding leader." This last title was given to Aflaq after he was ousted from the General Secretariat of the party.) The same conference elected also by acclamation Salahaldin al-Bitar, Jalal al-Sayyid, and Wahib al-Ghanim as the party's National Leadership. Moreover, the first conference adopted a Constitution of the Ba'ath Party (see Appendix A) which defined the three aims of the party in the following manner:

1. The Arab homeland is an indivisable political and economic unit, and it is impossible for any one of the Arab countries fully to realize the requirements of its life in isolation from any other Arab country.
2. The Arab nation is a cultural unity, and all the differences existing between its sons are accidental and spurious and will pass away with the awakening of Arab consciousness.
3. The Arab homeland is for the Arabs and they alone have the right to manage its affairs, dispose of its wealth, and direct its destinies.

The Ba'ath party, from its inception, has been strongly anti-communist. A communiqué issued by the Third National Congress of the party on October 10, 1959, published in *al-Sahafah* (Beirut), No. 283, stated: "We represent the Arab spirit against materialistic communism. This is why the party has always been engaged in a war against communism which strangles both the human being's freedom and his ethical values." Both Michel Aflaq and Salahaldin al-Bitar, the party's chief theoreticians, consider that there is a contradiction between

3. *Nidal Hizb al-Ba'th al-'Arabi al-ishtiraki 'abra mu'tamaratihi al-qawmiyah: 1947–1964* [The Struggle of the Ba'ath Arab Socialist Party through its Nationalist Congresses: 1947–1964], 2nd ed. (Beirut: Dar al-Tali'ah, 1972), pp. 18–19.

communism and Arab nationalism.[4] Elaborating on this, Aflaq has observed: "We consider the communist party to be destructive for two reasons. One, in its deceptive socialism, it promises the Arab nation the satisfaction of the achievement of its basic immediate needs, while its basic aim is to tie the destiny of the Arab people to the destiny of another state—namely Russia. Two, in its anti-nationalist stance [i.e., in its preoccupation with international issues, it negates the Arab nationalist thesis]."[5]

Notwithstanding the fundamental antagonisms between the nationalist orientation of the Ba'ath and the supranational orientation of communism, on the one hand, and between the essentially romantic values of the Ba'ath and the materialistic values of communism, on the other, socialist concepts in general, and scientific socialism in particular, have since the foundation of the party posed the major challenge to the party's ideology and stimulated its development and elaboration. Writing in 1974, Shibli al-'Aysami noted that: "In the intellectual legacy of the formative stage [of the party], we do not find detailed scientific analytical studies of the class situation in Arab society and certainly no advocation of the idea of class struggle. We do find in general terms attacks on feudalism, capitalism, and corrupt ruling elite, and a defense of the dispossessed classes. We also do not find any acceptance of dialectic materialism in the manner explained by Marxist theory."[6]

Socialist doctrines, indeed, posed the fundamental challenge to liberal nationalist ideas in the post–World War II era, and in 1952, the Ba'ath party demonstrated its viability as an essentially pragmatic ideology of Arab nationalism by merging with *Hizb al-Arabi al-Ishtiraki*, the Arab Socialist Party—a party established by Akram al-Hourani that had popular support in the Syrian district of Hamah and had several outspoken deputies in the Syrian Parliament. Thus, on November 13, 1952, the name of the merged party became the Arab Ba'ath Socialist Party.

With the exception of small groups of students at the Syrian University and the American University of Beirut (AUB), the party had no branches outside Syria. The first branch to be established was the

4. Michel Aflaq and Salahaldin al-Bitar, *al-Qawminyah al-'Arabiyah wa mawqifuha min al-shuyu'iyah* [Arab Nationalism and Its Stance Toward Communism] (Damascus, n.d.), p. 39.

5. Michel Aflaq, *Fi Sabil al-Ba'th* [For the Sake of the Ba'ath], 2nd ed. (Beirut: Dar al-Tali'ah, 1963), p. 210.

6. Al-'Aysami, *The Arab Ba'ath Socialist Party: 1—The Formative Forties Stage*, p. 69.

branch of Jordan in early 1948, followed by the founding of branches in Lebanon in 1949 and Iraq in 1950. At its inception the party was considered as a unified organization enocuraging the creation of regional branches in the various Arab countries, but subject to one "national leadership" seated in Syria.

This was formalized in 1954 by the creation of the National Command, established to direct and guide the various branches of the party, including the Syrian branch which had to this point exercised this overseeing function. The first National Command was appointed by consensus among the leadership of the various party branches.

Since this formative decade, the Ba'ath party has gone through several major stages of development that could be summarized as the Syrian-Egyptian union, establishment of the Ba'ath in Syria and Iraq, turmoil among Iraqi and Syrian Ba'athists, and the tripartite union and the sentencing of Aflaq.

THE SYRIAN—EGYPTIAN UNION

From its inception, the Ba'ath party was an active participant in Syrian political life. Michel Aflaq, Dean of the party, became Minister of Education in 1949, but resigned three months later in protest over alleged government tampering with the election. Until 1954, the party opposed the successive military governments ruling Syria in this period. In the popular election of 1954 that inaugurated the re-establishment of civilian rule, the party had seventeen members elected to the Parliament; in 1956, it gained the ministries of foreign affairs and economics in a National Union government. At this time, the party advocated a "liberated Arab policy" that supported resistance to colonialism. In the name of the Syrian government, the party established cordial relations with the Soviet Union and obtained Czech arms for the Syrian army.[7]

At this time, the fundamental political challenge in Syria to Ba'athist ideology came from the Syrian Communist party. Like the Ba'athist party, the Syrian Communist party was well organized and enjoyed a broad base of popular support. To forestall what the Ba'athists considered an imminent Communist takeover of Syria, in 1957–58, the party played an essential role in promoting and achieving unity between Syria and Egypt. All national forces in Syria saw in unity with Egypt a means of curbing and circumscribing communism and the

7. Amin Siba'i, "Lebanese Political Parties," *al-Jaridah* (Beirut), May 9, 1970.

Syrian Communist party which was becoming a strong force in the country's political life. To this, however, should be added that the leaders of the Ba'ath party saw in unity with Egypt a historical opportunity to achieve one of their basic goals—namely, Arab unity. The outcome was the creation of the United Arab Republic (UAR) in 1958.

In this stage of the party's development a violent controversy shook the pillar on which the party stood. The controversy was aroused by President Nasser's insistence on having parties in Syria agree to dissolve themselves as a condition for the unification of Egypt with Syria. The only organization Nasser would allow was the "National Union," to be copied from the Egyptian experience.

The Ba'athist leaders, assuming the new Syrian "National Union" to be an umbrella for their own activities, accepted Nasser's conditions and dissolved the party in Syria. The Third National Conference of the party, which convened in Beirut between August 29 and September 1, 1959, was convinced that the Syrian members of the party would lead the "Syrian National Union." Consequently, they supported the party leadership's decision to dissolve the party's branch in Syria.[8]

Seen in retrospect, the decision to dissolve the party's Syrian branch was a major cause of the divisions and dissensions that subsequently infested all branches of the party. With the subsidence of nationalist fervor following the union, opposition to the decision to dissolve the Syrian branch spread among both the cadre and leadership of the Ba'ath. Disclosure of Nasser's disagreements with the leadership of the Ba'ath party and the realization that it would be impossible to transform the National Union into a party base of power contributed to dissension. Soon, the first separatist movement, led by Abdullah al-Rimawi (the man responsible for the establishment of the Jordanian branch of the Ba'ath), appeared. Rimawi affirmed his loyalty to Nasserism and condemned the efforts of particular members to revive the party's Syrian branch.

Despite Rimawi's gestures, opposition to the dissolution decision increased and was prominent at the Fourth National Conference held in August 1960. Two of the resolutions adopted by the Fourth Conference indicate the strength of opposition to the decision to dissolve party branches in the UAR. The first resolution called on the party's national leadership to assert the independence of the Ba'ath from existing Arab regimes and to affirm the party's distinction from other Arab political movements. The second resolution rejected the decision of the Third National Conference to legalize the dissolution of party branches in the

8. *The Struggle of the Ba'ath Arab Socialist Party,* p. 56.

UAR, considering that step as "ideologically unacceptable and motivated by defeatist and naive considerations." It was maintained at the
conference that the loss to the party organization of its Syrian branch
was almost fatal, leading to loss of faith among members in the ability
of the party to maintain and continue its struggle, disenchantment with
the performance of the leadership, and a general alienation of supporters of the Ba'ath.[9]

The Ba'ath undertook an extensive criticism of the UAR.[10] Undemocratic practices in the UAR were openly condemned, and the
leadership of that country was accused of mistrusting the masses and
their organizations. UAR policies, it was maintained, had weakened
the Arab struggle for liberation and fortified reactionary forces. Criticism of the UAR intensified following the dismissal of party representatives and supporters from their government positions. The final *coup
de grâce* came when Salahaldin al-Bitar and Akram al-Hourani signed
the manifesto supporting the September 28, 1961, coup in Syria which
dissolved the union.

THE BA'ATH RULE IN SYRIA AND IRAQ

A new stage in the history of the Ba'ath party commenced following
the dissolution of the Syrian-Egyptian union. This stage was characterized by deep internal schisms and a reconsideration of the party's
basic ideological positions.

Of the slogans raised by the party, that of unity has been foremost
in the minds of the founders and members of the Ba'ath. By 1961, however, the party found itself in opposition to efforts made for renewing
the union with Egypt. Some of its prominent leaders had openly condemned the union and publicly supported a separatist Syrian movement. Because of this contradiction in party policy and practice, in the
new stage, the slogan of unity was repeatedly scrutinized.

The process of soul-searching began with the Fifth National Conference, which was held in the middle of May 1962 in Homs. Conference deliberations attested to the rise of a deep rift among members
as to the nature of the policy that the party should pursue. In its final

9. Ibid., pp. 98, 105.

10. For a detailed analysis see Munif al-Razzaz, *Al-Tajruba al-Mura* [The Bitter
Experience] (Beirut: Dar Ghandur, 1967), Chapter 2.

statement, the conference called for the eradication of the separatist disgrace and for the renewal of Syrian-Egyptian unity. Reunification was posited as the immediate objective of the Arab struggle. The September 28, 1961, coup in Syria was labeled as the greatest reactionary conspiracy. The conference made the revival of the union conditional, however, on the acceptance by UAR political leaders of the following: giving the masses their freedom, allowing parties to freely operate and allowing for regional differences that exist between the two countries.[11] The new position led to the final breakaway of Akram al-Hourani and his supporters from the party.

Thus, when the party was called upon to translate its avowed aims into action, the challenge exposed the contradictions that plagued the Ba'ath throughout, revealing the class and intellectual disharmony prevailing among Ba'ath members, the conflicting aims of the middle and small bourgeoisie that composed the party rank and file, and the existence of leftist and rightist factions within the party organization.[12]

The divorce of theory and practice in the party became more obvious in this stage. For instance, the resort to political and military intrigues was openly condemned by the 1960 Fourth National Conference.[13] In its communique that conference had noted with concern the increased reliance of party leaders on coups d'état as the means to power and had considered such attitudes contrary to the party's constitution and doctrine. It had also demanded that the Ba'ath national leadership work diligently to arrest this trend.[14] Despite the clarity of the directive, leaders of the Syrian and Iraqi party branches chose to ignore it and used military coups as the major, almost sole, means for assuming power. The effect of the series of coups that they undertook was the final splintering of the Ba'ath party into several parties fighting each other.

With the assistance of some nationalist elements, on February 8, 1963, the Ba'ath led a military coup against the regime of Abd al-Karim Qasim. Directly after, it mounted a policy of recrimination and physical liquidation against Iraqi Communists, Qasimites, and opponents to their rule. At the same time, it reasserted the party's commitment to

11. Ibid., pp. 123, 133.

12. This explanation is advanced by a number of leading Ba'ath members. In particular, reference should be made to *Azmat Hizb al-Ba'th al-'Arabi al-ishtiraki min khilal tajribatihi fi al-'Iraq* [The Crisis of the Ba'ath Arab Socialist Party as Based on its Experience in Iraq] (Baghdad: Dar al-sha'b, 1964).

13. For details, see al-Razzaz, *The Bitter Experience.*

14. *The Struggle of the Ba'ath Arab Socialist Party,* p. 98.

Arab unity. One month following the Iraqi coup, the Ba'ath party led another successful coup in Syria which similarly raised the banner of Arab unity. Both regimes of the Ba'ath undertook to negotiate a union with Egypt. The agreement reached with that country was soon discarded.

A Sixth National Conference, meeting in Damascus between October 5 and 23, 1963, to discuss the new developments, witnessed new organizational and ideological divisions. The conference directed its two branches in Syria and Iraq to announce an immediate union between the two countries. Though formally declared, the union was never implemented and led to disagreement between the Ba'athists on the one hand, and the Iraqi President Abdul Salam Aref (a self-proclaimed pro-Nasserite at the time), on the other. It also caused dissenison in the ranks of Iraqi Ba'athist and between Iraqi Ba'athists and the Ba'athist National Leadership which was headed by Michel Aflaq.[15] Another important consequence of the Sixth National Conference was the emergence of a strong leftist trend. Its proponents, adopting Marxist concepts and tools of analysis, subjected most party doctrines to critical re-evaluation and questioned—in particular—the thought of Michel Aflaq. The ideological line of those leftists was approved by the conference after bitter and lengthy discussion and was issued in a leaflet entitled *Some Theoretical Principles*.[16] The new publication was a serious attempt aimed at clarifying the party's socialist line and setting the principles that should guide the policy of Ba'athists to transform the Arab societies in which they rule to socialist ones.

The new document denounced the party's previous belief in the utility of private property and condemned it as a petty bourgeois socialism. The class of middle bourgeois, the document added, has proved itself incapable of the task of national economic construction. This class was discredited as a potential ally of neo-imperialism. Only the workers, peasants, and revolutionary intellectuals, the document argued, are able to forge the revolution in the first stages of socialism. The Ba'ath command was instructed to reflect this new line and to emphasize the need to recruit more peasants and workers into party ranks.[17]

Needless to say, the new ideological line did not go unchallenged.

15. An exposition of this conflict is available in *The Crisis of the Ba'ath Arab Socialist Party as Based on its Experience in Iraq.*

16. *Ba'd al-muntalaqat al-nazariyah* (Baghdad: Manshurat Maktab al-tawzi' wa al-nashr, 1970).

17. *The Struggle of the Ba'ath Arab Socialist Party*, pp. 161–62.

Early founders of the Ba'ath party, especially, found themselves at odds with the emerging leftist leadership. Clashes between the two groups outlasted the conference and became more pronounced in the period following the disestablishment of the Ba'ath in Iraq. An internal party newsletter, issued by the 1964 Seventh Party Conference, considered the situation sufficiently serious as to threaten party unity and confessed to a paralysis in party organs. "Locking themselves behind closed doors, party members find nothing better than to exchange accusations."[18]

TURMOIL AMONG IRAQI AND SYRIAN BA'ATHISTS

The extremely harsh measures adopted by the Ba'ath in Iraq to repress its opponents alienated local, regional, and international public opinion. Locally, their isolation helped crystallize differences between the military and civilian branches of the party and allowed Abdul Salam Aref to execute a coup with the assistance of some Ba'ath officers. After ridding himself of civilian Ba'athists, Aref dismissed a large number of Ba'ath members and supporters from the army. The role of the Ba'ath in Iraq collapsed and the confrontation between the civilian and military branches of the party in Iraq assumed contours of a rift between leftists and rightists.

In Syria, the dissolution of the party incumbent upon the Egyptian-Syrian union and Nasser's attempts to disperse party affiliates by transferring Ba'athist proponents among the Syrian military out of Syria had a singularly decisive effect on subsequent Ba'athist organization in Syria. According to al-Razzaz (an eminent Ba'athist intellectual, General Secretary of the Party in 1965, and at present a member of the National Command), Nasser "did not want the Ba'athists in the army. Therefore, he appointed some high-ranking Ba'athist army officers to the cabinet, transferred others to the diplomatic corp and transferred the rest to Egypt."[19] As a result, according to al-Razzaz, there emerged a clandestine organization of Syrian Ba'athist officers stationed in Egypt. This organization established its own internal leadership independent of and dissociated from the National Command. Among these leaders were Mohammed Umran, Salah Jadeed, and Hafiz Assad. Fol-

18. Ibid., pp. 260–61.
19. Al-Razzaz, *The Bitter Experience*, p. 87.

lowing the dissolution of the Syrian-Egyptian union in 1961, the Ba'athist Military Organization returned to Syria with well-organized cells;
and before even the nucleus of civilian Ba'athist reorganization emerged, it was collaborating in the abortive March 28, 1961, coup. The
National Command was left completely in the dark about the activities
of this military organization, including its successful March 8, 1963,
coup. Thus, al-Razzaz concludes that the Ba'ath party was decisively
split into military and civilian factions. The civilian faction in Syria,
in fact, was never able to regain control, and the National Command,
seated in Damascus, and the Syrian Regional Command eventually
came under the complete domination of the military faction.

Within the military faction, however, intense intrigues developed.
Ameen al-Hafiz, who became President in 1964, concentrated power in
his hands, gaining control over the state and the party. This alienated
other members of the faction. A February 22, 1966, military coup,
against him, led by Salah Jadeed, succeeded in assuming power. The
new leadership, accusing its opponents of being rightists, banished
Michel Aflaq, Salahaldin al-Bitar, and Ameen al-Hafiz from Syria and
dismissed them from the party.[20] A triumvirite leadership consisting of
Salah Jadeed, Nur al-Din al-Atassi, and Yousuf Ze'ayen was established
and soon initiated a policy of cooperation with the Syrian Communists
and other leftist groups and with the Soviet Union and countries of the
socialist bloc. Relations with Egypt, however, remained disharmonious.
After the Arab defeat of June 1967 and Nasser's acceptance of the UN
Security Council's peace resolution, Syrian-Egyptian relations became
more strained. Ba'athists opposing the Syrian regime, with the assistance of Nasserite elements, were accorded a better chance for plotting.
Meanwhile, the Iraqi branch of the Ba'ath, exploiting the social unrest
that followed in the wake of the June 1967 defeat, collaborated with
other nationalist officers and masterminded a successful military coup.
Once it was instituted, the Ba'ath rid itself of its previous associates
and exercised exclusive power.[21] The Ba'ath in Syria, however, refused
to cooperate with the new Iraqi leadership, which it viewed with sus-
picion. The National Leadership of the Ba'ath, led by Aflaq, sided

20. A rebuttal to the accusations of being rightists and the counter-accusations
of the Ba'ath National Leadership is offered in Amin Siba'i, "Lebanese Political
Parties," al-Jaridah (Beirut), May 9, 1970, pp. 6–7.

21. A triumvirate consisting of Ahmad Hasan al-Bakr (who assumed the position of President of the Republic), Hardan al-Tikriti (who assumed position of
Vice-President, and was later expelled from his position and assassinated in
Kuwait), and Salih Mahdi 'Ammash (who assumed Ministry of the Interior and
was later expelled from his position) were the leaders of the new movement.

initially with the Ba'athists in Iraq, but differences between the two soon surfaced. Aflaq, bitter and dispirited, secluded himself in Beirut to write a series of articles in which he reviewed the acrid experience of the party, attacked military coups, and called for the rejuvenation of the Ba'ath. The articles were collected and published in a book entitled *Niqtatal-bidayah* (The Starting Point). Shortly thereafter, differences were patched up, and Aflaq resumed his leadership position as the General Secretary of the National Command. Aflaq is now residing in Baghdad.

THE TRIPARTITE UNION AND THE SENTENCING OF AFLAQ

The inside struggle for dominance in the Syrian Ba'ath leadership crystallized into two camps; the first led by Salah Jadeed and the second by Hafiz al-Assad. A stalemate period ended on November 16, 1970, when al-Assad, backed by the army, gained the upper hand and arrested the leading figures in the other camp. Al-Assad nominated himself for the Presidency of the Republic and, to confer legality on his action, conducted a plebiscite. To extricate Syria from its forced isolation, al-Assad eased relations with the UAR and, on April 17, 1971, signed a declaration for a Tripartite Union between Syria, Egypt, and Libya. A universal plebiscite was conducted and the Union of Arab Republics was declared.

Following the signing of the union agreement, the Syrian leadership ordered the trial *in absentia* of the two founders and historical leaders of the Ba'ath—Michel Aflaq and Salahaldin al-Bitar.[22] Both were sentenced to death by hanging. The trial came in the wake of the extermination of Sudanese Communists and the arrest of a large number of Egypt's leadership who were charged with conspiracy to overturn the regime.

To further secure his position, Hafiz al-Assad convened a national conference of the Ba'ath Party in Damascus in late August 1971. The conference, calling itself the Eleventh National Conference of the Ba'ath party, hurriedly elected al-Assad as the Secretary-General of the party and endorsed all his measures and policies. The conference also labeled al-Assad's coup as a correctionist movement that revived the Ba'ath party's nationalist line and that has taken effective steps aimed at the realization of Arab unity.

22. Salahaldin al-Bitar fled to Beirut and subsequently ceased all political activities. In January 1976 he was pardoned. *Al-Ahram* (Cairo), January 16, 1976.

With the Eleventh National Conference, the tragic cycle of the
Ba'ath was completed. Divided along ideological and regional lines
and unable to harness the personal and conflicting ambitions of those
in leadership positions, the Ba'ath Arab Socialist Party has suffered
attenuation of its proponents. A large number of its skilled members
have joined other political movements, completely abandoned political
work, enlisted in commando organizations, or started new political
movements of their own. The Ba'ath became the single most important
source for recruitment to other Arab parties, blocks, cliques, and leftist
organizations. Within the latter, former Ba'athists are almost invariably
found in leadership positions. The stability of the party in Iraq, however, its successes in building socialism within Iraq and its vanguard
role in Arab issues is giving renewed vitality to the party and is re-
juvenating its image as a leading progressive nationalist party.

THE BA'ATH AND BASIC ISSUES

In the course of its history, the Arab Ba'ath Socialist Party has had to
define its position regarding the fundamental issues facing Arab society
not only as a party advocating an ideology but also as a ruling party
possessed with means for translating its ideals into practice. The
thoughts and performance of the Ba'ath in the areas of unity, the
Palestine problem, and social development will be examined.

The Ba'ath and Arab Unity

A cardinal point that dominated the literature of the party and occupied the minds and hearts of party adherents was the question of unity.
Writing in 1962, Michel Aflaq noted that "the aim of Arab unity is the
strongest and deepest motivation for the existence of the Arab Ba'ath
Socialist Party as a popular revolutionary and progressive movement."[23]
In the constitution of the Ba'ath, innumerable references were made to
the need and plausibility of unifying Arab countries. The existing divisions and frontiers were shunned as fabrications of colonial powers
with no substantive reality to them. Unity was considered an existing
reality that merely needs to be embodied in formal institutions. A

23. Michel Aflaq, al-Ba'th wa al-wihdah [The Ba'ath and Unity] (Beirut: The
Arab Institute for Research and Publication, 1973), p. 93.

primary object of the party was to break down and eradicate the barriers separating the Arabs.

The first principle in the Ba'ath constitution (see full text in Appendix A) stipulated that the Arabs constitute an indivisible, political, economic and cultural unity. Differences among them "are accidental and spurious." It also stressed that they should be the masters of their house. An ideal picture of the character of the Arab nation, one endowed by "a fertile vitality and creativeness, and a capacity for renewal and resurgence," was drawn in the second principle. The third principle imparted to the Arab nation an eternal mission which "aims at revitalizing human values, stimulating the progress of mankind and furthering harmony and cooperation between nations." The intensity and magnitude of nationalist feelings are most clearly observed, however, in Article 3 of the Constitution. To the Ba'ath, the article stipulated "the feeling of nationalism which closely binds the individual to his nation is a sacred feeling, charged with creative power, impelling to sacrifice, inspiring a sense of responsibility, directing the humanity of the individual along a practical and fruitful course." Based on the above, the party set three integrated objectives for itself:

(1) The struggle against foreign imperialism for the complete and absolute liberation of the Arab homeland.
(2) The struggle to bring together all Arabs in a single Arab state.
(3) The overthrow of the existing corrupt order by a revolution that shall embrace all aspects of life—intellectual, economic, social, and political.

Finally, Article 15 of the Arab Socialist Ba'ath Party Constitution stated: "The national bond will be the only bond existing in the Arab state—a bond that guarantees harmony between the citizens and their fusion in one nation, and that combats other and factious forms of solidarity such as the religious, the sectarian, the tribal, the racial, and the provincial."

From its earliest formulation, then, the Ba'athist concept of unity has been closely allied with the concepts of liberation and social transformation. It was the assumption of Ba'athist theoreticians that a unity fostered by progressive social forces would result naturally in liberation and social transformation. Hence, the heavy emphasis on unity. Writing in 1949, Michel Aflaq explained the relationship between unity, freedom and socialism accordingly:

The Arab Ba'ath became aware of the real national aims when it combined them in these principles and realized that they constituted a complete unit. Work towards unity is a natural necessity for the Arabs to safeguard their future, as well as efforts towards freedom—for what is the value of unity if it did not include a free people who are aware of their rights and capable of exercising them. . . . The third principle, socialism, is that there should be at this stage an industrious free people—destine to live and whose individuals are afforded great opportunities so that their strength and potentialities become apparent without any artificial obstacles imposed by one class upon another and without internal differences. It is then that the Arabs will give forth their great strength and their society will be destined to remain and to defend itself.[24]

In addition, he cautioned against the nationalist pretense of reactionary forces, as *al-Ba'ath* (Damascus), December 29, 1949, reported, noting that "there are some who serve imperial interests through the call to unity, republic and freedom. . . . [They] surrender to foreign interests but claim to carry the banner of unity."

For more than two decades, this Ba'ath notion of Arab unity remained almost unaltered. The experience gained by the 1958 Egyptian-Syrian union and its dissolution in 1961, however, enriched and transformed the theoretical formulation of this notion. In the 1963 Sixth National Conference of the Ba'ath, for instance, the conferees criticized the high-level abstraction in the concept of unity and the party's overemphasis of unity to the neglect of socialism. Such a practice, the conferees said, removed the notion of unity from its anti-imperialist, anti-feudalist and anti-bourgeois social class context. The new formulation, which appeared in the conference manifesto, made the struggle for unity synonymous with that of socialism. In *Some Theoretical Principles* the conference considered former attempts at unity as pointers to the socialist, popular, and revolutionary character of that movement and as the *cause célèbre* of workers, peasants, small bourgeoisie, and revolutionary intellectuals. This reformulation of the notion of unity, forwarded by Marxist-oriented Ba'athists and adopted by the Sixth National Conference, presents the general theoretical guidelines upon which the various elements, blocs, and Ba'athist parties remain in agreement.

Four attempts have been made by the Ba'ath to translate its ob-

24. Quoted by Shibli al-Aysami, *Unity, Freedom and Socialism* (Beirut: Arab Institute for Research and Publishing, 1975), pp. 17–18.

jectives of unity into practical schemes. In 1958, the Ba'ath was a principle architect of the United Arab Republic. The endorsement in 1961 by a part of its leadership of Syrian secessionism was later condemned and the party demanded a renewed unity. In 1963, the Ba'ath made a second attempt when it entered into negotiations with Egypt for a Tripartite Syrian-Iraqi-Egyptian union. The Charter of Unity was discarded only a few weeks after it was officially ratified. The third attempt at unity was made following the failure of the "rapproachment" with Egypt. The Sixth National Conference directed the Ba'ath provincial leadership in Iraq and Syria to unify the two countries. The directive, however, was not realized due to the internal disagreements and conflicts within the party. The assumption to power of Hafiz al-Assad in 1970 witnessed the last Ba'athist attempt at unity. Following negotiations between Egypt, Syria, and Libya, a Union of Arab Republics was declared in July 1971, but this, too, failed to materialize.

The Ba'ath Party and the Palestine Question

For the Ba'ath, the issue of Palestine has been viewed within the context of the advance and consolidation of the Arab revolution at the national level. No specific mention of the Palestinian cause was made in the Ba'ath Constitution because it was drafted in 1947. At that time, the entire Arab world was divided and under foreign domination of one kind or another, so the issue of liberation was pervasive throughout the area. However, the party organized volunteer units that participated in the Palestine War of 1948 and opened a permanent Palestine Bureau in the same year, reflecting the early and consistent concern with this issue.

The Fourth National Conference of the party (1960) held the view that only the progress of national revolutions in Arab countries could foster the degree of unity and strength necessary to destroy Zionism and return the Palestinians to their land. The party envisaged a protracted guerrilla struggle, the brunt of which would be borne by a popular front of Palestinian organizations; the role of Arab governments would be limited to prevention of further Israeli expansion. The party reaffirmed this position at its next two National Conferences in 1962 and 1964. The so-called leftist faction of the party, led by Ali Saleh al-Sadi, stressed the complex historical, cultural, and economic aspects of the Arab confrontation with Israel; nevertheless, its practical conclusions on strategy and tactics virtually coincided with the main-line of the party on the Palestine issue.[25]

The June 1967 War had profound effects upon the Ba'ath view of strategy. The war not only demonstrated the inability of Arab govern-ments for concerted action: it also demonstrated the imperialist strategy of broadening the geographic cleavage of the Arab world. Israel, then, was not just an alien entity, but a vital part of imperialist strategy. As noted an eminent Ba'athist philosopher: "The complete merger of Israel and the imperialist forces, particularly the U.S., makes Israel a power greater than its actual presence. . . . Thus, Israel is not only a state that can be dealt with through traditional warfare. Above this, it is Imperialism in its essence. The negation of imperialism is revolution."[26]

The Ninth National Conference in March 1968 resolved that the Palestinian movement was the crucible of the Arab revolution, and that therefore the party must exert all its energies in support of the move-ment. The party drew up slogans and programs, including the complete rejection of defeatist compromise solutions, denunciation of the Arab regimes responsible for the defeat, and a call for a protracted popular war with the unqualified support of all Arab countries.[27]

Only four months later, the Ba'ath came to power in Iraq. Im-mediately, the party was besieged with pleas to enact its Palestine program. An official source remarked: "The urgent pleas came from every direction, from the base of the party and its organizations, from the masses and from the Palestine Resistance Movement, some of whose sections had negative sentiments due to former relations with the Party." Not only were those circles pressing the party hard for action, but many suspect elements were doing the same in order to embarrass the party.[28] But the regime had to consolidate its domestic authority and deal with the Kurdish revolt before it could feel secure enough to act on the radical course charted at the Ninth Conference of the party. The embarrassment was severe: "We must confess that the gap was great between our slogans and our ability to translate

25. Leftist Socialist Party Arab Ba'ath, al-Bayan Al-Syasi lil-Moutamar Al-Sabie [Political Statements of the National Conference] (Baghdad, n.d.), pp. 169–71.

26. Munif al-Razzaz, Al-Sabil ila Tahrir Filistin [The Way to the Liberation of Palestine] (Beirut: The Arab Organization for Publication and Studies, 1971), pp. 27–29.

27. Revolutionary Iraq: 1968–1973, Political Report adopted by 8th Regional Congress of the Socialist Arab Ba'ath Party (Baghdad, 1974), p. 199.

28. Ibid., p. 200.

them into practical action."[29] Nevertheless, the regime kept up the radical slogans. The embarrassment reached its peak in September 1970, when Iraq was powerless to stop the Jordanian repression of the Palestinians despite repeated commitments of support in the period leading up to the repression. The Ba'ath regime lost a great deal of credibility among the Palestinians as a result of its repeated failures to act on its program. "When the Jordanian regime ruthlessly embarked upon the liquidation of the Palestinian Resistance, putting to the test all the slogans, the party and the revolution found themselves unable to deal in a way commensurate with the size and extent of the conspiracy and with the abovementioned promises. The reputation of the party suffered immensely among the Arab masses and in Arab and foreign political circles. For some time, the party was isolated and unable to move among the Arab masses."[30] Its relations with some resistance circles deteriorated. Ruefully looking back on the period from the Ninth Congress to the September 1970 debacle, the same official source commented that "the party had made major promises for temporary psychological advantage without considering the possibility that it might have to act on those promises."[31]

The Tenth Congress of the party was highly significant in the development of the party's policy on the Palestine issue. The party reaffirmed the assumption that the Palestine movement was one of the foci of the Arab revolution and that deviationist tendencies arising from a regionalist or opportunist outlook must be crushed, since it could break the dialectical relationship between the Palestinian and Arab revolutions.[32]

"Deviationist tendencies" and "opportunist outlook" referred to the tendencies of certain Arab government to seek specific, isolated settlements and thus fragment the overall issue. The Ba'athists viewed this fragmentation as an integral part of the imperialist strategy to break any unity of purpose among the Arab nations. According to Michel Aflaq, founder of the Ba'ath party:

The local mentality ignores not only the necessity of Arab unity, but enhances the unity of our enemies and endangers the unity of Arab destiny. . . . The local mentality considers withdrawal of the enemy

29. Ibid., p. 199.
30. Ibid., pp. 201–202.
31. Ibid.
32. See The Arab Ba'ath Socialist Party, *Political Report: Tenth National Congress* (Baghdad: National Bureau of Culture, n.d.).

armies from local areas to the 1967 boundaries is nationalist aim as it secures local independence. This ignores the meaning of the presence of Israel in the heart of the Arab nation and the Arab land and its integral alliance with imperialism and its evil aims once the war is over and stability imposed.[33]

Regional problems had to be solved only in the light of the strategy of resistance to Zionism. The Tenth National Conference also marked the launching of the Arab Liberation Front, an arm of the Ba'ath party in Palestine that was to insure the merger of the Arab and Palestinian revolutions. The Palestine revolution was vulnerable to compromising interests, and it therefore needed the support of those of the Arab revolution itself. "Theoretically, the Front has no separate ideology from the Party. The Front's thought emanates from the Arab revolutionary ideology whose banner was carried aloft. . . . Any . . . [thought] produced by the Front will only be an interpretation of the Party's thought on Palestine."[34]

The Arab Liberation Front was to recruit and organize support for the armed struggle in Palestine through which the Arab nation would be reborn. In effect, it was a military organization, organized and financed by the Ba'ath, for action in Palestine. Recruitment would be drawn from all Arab countries, particularly those surrounding the Zionist entity. Finally, the party recognized for the first time, the internationalist aspect of the Palestinian movement. So the most significant thing was the creation of a political organization aimed at implementing the militant views of the Ba'ath in Palestine. The party reaffirmed its pledge to struggle against all attempts to liquidate the cause of the Palestinians, whether by Palestinians themselves or by opportunists or reactionary Arab governments. Michel Aflaq viewed the formation of the Arab Liberation Front as fulfilling the basic need of the party to realize its revolutionary aims through armed popular struggle (in contrast to the pre-1967 passivity and contentment with radical declarations without substance): "The logical conclusion is that the Party is not only lacking in one aspect . . . but the Party has been lagging behind for a long time in all aspects and this was what made it unable to see the essential need for armed struggle and the importance

33. Michel Aflaq, *Niqtato al-Bidayah* [The Starting Point], 2nd ed. (Beirut: Arab Organization for Publications and Studies, 1971), p. 167.

34. Ibid., p. 118.

of the battle of Palestine. It was preoccupied with secondary matters, secondary in relation to the battle."[35]

During this period, Iraq deployed fifty thousand troops on the Jordanian and Syrian fronts with Israel, although the building up of the basic units of the Arab Liberation Front was slower than the pace indicated at the Tenth Party Conference. In June 1972, the Ba'ath government of Iraq proposed to sign a commitment with Syria and Egypt on a policy of continued confrontation with Israel.[36] In November 1972, Iraq became the first Arab state to make a direct link between the use of the oil weapon against Western Europe and the United States directly contingent on the latter's attitude to the Palestine question. The Saudis and Kuwaitis shied away from this overt linkage of their oil shipments with the most militant claims of the Palestinians.

Although it has become conventional to regard wars as benchmarks in the development of political trends in the Middle East, Ba'ath policy remained fundamentally unchanged in its basic assumption in the wake of the October 1973 War. The war caught the Iraqi government by surprise, and it moved quickly to nationalize the Basrah Petroleum Company, dispatch ground and air forces to Syria, and attempt to resolve differences with Iran in order to free its hand for participation in the Palestine struggle.[37]

Rejection of UN Resolution 242 and formation of the Arab Liberation Front, then, can be viewed as Ba'ath attempts to thwart an imperialist strategy aimed at fragmenting the unity of the Arab position vis-à-vis Israel while establishing the Palestine movement as the bridgehead of the Arab revolution. This may appear as mere leftist polemics, but the Ba'ath view of impending imperialist conspiracies has had a very real impact on policy. One major problem with American policies in the Middle East is the consistent failure of the U.S. State Department to consider opposing definitions of the situation. That American policies are identified as imperialist has been treated by the Western press as incomprehensible and mere polemics. But the relationship between Israeli aggression, Arab reactionaries, and American imperialism are very real to Arab minds, and not just the Ba'athists. As an ideology, however, Ba'athism has synthesized this relationship within an

35. Ibid., p. 100.

36. Ibid., pp. 201, 203.

37. Arab Ba'ath Socialist Party, *Report on the October War* (Baghdad: al-Thawra Publications, 1974), pp. 15–16.

analytic framework more consistently than any other Arab nationalist ideology:

> The struggle for the liberation of Palestine never was a nationalist struggle in the narrow sense. Rather, it is and will always be a national liberation struggle with a . . . content directed against international imperialism and local reactionary forces. Thus, recognition of the Israeli entity is not only a capitulation of a legitimate and natural right of the Arab nation. . . . It is also a great obstacle to the Arab struggle against imperialism and reaction, and an attempt to rob the struggle of its essence.[38]

Not only has this ideology served to analyze events *ex post facto* to confirm the consequences; more importantly, it has provided a framework for predicting events. Thus, in February 1973, the Ba'ath party official newspaper *al-Thawra* observed: "The region is now witnessing . . . secret and public activities . . . which prove that there are events of great importance [to the area] being cooked and events of great importance will be taken place."[39] Nine months later the 1973 Arab-Israeli war broke out, in effect confirming the Ba'athist view of impending conspiracies.

The 1973 war has been identified by the Ba'ath as a conspiracy on the one hand to force the Arab nations to accept settlement in terms of 1967 boundaries, with only minor withdrawals from lands occupied by Israel in 1967; and on the other, to break the growing coalescence of Arab views around the Palestine issue.[40]

The occupation of extensive Arab territory in the 1967 war had in effect shifted the issue from the question of Israel's existence to the question of Israel's boundaries. According to Ba'ath analysis this imperialist strategy of thereby gaining affirmation of Israel's existence had not anticipated the growth and viability of the Palestine liberation movement as a result of the 1967 war nor the intransigence of Israel in withdrawing from occupied Arab land. Hence, the necessity for imperialist strategy of the 1973 war which shifted the question from one of withdrawal to "how much" withdrawal. Israel's retention of occupied territory, then, became negotiable, further removing the issue

38. *Al-Thawra* (Baghdad), *Issues and Legitimate Questions,* p. 58.

39. From collected editorials of *al-Thawra* (Baghdad), in *al-Mintaqah . . Madha? . . Wa'ila Ayn?* . . . [The Area: Why? And Where is It Going?], 3rd tions] (Baghdad, 1973), p. 58.

40. Ibid., pp. 14–43.

from the original, and to the Ba'ath view, essential question of the right of Israel to exist at all within the heart of and at the expense of the Arabs. As the official organ of the Ba'ath party in Iraq assessed the relationship:

> An increase in the strength of the Arab struggle against Zionism is corollary to an escalation of the struggle against imperialism and the growing isolation of reactionaries. Any cessation of the struggle against Zionism, then, will negatively affect the struggle against imperialism and Arab reactionaries to their benefit. The Arab experience from June 1967 to October 1973 provide us with vivid lessons of this. . . . After June 1967, the American imperialist influence in the Arab nation was subjected to strong condemnation . . . which became the fertile base for the growth of the revolutionary progressive struggle. This struggle led to an awakening. . . . During the protracted war of 1970, the Arab liberation struggle against imperialism escalated and the role of the reactionary forces receded. The progressive Arab forces, particularly the Palestine resistance, gained impressive strongholds.[41]

From this view of the nature of the Arab-Israeli conflict and its relationship to Arab liberation, the Ba'ath policy of rejection of imposed settlement can be understood. At the outbreak of the 1973 war Iraq mobilized all its forces and sent them to Syria to fight in coordination with the Syrian army. Iraq boycotted the Algiers conference of November 1973 because of the Syrian and Egyptian decisions to negotiate with Israel by recognizing the UN ceasefire Resolutions 242 and 338 and agreeing to attend the Geneva talks on troop separation and disengagement.

Acceptance of the ceasefire and UN Security Council Resolutions 242 and 338 involve negotiations with the enemy and relinquishment of some Arab lands it had usurped. The Ba'ath also claimed that the compromising position of the Egyptians and Syrians jeopardized the morale of the Arab fighting forces.

To forestall the impending piecemeal settlements and consolidate the liberation movement, throughout 1974 and 1975, the Ba'ath leadership in Iraq undertook unification of the "Rejection Front" through continuous dialog and meetings with the four Palestinian organizations that rejected peaceful settlement and Libya and Algeria. The

---

41. *Al-Thawra, Qadaya wa Tasa'ulat Mashru'ah* [Issues and Legitimate Questions] (Baghdad, 1973), p. 58.

personal direction of this initiative by Iraq's Assistant General Secretary of the party, Regional Command, Saddam Hussein (vice chairman of the Revolutionary Command Council) emphasizes the importance the party has given to the issue.

In July 1975, the Secretary-General of the Arab Liberation Front called for the formation of an Arab front at the national governmental and public levels to oppose settlements and weld the Front with the Palestinian movement, as reported in the *Baghdad Observer* on July 23. The Arab Liberation Front opposed the scheme of setting up a state on the West Bank and in Gaza administered by the Palestine Liberation Organization, since this would be no more than a passport for the liquidation of the Palestine issue in a manner perpetuating the Zionist presence. He also urged greater cooperation among the leading Palestinian groups, among which he included the Arab Liberation Front.

The Ba'athist world-view is founded upon a conception of world order imposed by power relationships. Under the imperialist order, strong powers have consolidated and expanded their power by exploitation and division of nations. Only nationalist resurgence through revolution and unity can break the pattern of power relationships imposed by imperialism.

The emergence of a plethora of weak Arab states following the Second World War has further strengthened the stranglehold of imperialism on the area in the Ba'ath view, and has in effect affirmed the need for unity. Palestine is the ultimate symbol of both disunity and the aims of imperialism—obliteration of the Arab national identity. According to Michel Aflaq, "The road to unity passes through Palestine."[42]

The Ba'ath and Socialism

Among the nationalist (that is, non-Communist) Arab parties, the Ba'ath was the foremost in raising the banner of socialism. Ba'ath notions of socialism, however, have evolved from utopian, undefined teachings whose hallmark was their opposition to Marxism and communism, to Marxist-oriented formulations that borrow from the ideas of scientific socialism and assimilate them to the nationalist ideas of the old Ba'ath.

42. Aflaq, *The Ba'ath and Unity*, p. 10.

In Article four of the 1947 constitution (see Appendix A), the Ba'ath was defined as a socialist party believing that "socialism is a necessity," and that socialism constitutes, "the ideal social order." As to the means for the establishment of socialism, Article six of the same constitution, stipulates that "The Arab Ba'ath Socialist Party is a revolutionary party believing that its principal aims—resurrecting Arab nationalism and building Socialism—cannot be realised except by resolution and struggle, and that reliance on slow evolution and contement with superficial and partial reforms threaten these aims with failure and extinction."

The constitution does specify the economic plan of the party. Article 26 described the Ba'ath as a socialist party claiming that all the economic resources of the Arab nation should be owned by Arabs themselves. Article 27 declared that this economic wealth had been distributed unjustly; hence, it should be redistributed equally among the people. It followed in Article 28 that the exploitation of man by man was condemned, for all citizens are equal. The state manipulation of the means of production was also approved by virtue of Article 29. The aforementioned article clearly stated that the state should run cooperations of public interest, natural resources, factors of production, and the means of transportation.

Nevertheless, private property was not abolished, for Article 34 of the constitution considered it a natural protected right, but limited it in Articles 30, 31, and 33. According to these articles, private land ownership was limited to the ability of the owner to utilize the land efficiently without the exploitation of others. The state would supervise that and it would be carried out according to the general economic plan. Entrepreneurship was limited to the economic standard of the rest of the population. Ownership of real estate was open to all citizens, provided that they did not accumulate more than they could directly utilize and did not utilize it to exploit others. Thus, the state would enforce the minimum ownership of real estate.

With respect to social classes, the constitution in Article 42 considered the separation and differentiation among classes as "the consequence of a faulty social order." A more just and equitable social order, it was felt, would eradicate class differences.

The Ba'athist call for socialism was, until recently, invariably accompanied with an emphasis by the party that its teachings contradict those of communism and that it could even be characterized as an anti-Communist party. In its political statement the Third National

Conference (1959), in a section entitled "Position of the Party on Communism" had the following to say:

> The party has, since its founding, clearly defined its ideological position on communism and revealed the latter's errors and dangers to the Arab liberation movement. We will continue our intellectual ideological struggle against communist revisionism, elaborate the difference between the theoretical and practical premises of Arab liberation which we advance, from those advanced by the communist movement and explain how the movement for Arab liberation surpasses the shortcomings and limitations of communism.[43]

Michel Aflaq had written earlier that communism was a product of abstract eighteenth-century philosophy and that its practice in Russia seems to be the product of Russian spiritualism and scientific European thought. To him, communism had no semblance to any Arab intellectual traditions or to the past and present life of the Arabs.[44] The insistence of the Ba'ath on differentiating its socialism from Marxist scientific socialism has led to the coining of the term "Arab Socialism," not as a derivative of Marxism but as an opposing and contradictory ideology.

Despite its outward criticism of Marxism, the Ba'ath party was not content with its own brand of socialism. As early as 1960, the party circulated an internal memo which admitted to the general nature of the party's notions of socialism and to the lack, within party literature, of any specifications as to the means and stages for establishing a socialist order. This memo also criticized party doctrine for its vagueness on private property, means of production and the role of individuals, unions, popular institutions, and the state in social organization and economic development. The report submitted by the Ba'ath national leadership to the Fourth National Conference (1960) presents another illustration of the dissatisfaction with the party's position on socialism. Lamenting the negligence in party writings of the subjects of socialism and democracy, the report observed the hesitancy of socialists to join party ranks.[45]

Deliberations of the Sixth National Conference (1963) significantly enhanced the Ba'ath notion of socialism and subjected all past

43. *The Struggle of the Ba'ath Arab Socialist Party*, p. 57.
44. Aflaq, *For the Sake of the Ba'ath*, pp. 153, 158.
45. *The Struggle of the Ba'ath Arab Socialist Party*, pp. 64, 65, 108.

beliefs to critical re-evaluation. In *Some Theoretical Principles*, the conference explained the adoption of the slogan "Arab Socialism" as a negative and incomplete response to the challenge of local communism. It warned that such an attempt might lead to a nationalist chauvinism which rejects the universal intellectual heritage of socialist thought. Arab socialism, the conference added, has remained, on the whole, partial and without any scientific content. Assessing the impact of the party's distorted image of socialism, the conference pointed to the dominance in the party organization of bourgeois elements and the prevalence of the petit bourgeois mentality in party ranks. Middle-of-the-way practices govern party activities, the conference cautioned. A new conception of socialism was formulated by the Sixth National Conference, which also visualized the nature of the process of socialist transformation in the Arab world.

In the new formulation, socialism aims at the establishment of a new social order in which objective economic, social, intellectual, and political conditions are established that free the individual from all forms of exploitation, subjugation, and stagnation and allow him to become a completely free human being. The new socialist order will eradicate material exploitation, deepen the democratic content of socialism, and give the citizen a socialist and scientific education that frees him from the yoke of inherited backward social customs and traditions. Meanwhile, the process of socialist transformation will necessitate public ownership of the means of production, completely abolish the need for the capitalist middleman, make the income of the individual dependent on his labor and abilities, mold the various social classes into one class, and, finally, anul the profit economy and replace it with one based on need. Automation, the role of the small bourgeoisie, state capitalism, the changes of bureaucratization, land ownership, socialist planning, and the functions of an organized popular, revolutionary vanguard were among the many issues on which the conference voiced its opinions.[46] This new conception of socialism which the Sixth National Conference had approved was soon to be attacked by both rightist and leftist elements within the Ba'ath. The former discredited it as being extremist and the latter condemned it as being selective and not sufficiently radical.

In the area of actual policy, the Ba'ath, after assuming power in Syria and Iraq, conducted a series of unplanned nationalizations and reforms. These augmented the measures adopted by Gamal Abdul-

46. Ibid., pp. 205–11.

Nasser in Syria and Abd al-Karim Qasim in Iraq. The basic guidelines adopted by the Sixth National Conference, however, remain in need of elaboration into a concrete program.

As for Iraq, great changes have occurred in various facets of life since the Ba'ath assumed power in 1968. In 1974, a whole program was published whereby the stages of socialist development were defined, and the shortcomings of the government institutions were acknowledged.

What kind of changes did the new program bring about in Iraq? To what extent was the Ba'ath concept of socialism implemented?

Ba'ath socialist ideology could be summed up as opposition to class distinctions and a commitment to establish an equitable social order. Thus, armed with an ideology vague enough to be highly flexible in practice and a nationalist position militant enough to counter the popular disillusionment following the decisive defeat of the Arab-Israeli 1967 war, the Ba'ath came to power in Iraq by military coup d'etat on July 17, 1968. The internal problems they assumed were indeed grave. A Kurdish rebellion in the north was in progress; Shi'ite dissatisfaction in the south was polarized between a reactionary traditional leadership and popular radical movements; and the general disarray of the economy was compounded by the Syrian action in closing the pipeline which carried Iraqi oil (from December 1966 to March 1967), seriously affecting Iraq's balance of payments.

On July 30, 1967, the Revolutionary Council stated that the best way to achieve progress was through a revolutionary democratic regime. The regime announced it would carry on a policy of radical agrarian reform and creation of an oil policy through the National Petroleum Company. On the first anniversary of the revolution, President Ahmed Hasan el Bakir enunciated the following steps for completion of the socialization of Iraq: Strengthening the revolution by elimination of competition and external interference in Iraq; formation of trade unions, new levels of military preparedness, plus the use of a "people's militia"; increased economic progress through scientific planning and conservation of natural resources; increasing reform of land use, thus increasing cash flow to the peasantry; equal opportunity and the strengthening of the individual through ideology; and, finally, a solution to the Kurdish question.[47]

The party proceeded to implement the aforementioned policies as

47. Iraq, President's Speech, June 17, 1969 (Baghdad, Public Institution for Press and Printing, 1969), pp. 8–11, in Arabic.

quickly as possible. Political prisoners were freed and civil servants dismissed for political reasons under previous regimes were reinstated. In industry, however, grave difficulties existed. Contrary to the practices of previous regimes which generally abandoned projects of the deposed government, the Ba'ath's first task, it was decided, would be the conclusion of the current five-year plan (1964-69) and other industrial projects begun long ago but never completed—the glass factory of Ramadi and the textile factory in Hulla are examples. The percentages of completed projects during the first four years of the plan had been a lamentable 50 percent; by 1969 this figure had increased to 86 percent. In this period an annual growth rate of 6.8 percent in the GNP was achieved.

The result of this was a new five-year plan to conclude in 1974 which called for a series of projects, the most important of which were the use of modern techniques in production; the presence of a healthy equation of consumption; savings and reinvestment; finding an equilibrium between the needs of the populace and that of industry; finding and persuading the investment of capital in important projects while seeking skill, expertise, and other essential resources from friendly governments.[48] In order to administer this program the Ba'ath wished to establish a center for economic planning and programming. They also, it appears, hoped to establish a master plan of coordinated economic and social development. Unlike the central planning found in many Western socialist economies the Ba'ath hoped to have a guiding authority at the center, but multi-centrism for administration so that a form of regional autonomy would be achieved in the nation's economy. This is a basic difference between Ba'ath socialism and European Social Democracy or Marxism. Total expenditure for the plan was calculated to be 1,144 million dinars (one ID = $3.37)—the largest expenditure since the first five-year plan.

The Ba'ath did not plan to exclude private investment; in fact they encouraged it in such areas as the agricultural sector, transportation, services such as theaters, casinos, and restaurants. This is in keeping with the attitude of the party to private ownership as stated in their constitution of 1947. Still, private investment has set clear guidelines in the agricultural sector to prevent a renewal of "exploitation." It was allowed to loan farmers money for machinery, to set up services for pest control, and to strengthen trade and transportation in order to assist the marketing of goods.

48. *Al-Tatawur al-Iqtisadi fi al-'Iraq* [Economic Development in Iraq] (Baghdad: al-Thawrah Publications, 1972), pp. 53-54.

In the industrial sphere the government attempted to give incentives to increase investment capital through a tax exemption on machinery and expensive equipment. Also, an Industrial Bank was established to assist in financing very costly projects. These measures and the great increases in demand of Iraqi oil have dramatically increased the national wealth of Iraq. Whereas in 1969 the GNP stood at 896 million dinars, by 1972 it had reached 1,218 million dinars; estimates for 1974 are 2,550 million dinars which would translate into a 185 percent increase in the GNP since the beginning of the last five-year plan.

Individual income has increased from 100 dinars per capita in 1969 to an estimated 236 dinars per capita at the end of 1974.

In the agricultural sector growth averaging 15.5 percent per year was realized in the period 1969–72. Growth in this sector, however, continues to be hampered by a lack of adequate irrigation facilities and soil exhaustion.

In the industrial sector growth was also pronounced, the average increase for the period 1969–74 being 14 percent per year. The labor force employed in manufacturing has risen to 3.2 million by 1974 compared with only 2.5 million in 1969. The high prices Iraq receives for its petroleum products has done much to bring about this state of affairs. Western nations concerned with a balance of payments problem have been able to sell entire plants to the Iraqi government. Examples are an Italian company which has contracted to build a tire and rubber plant for 11 million dinars and a French company which is proceeding with construction of an iron and steel complex, the first stage alone of which will cost 40.5 million dinars.

Agricultural reform was one of the chief pillars of the Ba'ath's economic ideology, and upon their assumption of power reform in this sector was speedily undertaken. The Iraqi government is of the opinion that the most effective method for increasing production in the agricultural sector would be to collectivize and thereby pool the technical and material resources of the farmers, permitting them in this way to take on management of their production themselves. The Ba'ath hope that by pooling resources on certain collective farms to turn them into showcases of development for the more conservative small farmers who would then be encouraged to collectivize. This is being done because the party feels individual production will only continue to deteriorate as the small farmer cannot hope to benefit from financial loans and increased mechanization. With this in mind the government formulated a new plan for rural reform which was mainly concerned with the expansion of the collectivist system. *Al-Thawrah* (Baghdad) reported on August 29, 1969, that new cooperative organizations would be established to coordinate all areas of agriculture, production, marketing, and transportation.

In 1974–75 investment programs, the Ministry of Agriculture and Agrarian Reform stressed coordination between the General Federation of Agricultural Societies and the General Federation of Agricultural Cooperatives in order to mobilize the forces of the peasants, direct them in carrying out programs, and coordinate agricultural and industrial output with the Ministries of Irrigation, Industry, and Economy. The ministry's plan concentrated on modern techniques for following a suitable agricultural cycle, for expanding mechanization, and for using improved seeds, chemical fertilizers, and other services, as *al-Thawrah* reported on August 27, 1973.

The new marketing system attempts to provide stable prices to both producer and consumer by paying a high price to the producer and subsidizing the price to the consumer through oil revenue. The question of land distribution is also associated with marketing procedures in that the larger a farm invariably the more profitable it shows itself to be. The Minister of Agriculture stated that land for individual farmers would be confined to areas where large cooperatives would not work. *Al-Thawrah* reported that the government had no plans to expropriate the land of these small farmers; it merely hoped to encourage them to form cooperatives. In the northern part of Iraq, however, the government has moved to establish state farms. The nagging problem of migration to the cities the government hopes to solve by making agriculture more profitable and at the same time more attractive through creation of what it terms "ideal rural communities." By 1973 the policy of agrarian reform seemed to be proceeding but at a slow rate considering the number of people and amount of land involved. In October 1973, an official of the Ministry of Agriculture related to the author that by February 1973 his ministry had reported only fifty-six collective farms in operation and only twelve hundred cooperative societies. Resistance among traditionally conservative farmers seems to be high indeed.

The 1976–80 Plan announced in January 1973 allocated $10 billion for agricultural development. Dr. Hasan Fammi Jum'a, Minister of Agriculture and Agrarian Reform, revealed that the new plan will concentrate on "expanding agriculture both vertically and horizontally for

certain products and regions in orders to meet Iraq's demand for foodstuffs and the requirements of the industrial and export sectors."[49]

The main features of the plan are:

—Production of large quantities of foodstuffs, including rice, meat,
fruits, and animal fodder.
—Implementation of irrigation and drainage systems for an area of
1,250,000 dunums of agricultural land.
—Leaching and cultivation of 1,250,000 dunums of reclaimed land.
—Surveying of 12,900,000 dunums of agricultural land.
—Building of 96 experimental stations for research and six soil labs, and
training of 5,000 technicians.
—Raising the water storage capacity by 25 percent.
—Construction of 450 new agricultural cooperatives in the areas covered
by the agrarian reform and 335 new cooperatives in the areas outside
the agrarian reform.
—Increasing the areas of state farms to a million dunums.
—Raising total cultivable land to 17 million dunums by 1980.

The Ba'ath's main concern, of course, is to socialize the state and
improve the lot of the citizens, and since 1968 an intensive program
has been aimed at carrying out this program to increase the quantity
and quality of social services. According to government statistics ex-
penditures on medical services have increased 40 percent since 1968.
The ratio of doctors to population has improved from 1:4,200 to 1:3,200
(in 1972). Seventy percent of the population is now covered by free
health-care services. The number of beds in hospitals also increased
from 12,300 beds in 1968 to 20,322 in 1973. The number of medical
assistants had increased by 57.8 percent by 1972.

In education the increases have not been as dramatic. Expendi-
tures increased only 10 million dinars between 1967 and 1970. The
number of students at the elementary level have increased from 990
thousand pupils in 1967 to 1,110 thousand in 1970. The number of students at the university level increased from 30,000 in 1967 to 38,000 in
1970. The students attending technical schools increased from 10,000
in 1967 to about 12,000 in 1972.

Before the Ba'ath took over, 96 percent of the villages in Iraq did
not have clean drinking water supplied to homes. Hence, the Iraqi
government planned a huge project that will cost more than $80 mil-

49. *Middle East Economic Survey* 18 (13) (January 17, 1975): 1.

lion to provide drinking water to most villages. However, this project will take many years to complete. For the near future, the government has allocated 28 million dinars to be spent on similar minor projects. These minor projects will cover 90 percent of the needs of the cities and suburbs and only 5 percent of village needs.

The Iraqi government admits that its progress is fueled mainly by Iraq's vast oil reserves and production. Before Law No. 80 of 1961 which deprived the oil companies of 90 percent of their concession areas, Iraq received very little indeed of the old revenues generated by her diminishing natural resources. The Ba'ath sought to change this state of affairs and did so in accordance with their new platform at the Sixth Party Congress. The companies were progressively nationalized, and by June 1, 1969, the process was complete. In spite of local ownership, distribution is still in the hands of the companies rather than the Iraqi National Oil Company which now has all oil rights in Iraq.

In light of its nationalist bent it is hardly surprising that the foreign relations of the Ba'ath have taken on a decidedly anti-Western look. The foreign relations of Iraq prior to 1968 were motivated mainly by much anti-Zionist, anti-Western rhetoric but quite little action. Once an Iraqi armored division was dispatched to aid Jordan but it did not arrive in time to be of any use.

◆◀ 3 ▶◆

AL-HIZB AL-TAQADDUMI AL-ISHTIRAKI
(The Progressive Socialist Party)

THE effectiveness of the Progressive Socialist Party in the political life of Lebanon is highly dependent on the personality of its unchallenged founder and leader, Kamal Jumblat.[1] The popularity of Jumblat derives not only from personal qualities but also from the enjoyment of a communal power base whose leadership he inherited. A leading feudalist family, the Jumblats have exercised deep influence on the Druze religious community for centuries. Not surprisingly, therefore, the decision to treat the Progressive Socialist Party as a leftist political organization may be contested by many. We have chosen to treat it thus for several reasons. First, the party professes to be socialist, and in practice has aligned itself in Lebanese politics with other socialist and communist parties. Second, refusal to consider the Progressive Socialist Party as leftist is usually based on an absolute criterion that does not take into consideration results from the socio-economic environment of political parties. Third, decisions made not to include the Progressive Socialist Party among the leftist organizations of the Arab world do not take into sufficient consideration the anomalies and peculiarities of Lebanon's political processes and structures. The programs, organizations, and leadership of the Progressive Socialist Party are strikingly leftist when contrasted with such other Lebanese parties as the Phalangists, Najjadah, National Bloc, Constitutional Bloc, and National Liberals. Finally, recent changes in the ideology and organization of the party have helped to make the party more distinctly leftist.

1. In the Arabic language the name is written *Junblat* but pronounced in colloquial *Jumblat*. The latter spelling will be used in this book.

This was exemplified during the political crises in the summers of 1973 and 1975 when Jumblat represented the demands of the left, consulting continuously throughout the crises with leaders of the independent socialist parties, the Ba'athists, and the Communists. All leftist groups rallied around Jumblat's leadership, and he accepted the role with acumen.

The Progressive Socialist Party was formed in 1948. Ever since, it has operated openly, has participated in parliamentary life, and has been actively engaged in the power game. It is viewed as the only leftist force to make inroads on the establishment.

No valid figures as to the number of members in the Progressive Socialist Party exist. Such matters are considered a party secret. Most likely card-carrying members do not exceed a few hundred. It would be a mistake, however, to judge the Progressive Socialist Party's effectiveness and popularity by such a criterion.[2] As mentioned earlier, the leader of the party commands a wide communal power base, consisting of the Druze peasants of the Shuf, Metn, and West Beqa' areas. These are natural supporters of Jumblat and, hence, the party. This sector is augmented by some of the Shuf's Maronite peasantry, which traditionally supported the Jumblati cause in the Jumblati-Yazbaky feudal right. An additional segment of the population, cutting across religious lines and of middle class and peasant backgrounds, cherishes the causes upheld by the Progressive Socialist Party and could be motivated to action by the party. Finally, the party enjoys popularity among that portion of Lebanon's intelligentsia which is alienated from the system and advocates change, yet is not sufficiently radical to join the Pan-Arab revolutionary movements or the Communist Party.

The dominant features of the Progressive Socialist Party's ideology are its eclecticism and reformism. With respect to the former, the party draws on the thoughts of Gandhi and the heritage of old Indian philosophies, as well as on the thoughts of Rousseau, Carlyle, Marx, Middle East sophists, and Jamal Abdul-Nasser. This assorted mixture of currents, divergent and at times conflicting, has imprinted itself on

2. This figure represents the author's conviction and has been arrived at following many informal discussions with members of the Progressive Socialist Party. In 1959, the Progressive Socialist Party claimed 6,800 members. If the number is accurate, it is due, in all probability, to the soaring popularity of Jumblat among the dissidents of the 1958 civil war. It is extremely doubtful that the party had been able to maintain such members after tensions had eased. See Toufic Mokdessi and Lucien Georg, al-Ahzab al-siyasiyah fi Lubnan [Political Parties in Lebanon] (Beirut: L'Orient, n.d.), p. 14.

the party's teachings and course of action.[3] Being responsible for a high
degree of intellectual confusion, this eclecticism has led to the withdrawal from the Progressive Socialist Party of several noted personalities such as Abdullah al'Allayli, George Hanna, Albert Adeeb, and
others.[4]

In its social conception of man, the Progressive Socialist Party is
influenced by elitist principles. It emphasizes the need for a vanguard
that would lead the process of social change and stresses the role of
the leader.[5] In the areas of human cooperation, participation, and the
economy, the party advocates the Marxist line and calls for a system
of distribution based on need and labor. In international relations, the
party, reflecting the influence of Abdul-Nasser, calls for a policy of
nonalignment with either of the two world blocs. Following the June
1967 War, and again under the influence of Nasserism, the party advocated a policy of close cooperation and friendship between Arab
countries and those of the socialist bloc that would act as a deterrent
to Israel and counter pro-Israeli policies of Western countries.

As to its reformism, the party voices and defends the demands of
Lebanese leftist groups and political organizations, and constantly re-
minds government of the need to conduct reforms in the civil service,
legislation, public life in general, and the realization of labor union demands. The party has warned that unless such measures are taken, the
regime and system stand in peril. Within this general policy line, the
Progressive Socialists have been instrumental in the recurrent crises
leading to the disestablishment of some power groups and the coming
to power of others. With other groups and political personalities, they
succeeded in 1952 in overturning the regime of Bishara al-Khuri and
the election of Camille Shamoun to the presidency. In 1958, the party
was a leading force in the armed rebellion against the regime of
Shamoun, and actively supported the regime of Fuad Shihab. During

3. For a leftist critique of the party's ideology and the thoughts of its leader see
'Afif Farraj, *Drasat Yasariyah fi al-fikr al-yamini* [Leftist Studies in Rightist
Thought] (Beirut: Dar al-Tali 'ah, 1970), pp. 39–72.

4. In a newspaper interview, Jumblat was asked why most of those who played
a notable role in founding the party have deserted its ranks. Despite the many
reasons given by the interview it seems that opposition to the high-handed practices of the leader himself was chiefly responsible for this situation. For the text
of the interview see *al-Jaridah* (Beirut), March 1, 1970.

5. Addressing itself to its student members, a Party leaflet stated: "We regard
ourselves as the vanguard of all the aware, responsible elements in our society . . .
and our role will be one of vanguard leadership," ibid.

the regime of Shihab's successor, Charles Helou, the party assumed the role of the opposition again, successfully blocked the election to the presidency of a Shihab nominee, Elias Sarkis, and cast the votes responsible for the seating of Suleiman Franjieh. The Progressive Socialist Party accurately described its role in Lebanese society as that of an intellectual, social, and political pressure group.[6]

In recent years, the Progressive Socialist Party has been increasingly attracted to Marxist ideology and to the Soviet experiment in socialist construction. The shift in party alliances reveals this new influence. It has led to close working relations with the Lebanese Communist Party, to a spirited defense of Arab-Soviet friendship and to advocacy of Arab-Eastern bloc alliances. The impact of scientific socialism is seen in the many recent statements of Jumblat and in the writings of the other leading members of the party. In a lecture given at the Arab Cultural Club, Khaleel Ahmad Khaleel explained the party's policy in the following manner: "The party adopts a dynamic, experimental and progressive political philosophy. Progressiveness means an open and active movement that renews personal, group and national abilities and converts them into effective forces. Socialism is the assertion of the quality of progressiveness in the complete liberation of man and the masses from all forces aimed at the exploitation of resources and potentialities of a people."[7]

The Progressive Socialist Party remains the only leftist party in Lebanon that has been able to seat some of its members in Parliament. Its ultimate objective has been defined as the assumption of power in order to initiate basic changes in the socio-economic and political structures of the country. Jumblat put it in the following words, carried in the July 29–August 5, 1971, issue of Assayad (Beirut): "If our party comes to power, we will immediately realize our plans. We have our specific notions of the state and its social function, political freedoms, duties and responsibilities, popular representation, governing, etc. We also have an organizational framework ready for immediate implementation."

As to the means for coming to power, through pacific and legally prescribed ways or through violence, in 1971 the Progressive Socialist Party favored the former course but did not rule out the latter. If

6. From a statement issued by the party on the occasion of its Seventeenth Anniversary, quoted in Progressive Socialist Party, Mawaqif wa 'Afkar [Positions and Opinions], May 1, 1965, pp. 7–8.

7. Arab Cultural Club, al-Qiwa al-siyasiyah fi Lubnan [Political Forces in Lebanon] (Beirut: Dar al-Tali-ah, 1970), pp. 64–65.

peaceful methods do not work, Jumblat asserted, then the party methods might then include the resort to violence.

THE PROGRESSIVE SOCIALIST PARTY AND ARAB UNITY

Of Lebanon's leftist and nationalist political parties, the Progressive Socialist Party is perhaps the one that shows least concern with the question of unity. In its ideology and political work, the emphasis is on Lebanon and the features distinguishing it from its environment. There are few writings in the literature of the party on the subject and all such writings make continuous reference to an Arab but independent Lebanon, in solidarity with sisterly Arab countries.[8]

A spokesman explained the party's attitude to Arab nationalism in the following manner: There is an Arab nationalism but no Lebanese nationalism. The Lebanese, however, have their own objective conditions and they would like to preserve their political independence in order to develop their internal unity. Arab nationalism needs yet to rid itself of some ethnocentric attributes and be endowed with a secular spirit. Its relevance depends on its ability to perform the function of aggregating the popular forces of the Arab world in their struggle against underdevelopment and imperialism.[9]

The linking of unity to national development betrays, again, the influence of Nasserism. To Jumblat, Nasser's leadership was historic because it merged the two objectives: unity and socialism. As he stated in *al-Anba'* (Beirut), October 9, 1971: "Nationalism's basic objectives of unifying citizens and destroying the psychological boundaries and barriers among them cannot be attained unless it adopts socialism, with

8. Among the reasons given by some of the early founders of the party for their desertion of party ranks was the existence in the Progressive Socialist Party "of a lukewarm or noncommittal attitude" concerning Pan-Arabism. See Michael W. Suleiman, *Political Parties in Lebanon* (Ithaca, N.Y.: Cornell University Press, 1967), p. 215. In an effort to become more appealing to Pan-Arabists, in and outside of Lebanon, the Progressive Socialist Party seems to be taking a more sympathetic view of Arab unity. In what seems to be a new move, the party issued a leaflet calling for a decentralized and federated union among Arab countries that would include Lebanon. See Progressive Socialist Party, *Ra'y al-Hizb fi al-qawmiyah al-'Arabiyah wa al-wihdah* [The Party Opinion Regarding Arab Nationalism and Unity] (Beirut, n.d.).

9. Arab Cultural Club, *Political Forces in Lebanon*, pp. 65–66.

its basic objectives of equating citizens and melting their differences in the bond of social unity."

THE PROGRESSIVE SOCIALIST PARTY AND THE PALESTINIAN PROBLEM

Like most other leftist groups in the Arab World, the Progressive Socialist Party considers the Palestinian question as the foremost concern of the Arabs. A solution to this question, it asserts, would release potentialities for Arab freedom, development and a common struggle. This solution, however, cannot be based on lines similar to those proposed by West European and American powers: namely, financial compensation for the refugees and their resettlement in the Arab World. Neither can it be a return to the 1948 UN partition resolution, which some Arab countries accepted and Western powers refused to implement. The acceptable solution would have to allow the repatriation of the Palestinians and the restoration to Palestine of its Arab identity.[10] Unlike other leftist groups, however, the Progressive Socialist Party does not seem to believe that a people's war of liberation, or guerrilla warfare, is the means to attain such a solution. The Palestinian resistance movement, which employs guerrilla tactics, performs a different function. It raises Arab morale, helps to quench the irrationality, tribalism and sophistry in Arab actions, allows the masses to gain better knowledge of the Palestinian cause and finally, encourages in the Arab personality such traits as courage, daring, discipline, sacrifice and consistency. Arab armies must still be relied upon to impose the required solution.

THE PROGRESSIVE SOCIALIST PARTY AND SOCIALISM

The Progressive Socialist Party seems to lack a uniform notion of socialism and a program defining the ways and means necessary for its successful application to Lebanon. The eclecticism of the party's ideology is perhaps the factor responsible for this. A trend in the attitudes of the party's leader, Jamal Jumblat, toward Marxism is evident. He has

10. Progressive Socialist Party, *Positions and Opinions*, pp. 15 and 59–60.

moved from a position of caution, criticism, and advocacy of a "Lebanese" or "Arab" brand of socialism to one of greater acceptance of
Marxism and the assertion that there is only one socialism—scientific
socialism.

In its literature the party advocates public ownership of the means
of production, nationalization of all institutions that play an important
role in the economic, social, and political life of the country, and centralized planning. To popularize the party's notions of socialism the
following political slogans were employed: Ownership is a social function and not an individual right; socialism cannot be accomplished unless the idea of work for gain is replaced by the idea of a classless and
non-feudal society; victory to the peasants, workers, and intellectuals;
there can be no national unity under the banner of factionalism, political confessionalism, and capitalist monopoly; all citizens should be
owners.[11]

In the socialist order visualized by the Progressive Socialist Party,
three types of ownership exist. The first consists of small holdings,
privately owned, such as houses, small parcels of land, and shops. The
second, which is collective cooperative ownership, will extend to all
middle sectors of agriculture and industry. In this type of ownership,
the state is a partial owner and provides guidance. The third and final
type of ownership is public ownership. To Jumblat, private property
must be tolerated since it answers some of man's basic needs. Human
nature has both altruistic and selfish aspects, the former encouraging
public ownership and the latter demanding, for its satisfaction, the
private ownership of property.[12]

By 1971, Jumblat denied that there could exist a "Lebanese socialism." He referred to a socialist experiment in Lebanon and asserted
that the distinction between a Marxist and a non-Marxist socialism is
fictitious. Socialism is one, and it consists of the means for the realization of public ownership of the means of production in society.

How would the Progressive Socialist Party go about creating a
socialist order in Lebanon if it assumes power? The first step, Jumblat
explains, is to found a council that will coordinate economic relations
with other Arab countries, especially with Syria, Jordan and Iraq.
Lebanon would also become a member of the Arab Common Market,
and other Arab countries would be encouraged to establish industries
in its territory. Arab citizens would be free to work in Lebanon in ex-

11. Ibid., pp. 66–67.
12. Al-Nahar Economic Supplement, July 25, 1971.

change for a similar freedom for the Lebanese. Domestically, industry will be forced to disperse into the country in order to offset its present concentration around Beirut. Model cities would be constructed, and in order to instill a unified social spirit the student youth would be required to spend one day a week in factories and farms. In the agricultural sector, private and cooperative holdings would coexist and any unused land would be reclaimed by society. The public sectors in the economy would, however, be expanded and would dominate the private sector.[13]

Jumblat's elusive style of writing makes it difficult to establish exactly his conception of socialism. The nearest to a definition that we found, when surveying his writings, occurs in a lecture he delivered in September 1964 at a local party meeting. In it he listed six principles which, he argued, form the *sine qua non* of all socialisms:[14]

(1) Planning.
(2) Level of production based on need, not profit.
(3) Public or communal ownership of the means of production and financial institutions.
(4) Income based on the amount of labor.
(5) Distribution of goods to consumers dependent, in the first stage of socialism, on merit, and in the second, on need.
(6) All forms of social securities (e.g., housing, education, health, unemployment, old age pensions) provided.

The founding of a society adhering to the above six principles is the professed aim of the Progressive Socialists. Jumblat believes that they are the cure for Lebanon's perennial social problems, which he enumerates as follows:[15]

(1) Inherited factionalism characteristic of the Lebanese village and city.
(2) The foreign intruders who came to settle in Lebanon and were granted Lebanese citizenship but whose integration into society is not likely.
(3) The influence of the Moslem brotherhood and other calls for Mos-

13. Ibid. See also his interview in *Assayad* (Beirut) July 29–August 5, 1971, and *al-Muharrir* (Beirut), September 20, 1971.

14. Kamal Jumblat, *Thawrah fi 'alam al-'Insan* [A Revolution in the Life of Man] (Beirut: Dar Sadir, 1967), pp. 27–30.

15. Ibid., pp. 120–23.

lem solidarity which, in Lebanon, have invoked an opposing confessional attitude among Christians.

(4) The emergency regulations effective in half of the country which have impeded the political and administrative unification of the people.

(5) The adoption of the principle of confessional representation at all levels of the state.

CONCLUSION

The leftist nature of the Progressive Socialist Party has been challenged on two accounts: ideological ambiguity and the strong dependency on a leader who, within the party organization, enjoys vast powers. Both accusations are valid and are rather self-evident. Yet the Progressive Socialist Party merits consideration as a leftist political party due to the following: it upholds socialist doctrines, has allied itself for the past decade with leftist organizations, sponsors platforms that appeal primarily to workers and peasants, and is the only effective Lebanese party to become the spokesman of dissent and opposition to establishment politics. Furthermore, the Progressive Socialist Party seems to be increasingly aware of the two drawbacks cited above. With respect to ideology, it has begun doctrinal training courses for its members and has recently established a party research institute specializing in socialist studies.[16] In the twenty-second annual convention of the Progressive Socialist Party in 1971, the party leader, in his annual message, reported that the policy of the party now is "to broaden the base of representation in the General Assembly in order that a larger number of workers, peasants and students should participate, so that the leftist nature of the party would be decisively rooted."[17] As to the monopolization of power by the party leader, he has gradually, albeit slowly, been delegating authority. In 1962 and 1963, the party amended its constitution so that its General Assembly and Management Council

16. This research institute is already in operation and has put out its first publication. See Khalil Ahmad Khalil, *Qadaya al-Fallahin wa al-'Ummal al-zira'iyin fi Lubnan* [The Problems of Peasants and Farm Workers in Lebanon] (Beirut: Progressive Socialist Party Center for Socialist Studies, 1971).

17. The complete text of Kamal Jumblat's report to the 22nd Annual Convention of the Progressive Socialist Party appears in the party newspaper, *al-Anba'* (Beirut), No. 1013, November 16, 1971, p. 13.

might enjoy larger powers.[18] In the 1971 party convention, other reforms were introduced and authority was delegated further. Despite this, it would be fair to say that the party has yet to prove itself as an entity independent of the personality of its founder.

18. See Suleiman, *Political Parties in Lebanon*, p. 216.

❖❮ 4 ❯❖

HARKAT AL-QAWMIYIN AL-'ARAB
(The Arab Nationalist Movement)

HISTORICAL BACKGROUND

THE Arab Nationalist Movement[1] constitutes a phenomenon that merits the attention of the political, social, and ideological analyst, because the history of the movement reveals the transformation of a nationalist non-socialist organization into several leftist offshoots that have all adopted the Marxist-Leninist ideology. The most important among these offshoots are (1) Munazzamat al-ishtirakiyin al-Lubnaniyin (the Organization of Lebanese Socialists)—OLS; (2) Hizb al-'amal al-ishtiraki al-' Arabi (the Arab Socialist Action Party)—ASAP; (3) al-Jabhah al-Sha'biyah li-tahrir Filastin (the Popular Front for the Liberation of Palestine)—PFLP; (4) al-Jabhah al-Sha'biyah al-dimuqratiyah li-tahrir

---

1. The history of the Arab Nationalist Movement, as it might be expected, has been the victim of the cold war between the two major wings that emerged after June 1967. The confusion as well as the different stories about the history of the movement necessitated two fact-finding trips to the Middle East by the author. The following few pages present the author's version of the history of the movement as he managed to gather it from his own independent research. Those interested in the two major contradictory stories of the two wings should consult the following sources: The Organization of Lebanese Socialists, with an introduction by Muhsin Ibrahim, *Limadha Munazzamat al-ishtirakiyin al-Lubnaniyin? Harakat al-qawmiyin al-'Arab min al-Fashiyah ila Nasiriyah* [Why the Organization of Lebanese Socialists? The Arab Nationalist Movement from Fascism to Nasserism] (Beirut: Dar al-Tali'ah, 1970). Referred to hereafter as *Why the OLS?* Also see, Popular Front for the Liberation of Palestine, *al-Jabhah wa qadiyat al-inshiqaq* [The Front and the Secession Question] (Beirut: Lajnat al-'I'lam al-markaziyah, 1970).

Filastin (the Popular Democratic Front for the Liberation of Palestine) —PDFLP; (5) al-Jabhah al-Sha'biyah al-thawriyah li-tahrir Filastin (the Revolutionary Popular Front for the Liberation of Palestine)— RPFLP.

These offshoots are by no means the only ones. More than ten factions have been enumerated by Ilyas Murqus, and all were either ex-members or branches of the Movement.[2]

Stage I: The Rightist Orientation in the Fifties

The Arab Nationalist Movement first appeared at the American University of Beirut in the early fifties as a current of disillusionment with the Arab situation in general and Arab political parties in particular. Informal groups known as the Young Arab Nationalists (al-Shabab al-Qawmi al-Arabi) and the Arab Nationalists (al-Qawmiun al-Arab) organized themselves into the Arab Nationalist Movement in 1954. Dr. George Habash established a weekly paper, al-Raay, in Amman, Jordan, which functioned as the new movement's organ. (Within months of its opening, the paper was forced by Jordanian authorities to close because of its outspoken positions, but it reopened in Damascus). Composed primarily of students and professors drawn from all over the Arab world, the new movement was affected by Western trends in political thought. In consequence, the movement was not only anti-communist, but it also lacked the social reformist tendencies that characterized nationalist trends at that time.[3] During the fifties the movement emphasized national unity rather than class struggle. Its anti-colonialist position lacked clarity and was void of theoretical content. Moreover, the movement's program at that time was characterized by a vague, romantic advocacy of Arab unity that was envisaged to follow the German pattern of national unity. Finally, the movement took an anti-Communist stance that rejected any attempt at alliance with the "secessionist communists."[4] In consequence, the movement ap-

2. Ilyas Murqus, *Afawiyat al-nazariyah fi al-'amal al-fida'i* [The Spontaneity of Theory in the Commando Action] (Beirut: Dar al-Haqiqah, August 1970), pp. 12–13.

3. *Why the OLS?* p. 17.

4. For a detailed and expressive picture about this consult the following: *al-Hakam Darwazah, al-shuyu'iyah al-mahalliyah wa ma'rakat al-'Arab al-qawmiyah* [Local Communism and the Arab National Battle] (Beirut: Maktabat Munay-

pealed mainly to elements of the prosperous bourgeoisie and to those from more or less aristocratic origins. As it failed to attract the masses, it remained very small. Up till 1960, for example, because of both the movement's lines of policy and the attitude of UAR authorities (as was pointed out earlier), the movement could not claim more than tens of members in Syria. Until 1958 the size of membership was no better in Iraq. In Beirut, however, the movement managed to spread among the Islamic community, on the one hand, and the students of the American University (in particular), on the other. The commercial bourgeoisie elements who were out of sympathy with the obsolete tribal structure in Kuwait constituted a spring from which the movement drew some members. The Jordanian-Palestinian branch of the movement was mainly dominated by non-radical upper bourgeois elements. Despite the contention of the later splinters that the movement was nothing but the backward right wing of the then national movement,[5] it must be realized that the movement at that time was, in relative terms, a faction of the radical wing of Arab nationalism.

Stage II: Petty Bourgeoisie Orientations in the Sixties

During the second stage in the development of the Arab Nationalist Movement major changes in the Arab world took place, which, in turn, resulted in many conflicts, debates, and splinters within the various political parties. In this regard, the basic change was the reformist trend that the UAR regime demonstrated by its 1961 nationalization laws as well as by its National Charter which gave a more progressive cast to the 1952 military movement. The close relationship between the Arab Nationalist Movement and UAR authorities at that time exposed the movement to the influences of Nasser and his regime. Furthermore the movement lacked political philosophers who could establish it on a theoretical basis. Without an established theory, each member in effect participated in the development of a political phiolosphy through group discussion and study. The result was that members of

---

manah, 1963), 3rd ed. Also see the Arab Nationalist Movement's Branch in Iraq, 'Ayyuha al-shuyu'iyun: Ayna imanukum bil-Ittihad al-Fidrali [You Communists: Where is Your Faith in the Federal Union] (Baghdad: n.p., 1959), pp. 3–24; also see the Arab Nationalist Movement, al-'Iraq wa 'a'da' al-wihdah [Iraq and the Enemies]; see also Why the OLS?, pp. 17–21.

5. Why the OLS? pp. 23–25, 45.

the Arab Nationalist Movement familiarized themselves with a variety of political philosophies in seeking to define their own, and the level of political sophistication within the movement grew rapidly. Because of Nasser's clashes with Britain and the United States, the movement took an anti-imperialist position which led ultimately to anti-Westernism.

The experiences of the Arab Nationalist Movement in the sixties were then both concomitant with and highly influenced by those of the UAR. The outcome manifested itself in a closer identification with Nasserism to the degree of demanding organizational ties with the Nasserist movement, particularly after the emergence in Egypt of the Arab Socialist Union (ASU) on December 2, 1962.[6] After 1962, however, two trends within the movement began to emerge, one led by Muhsin Ibrahim, Mohammad Kishly, and Nayif Hawatmeh and the other led by Dr. George Habash, Dr. Basil al-Kubaisi, Hani al-Hindi, Dr. Ahmad al-Khatib and Dr. Wadi Hadad. While both trends were pro-Nasserist (in the belief that Nasserism at that time represented the most progressive sector of Arab nationalism), the two groups differed on the future of their own movement. Dr. Habash's group was not enthusiastic about the idea of dissolving the movement into the wider and stronger, but completely unorganized, Nasserist tide which dominated the political scene at that time. The Ibrahim wing, which considered itself more leftist, advocated gradual assimilation of the movement into the Nasserist tide. One analyst considered that the first rift in the Arab Nationalist Movement appeared in the 1962 Party National conference and described it as follows:

> The 1962 conference witnessed the first clear split between two factions within the movement's central command cadre. The progressive faction aspired to impart to the movement a nationalist, revolutionary, socialist, petit bourgeois horizon, and aspired to undertake the progressive political program of the Arab liberation movement, embodied by the Nasserist formula. Consequently, this faction sought to change the movement's traditional class and ideological structure and transform it into a progressive petit bourgeois group. This progressive

6. The best manifestation on this can be seen through publications like these: Muhsin Ibrahim, *Fi al-Demuqratiyah wa, al-Thawrah wa al-Tanzim al-Shabi* [On Democracy, Revolution and Populist Organization] (Beirut: Dar El-Fajr El-Jadid, 1962). Also, ———, *Munaqashat hawla Nazariyat al-Amal al-Arabi al-Thawri* [Discussions on the Theory of Arab Revolutionary Action] (Beirut: Dar al-fajr al-jadid, 1963). Finally, consult the Organization of Lebanese Socialists' *Why the OLS?*, p. 46.

faction contains a number of leadership elements, including Nayif Hawatmeh, Muhsin Ibrahim, and Mohammad Kishly.

The right-wing faction represented the established traditional leadership and was tied to ideas of the Fascist origin and the movement's original right-wing political program. The most prominent elements of this faction included Dr. George Habash, Hani al-Hindi, Ahmad al-Khatib, and Dr. Wadi Hadad.

The conference was a wrestling arena for those two factions. However, with the progressive faction bowing to traditions and bureaucratically united Fascist organizational relations at the head of the movement, the conference wound up with a behind-the-scenes agreement on theoretical and joint political stands that were submitted in an internal report that, of course, did not give the members a real picture of the discussions that took place or the stands and opinions that were adopted and voiced by both factions. It was content to submit to the movement's organizations and all its branches the drafting of the unified results in which the conference ended. Those unified results were really nothing but an abortion of the issues raised by the progressive faction in criticising the Fascist concept of the movement and its right-wing political program.

Thus the 1962 conference failed to effect any real change within the movement because the right-wing faction representing the established leadership imposed its inherent reservations on the petit bourgeois, socialist, revolutionary, nationalist line and rejected any radical criticism of the Fascist ideological horizon and the right-wing political program of the movement. It was generally agreed that the conference was only to inject the trends coming out of the 'fifties with a few verbalizations of socialist thinking.[7]

The two national conferences of the movement between 1963 and 1965 witnessed heated debates which widened the rift between the two wings and resulted in the adoption of what was condemned later as a petty bourgeois program, similar to Nasserism. The national conference of 1965 completed the semi-merger of the movement with Nasserism. Muhsin Ibrahim's wing admitted later that

the "socialist ideas" which [his wing] advocated in the National Conference of 1965 and which were, in turn, adopted by the Conference, were eclectic, idealistic, and petit-bourgeoisie ideas which imagined that socialism could be built through 'peaceful class' [relations] and

7. Amin Saba'i, "The Arab Nationalist Movement Originated in the Universities," *al-Jaridah* (Beirut), March 15, 1970, p. 4.

without the leadership of the working class. . . . In consequence the Movement's attempt ended by adopting a political and organizational strategy that believed that the path of the Socialist revolution in the Arab world passes through a blue print of the Egyptian political organization, namely, the alliance of the forces of the working people.[8]

In consequence, the movement's branches in both Iraq and Syria dissolved themselves and joined the nascent and almost nonexistent Arab Socialist Union. The same policy was implemented by the branch in Egypt. The branch in Southern Yemen froze its membership in the Union and opted to work independently.

In Lebanon, where there was no "Arab Socialist Union," the developments of the movement's branch took a different direction. The branch demanded a premature merger with the Lebanese Communist Party which had been, since 1964, on good terms with the UAR regime. The Communists, however, rejected the offer because of the major differences between their Marxist-Leninist ideology and the movement's Nasserist ideology. These efforts, nevertheless, ended in establishing "the Front of National and Progressive Parties, Institutions and Personalities in Lebanon." This included the Arab Nationalist Movement, the Lebanese Communist Party, the Progressive Socialist Party of Kamal Jumblat, and a number of progressive political personalities in Lebanon. Under the strains of the severe differences among its constituting partners, the front collapsed after the 1967 defeat.

The years 1965–67 proved that the attempted incorporation of the movement with the Nasserist forces was not only premature but also unfeasible. The various clashes with the "Nasserist" governmental agencies led the movement at first to justify its decision by laying the blame at the doors of some rightist Nasserist agencies which were accused of blocking the way of fruitful cooperation and incorporation with the UAR regime. Later, the movement (particularly Ibrahim's wing) went back to the original independence-maintaining stance of Dr. Habash, though with one difference: the earlier excessive enthusiasm of Ibrahim's group for incorporation of the movement into the Nasserist tide resulted in alienating that group from Nasserism. In consequence, the movement regained the independence of its organizations in Iraq and Syria and advocated special cooperation with Nasser, but not the "rightist Nasserites" and the UAR bureaucratic agencies.[9]

8. *Why the OLS?*, p. 56.

9. Nayif Hawatmeh, *Azmat al-Thawrah fi junub al-Yaman* [The Crisis of the Revolution in the Southern Yemen] (Beirut: Dar al-Tali'ah, June 1968), pp. 40–52;

In 1966, however, the group of Muhsin Ibrahim published some articles in *al-Hurriyah* (then the movement's official organ) that proved to be markedly antagonistic to UAR authorities. This year also witnessed the beginning of an increasing deterioration in the relations between Nasserism on the one hand and the Arab Nationalist Movement on the other.

Stage III: A Marxist Movement After June 1967

The third stage in the life of the Arab Nationalist Movement is characterized by the rapid political, ideological, and organizational transformation of the movement. The first manifestation of these transformations showed itself immediately after June 1967 when Muhsin Ibrahim wrote his now famous article: "No: Nasser Did Not Make a Mistake Nor Were the Arabs Defeated." Ibrahim's attempt at restricting the 1967 defeat to a military one aroused outraged reactions among the members of his group who considered the article as "the incarnation of the ultimate bankruptcy of the [socialist] eclectic thought which had nothing to give but artificial encouragements based on emotional stubbornness and sedative demagogic stands."[10] Later, in 1969, this wing declared its adoption of Marxism-Leninism after it was convinced that the petty bourgeoisie had abandoned all of its progressive roles and consequently become a counterrevolutionary force that was stifling the struggle and aspirations of the masses. The Palestinian organizational manifestation of this political and ideological metamorphosis resulted in the breaking off of a "leftist" group to form the Popular Front for the Liberation of Palestine, which was the armed wing of the Arab Nationalist Movement after June 1967. The other Lebanese organizational manifestation was the establishment of the Mundhmat al-Ishtrakieen al-Lubnanieen ("Organization of Lebanese Socialists") under the leadership of Muhsin Ibrahim and Mohammed Kishly. The Palestinian "leftist" splinter (the Popular Democratic Front) came under the leadership of Nayif Hawatmeh. These splinter groups astonished the other members in the Arab Nationalist Movement's leadership by

also see Organizational Committee for the National Front, *Kayfa nafhamu tajribat al-Yaman al-janubiyah al-sha'biyah* [How Do We Understand the Experience of the People's Republic of Southern Yemen] (Beirut: Dar al-Tali'ah, April 1969), pp. 52–70; finally see Muhsin Ibrahim's Introduction to *Why the OLS?*, p. 77.

10. *Why the OLS?*, p. 80. Also see Amin Sibai, "The Arab Nationalist Movement Originated in the Universities," *al-Jaridah* (Beirut), March 15, 1970, p. 4.

labeling the latter rightist and by viewing themselves leftist. In this regard, it is very difficult for an outside analyst to understand the mutual and confusing accusations and counter-accusations between the two wings. Both groups now claim to adhere to Marxism-Leninism; while Ibrahim's group calls the others "rightists" we find the group led by Dr. Habash accusing the splinters of being "opportunist leftists." Though the author does not want to take sides in this war of words, it must be mentioned that the many interviews he conducted with many former leaders of the Arab Nationalist Movement during 1970–71 in Beirut convinced him that Muhsin Ibrahim's group either made a deliberate attempt to distort fact or had unfortunately allowed themselves to be carried far away from facts while trying to justify their break away from the movement. In brief, it is very difficult to accept the "evidences" that allowed Ibrahim's group to claim exclusively the credit for the transformations mentioned above. The credit or, perhaps, the blame for that rather hasty transformation should go to the more powerful circumstances that emerged after June 1967.

Stage IV: The Organization of Communist Action in Lebanon and the Arab Socialist Action Party

The Organization of Lebanese Socialists spent the first year of its life working in two directions—first, to attack the Lebanese Communist Party and claim that the organization itself is the rightful party of the working class; and second, to intensify its relations with another former Ba'athist leftist group (Lebanon the Socialist) to pave the ground for future merger with the latter. The first trend resulted in widening the gap with the Lebanese Communist Party, which waged its own counter campaign against the organization and accused it of leftist adventurism.[11] The organization's effort on the second level, however, resulted in its gradual merger with "Lebanon the Socialist" (Lubnan al-Ishtraki) and the consequent establishment of the "Organization of Communist Action in Lebanon" in May 1971, as noted in al-Hurriyah (Beirut), July 5, 1971. Finally, as reported in al-Muharrir (Beirut), October 7, 1971, factions appeared within the new organization, one led by Mohammed Kishly, and the other by both Muhsin Ibrahim and Fawaz Tarabulsi.

11. See Anonymous, al-Yasar al-haqiqi wa al-Yasar al-mughamir [The True Left and the Adventurous Left] (Beirut: Dar al-Farabi, 1970).

On the other hand, the group of Dr. Habash, who managed to maintain the loyalty of the majority of the members of the Arab Nationalist Movement, had undergone major ideological, political, and organizational transformations. This group adopted Marxism-Leninism and announced the establishment of the "Arab Socialist Action Party" (Hizb al-'Amal al-Ishtraki al-Arabi), a party that was to shoulder the responsibility of transforming "the petty bourgeoisie party [The Arab Nationalist Movement] into a proletarian Marxist-Leninist one."[12] This party however, differed from the other wing led by Muhsin Ibrahim in its position vis-à-vis the Arab Communist parties. While Ibrahim's group consider themselves *the* true Communist party, the Arab Socialist Action Party led by Dr. Habash, view themselves as an ally of the Arab Communist parties and categorically deny any intention to replace these parties.[13]

Though Habash's group was very critical of the mistakes and shortcomings of the Arab Nationalist Movement, it nevertheless refused to accept the analysis of the splinter-group, which totally discredits the movement.[14]

In brief, the Arab Nationalist Movement *per se* is now defunct. Neither of the two wings was willing to keep the original name ("Arab Nationalist Movement") of the organization, which had given birth to the most of the neo-leftist parties and groups in the Arab East.

THE ARAB NATIONALIST MOVEMENT AND ITS SPLINTERS vis-à-vis ARAB UNITY

A critical analysis of the Arab Nationalist Movement's stance *vis-à-vis* Arab unity was first given by the Organization of Lebanese Socialists in 1970. This first splinter of the movement maintains that

> The movement had practiced a pro-unity policy that was romantic and foggy. [This policy] was characterized by severe verbal persistence [in advocating] unity. Such an attitude manifested itself in slogans like "Unity regardless of the Price," or "Unity Comes First and Last" and/

12. *Tariq al-thawrah* (Beirut) 2 (April 1971): 80.

13. Ibrahim, introduction, *Why the OLS?*, p. 73. *Tariq al-thawrah* (Beirut) 2 (April 1971): 81.

14. Popular Front for the Liberation of Palestine, *al-Jabhah wa qadiyat al-inshiqaq* [The Front and the Issue of Secession], p. 107.

or "Unity is the Path to Liberation and the Key to all Problems Confronting the Arab Society." This made the movement unable to see the Unity slogan in its proper historical context. It stripped the slogan of all progressive class contents. . . . Moreover the Jordanian Branch of the Movement proved incapable of taking immediate measures against the Hashemite Union [in 1958]. Instead, it slipped into supporting it with the conviction that every step toward unity, regardless of its political and class contents, is necessarily a step forward. . . . Again, when the movement declared its full support of the establishment of the United Arab Republic, it failed to see its petty-bourgeois contents.[15]

The other major splinter of the Arab Nationalist Movement introduced a more or less similar analysis. In the words of the Arab Socialist Action Party: "in its formative years, the Arab Nationalist Movement uesd to carry on activities in accordance with its idealistic contention that the unity of the Arab nation can follow the Italian and German patterns . . . in which . . . the national bourgeoisie acted as the instrument of achieving [that unity]."[16]

These criticisms, however, are not only too generalized but also unfair. For as early as 1964, and under the influence of Nasser's own evaluation of the UAR experience, the Arab Nationalist Movement adjusted its earlier romantic attitudes by becoming aware of the socialist dimensions of any political union. Muhsin Ibrahim, the contemporary philosopher of the movement, wrote: "the answer to the [Arab unity] question lies in socialism and in having the socialist forces assume the responsibility of achieving unity. . . . This opens the door wide for the achievement of Arab unity."[17]

Finally, the June 1967 defeat and the leftist orientations of all the offshoots of the Arab Nationalist Movement drastically changed the tone of these offshoots vis-à-vis Arab unity. Attention to social and class problems dominated their publications; consequently their concern about Arab unity ranked second in importance. A clear example in

15. Why the OLS?, pp. 20–21.

16. Tariq al-thawrah 2 (April 1971): 64. For a vivid picture of the stance of the Arab Nationalist Movement vis-à-vis Arab unity the reader is advised to consult the primary sources of the movement in this regard. These are: Arab Nationalist Movement, al-wihdah: thawratun wa mas'uliyah [Unity: A Revolution and Responsibility] (February 1959), pp. 3–70. Also, the Arab Nationalist Movement's Branch in Iraq, al-wihdah tariquna [Unity is Our Path] (October 1958), pp. 3–45.

17. Muhsin Ibrahim, "On the Unity of the Arab Socialist Movement," al-Thaqafah al-Arabiyah 6 and 7 (October 1964): 20–21.

point is the various attitudes of the several offshoots of the Arab Nationalist Movement in regard to the four-sided union declared between Egypt, Libya, Syria, and the Sudan in 1971. All factions took similar passive attitudes toward the newly declared union. The Arab Socialist Action Party, for example, declared in *Tariq al-thawrah* (Beirut), No. 2:

> Any scientific and objective glance at the union . . . is bound to assert the disharmony of this union with the interests as well as the aspirations of the masses. In consequence, the [union] constitutes a step backward because it sustains the important rightist institutions in the area. . . . The justification for the establishment of the union is negated by the fact that its actual function came to be negotiating a truce with the enemies rather than mobilizing the Arab forces to fight Israel, inperialism and [Arab] reaction. [The union] came to be a device to end the state of war [with the enemies], to suppress the leftist forces of the Arab national liberation movement in general, and to liquidate the [Palestinian] resistance movement in particular. . . . The union increases the circle of terrorization and suppression of the masses and represents an alliance of impotent petty-bourgeois [regimes] that are kneeling at the thresholds of reaction, imperialism, and Zionism. (pp. 129–30)

THE ARAB NATIONALIST MOVEMENT AND THE PALESTINIAN QUESTION

The leftist transformation of some sectors of the Arab Nationalist Movement[18] introduced major changes in the movement's position *vis-à-vis* the Palestinian question. The early positions of the movement did not escape criticisms from its former members and leaders. The Organization of Lebanese Socialists, for example, leveled basic criticisms that could be summarized in the following manner:

1. In the Arab-Israeli conflict the Arab Nationalist Movement failed to understand the dialectical relations between Zionism and capitalist imperialist interests and their implication in the Arab world.

18. The early stance of the Arab Nationalist Movement *vis-à-vis* the Arab-Israeli conflict was portrayed in Hani al-Hindi and Muhsin Ibrahim, *Isra'il fikrah, harakah, dawlah* [Israel: An Idea, a Movement and a State] (Beirut: Dar el-Fajr al-Jadid, 1958).

2. The movement failed to discriminate between Jews on the one hand and Zionists on the other. The movement used to believe that "every Jew is a Zionist" without realizing that some progressive Jews may become relentless enemies of Zionism.

3. The movement insisted that there are basic differences (or contradicitions) between the Zionist movement on the one hand and the imperialist capitalist camp on the other. In consequence, the movement differentiated between Zionism and world imperialism.

4. The movement, moreover, occasionally emphasized that the Arab struggle against Israel is exclusively national and has no class bases.[19]

The 1967 defeat, once again, brought about major changes in the stances of the leftist organizations that were once parts of the Arab Nationalist Movement. The Popular Front for the Liberation of Palestine, which was originally the Palestinian aspect of the Arab National Movement, introduced a well-defined position as far as Israel is concerned. The new stand, as shown below, stems from a Marxist-Leninist analysis of the Zionist state. In the words of the Popular Front for the Liberation of Palestine:

Thus, in our battle with Israel, we are facing not the State of Israel alone, but an Israel whose structure is founded on the strength of the Zionist movement. . . . [However] it must be pointed out that the enemy facing us and represented by Israel and Zionism is naturally governed by a number of conflicts both inside Israel, as in any other society, and between Israel and the world Zionist movement. . . . Now, does our perspective of the enemy stop at this limit? Is this the picture of "all the enemy" we are facing? . . . In the battle for the liberation of Palestine, we are facing a third force, that of world imperialism led by the United States of America. . . .

Here imperialism finds itself in the best position in this part of the world, because through Israel it is able to fight the Arab revolutionary movement which aims at eliminating it from our homeland, with Israel becoming the force and the base used by imperialism to protect its presence and defend its interests in our land. Such a situation creates an organic unity between Israel and the Zionist movement on the one hand and world imperialism on the other, because they are both interested in fighting the Palestinian and Arab national liberation movement. [Once more] is this "all the enemy" facing us? There is a fourth force which substantially stands on the side of the enemy camp and which we must view and define clearly. [This fourth force is Arab

19. *Why the OLS?*, pp. 19–20.

reactionary forces]. . . . Arab reaction cannot but be on the side of
its own interests, the continuation of which depends on the persistence
of imperialism.[20]

The other major offshoot of the Arab Nationalist Movement maintains almost the same position. In the words of the Popular Democratic
Front for the Liberation of Palestine which is, as mentioned earlier, the
Palestinian manifestation of the "leftist" splinters from the Arab Nationalist Movement:

> Israel represents the spearhead and base for neo- and traditional im-
> perialism in the Arab countries and the Middle East. Israel is supported
> by imperialism, which gives it the freedom—according to imperialist
> plans—to participate in quelling the national liberation movement which
> threatens the interests of imperialism in the Arab world. . . . Israel
> represents a dynamic society which has expansionist aims in the area
> in addition to Palestine. As a society it is superior to the underde-
> veloped Arab countries in the educational and technical fields. This
> makes its expansionist policy easier. The relationship between Israel
> and American imperialism necessitates the amalgamation of the na-
> tional Palestinian and Arab liberation movements. In addition, Palestine
> is a part of the Arab world and its future is related to that of the Arab
> countries.[21]

In brief, none of the offshoots of the Arab Nationalist Movement adhere any longer to the old analysis of the Arab-Israeli conflict. The
early apologetic approach has been dispensed with, and the relationships among Israel, Zionism, imperialism, and Arab reactionary regimes
and elites are vividly portrayed. This, according to the New Arab Left,
rendered a fatal blow to a long process of self-deception on the part of
the Arab revolutionary movement which has always tried to minimize
the number and strength of its enemies by indoctrinating its members
with illusions.

20. Popular Front for the Liberation of Palestine Information Department, *A
Strategy for the Liberation of Palestine* (Amman: Information Department, 1969),
pp. 9–14.
21. Democratic Popular Front for the Liberation of Palestine, *The August Program and a Democratic Solution* (np., n.d.), pp. 160–61. See Appendix D for
complete text.

THE ARAB NATIONALIST MOVEMENT AND SOCIALISM

Throughout the fifties one cannot find any commitment to either socialism or socialist transformation in the movement's documents and literature. In fact, during the first ten years of the movement's life the relationship of such solutions to the Arab problems was never examined
by the movement's leadership. Instead, the available documents attest
to the fact that the movement was not only anti-Communist but also
anti-socialist.[22]

It was not until the beginning of the sixties that socialist ideas
began penetrating the movement. As mentioned earlier, this occurred
as a direct consequence of the influences of Nasser and Nasserism on
the movement. In discussing the socialist transformation of the movement, Dr. Habash's Arab Socialist Action Party stated, in *Tariq al-
thawrah* (Beirut), No. 2, 1971:

> The Arab Nationalist Movement has been exposed to influences from
> both the continuous movement of the masses and the influences coming
> from . . . the Communist parties. . . . The Arab Nationalist Move-
> ment was ignorant as far as Marxist-Leninist theory is concerned. Any-
> thing the Movement knew [about that theory] was taken from sources
> that were against it. . . . It was not until 1967 that the Movement de-
> clared its adherence to the ideology of the working class.

The early sixties, however, were the years during which the Arab
Nationalist Movement showed an impressive drive toward acquiring
socialistic orientation and thought. Such developments are best reflected in one of the lectures given by Muhsin Ibrahim on behalf of
the movement, in Beirut, in mid-1964. The basic themes introduced in
that lecture are the following:

1. The bourgeoisie is completely incapable of achieving the national democratic revolution in the developing countries. The alliance
of this class with feudalism and neo-imperialism sets limits on its ability to achieve economic development, agricultural reform, and industrialization. This is why the Arab Nationalist Movement maintained
this tripartite alliance should be demolished by revolutionary means.

22. For a better appreciation of this attitude consult al-Hakam Darwazah and
Hamid al-Juburi, *Ma'a al-Qawmiyah al-Arabiyah* [With Arab Nationalism] (Cairo,
1959), 3rd ed. Also al-Hakam Darwazah, *Local Communism and the Arab National Battle*.

2. The very poor classes are the only classes qualified to shoulder the responsibility of implementing the national democratic revolution. It is imperative, therefore, that these classes find their way to power through an alliance with the middle class.

3. The latter alliance is entitled and expected not only to achieve the national democratic revolution but also to pave the ground for socialist transformation.

4. Finally, the leading national movement itself should experience a concomitant transformation that will make it a revolutionary socialist movement. Such leadership can then lead the society onto the path of "the permanent revolution."[23]

When Muhsin Ibrahim's wing of the movement finally adopted Marxism-Leninism, it made a new analysis of the economic-social situation in Lebanon at a provincial conference in 1968. The analysis reads:

> Workers, poor peasants and the petty-bourgeois masses in the city and the countryside (including the revolutionary and democratic intellectuals) constitute the base of the class national alliance that is capable of . . . confronting the ancient regime over which the commercial banking class dominates. . . . This alliance referred to, however, is nothing now but a theoretical hypothesis. The working class, which is still weak, unpoliticized, and unorganized in a real syndicate movement, together with the peasantry, which is . . . still subjugated to the domination of political, confessional, and tribal feudalism is like the (bribed) petty-bourgeois class in need of more suffering to become conscious of their . . . class interests.[24]

Finally, the other major wing of the movement, led by Habash, utilized the newly adopted Marxist-Leninist analysis and advanced its own formula for the socialist transformation in the Arab world. According to the Arab Socialist Action Party's publication, *Tariq al-thawrah* (Beirut), No. 2, 1970:

> The working class is the most revolutionary class in Arab society. It is the class that is historically qualified to lead the Arab poor and populist masses. Its revolutionary Marxist-Leninist party is the party equipped to mark out the path of revolutionary struggle for the masses and lead

23. Ibrahim, "On the Unity of the Arab Socialist Movement," pp. 11–13.

24. *Why the OLS?*, Ibid. pp. 109–10. Also see M. Kishly, *Hawla al-nizam al-ra'smali wa al-yasar fi Lubnan* [On the Capitalist System of the Left in Lebanon], pp. 77, 95.

its class struggle to achieve the Arab national democratic revolution in the Arab countries that have not witnessed this revolution. [On the other hand] the party will direct the struggle in the other countries . . . where the petty-bourgeoisie leadership has proved unable to fulfill that revolution. . . . [All this] is a prerequisite for the socialist revolution . . . which we have not experienced yet and which is the first stage in building the communist structure.

THE ARAB NATIONALIST MOVEMENT IN PERSPECTIVE

In conclusion, the Arab Nationalist Movement, which emerged from a cultural-political pressure group, managed to transform itself in the late fifties and early sixties into a party that, in one way or another, represented one wing of the more general modern Arab nationalist movement. Contrary to many evaluations, the movement has not yet sunk into political oblivion and history. The *manifest* disintegration of the *original* movement did not put an end to the existence of this political force. The end of an *era* in a movement's life should not be confused with the end of the movement. The life of the Arab Nationalist Movement has been a *chain* of continuous transformations. While it is admitted that the post–June 1967 changes have been drastic ones, they are basically an integral part of a series of transformations through which the original movement has been going for the last twenty-five years. One of the offshoots of the movement constitutes the ruling group in the Republic of Southern Yemen. Another former Arab nationalist branch is busy waging a liberation war in Dhufar. A third branch constitutes the major opposition group in the Kuwait parliament in particular and the whole political system in Kuwait in general. A fourth and a fifth offshoot of the movement compose the leftist wing of the Palestinian Resistance Movement. Finally, other offshoots represent important sectors of the opposition groups in many Arab countries in general, and in Lebanon in particular. In brief, the final judgment about the Arab Nationalist Movement depends on the future of its offshoots, and this particular future cannot be determined for some time.

NASSERISM

O<small>NCE</small> Nasserism began to crystallize as a distinctive current among Arab masses, to propose and translate into action slogans that had been highly popular among these people, to challenge European imperial powers, and to conduct fundamental changes in society and the economy, it commenced to deeply influence the thought and even the structure of national and leftist Arab parties. The sources of this influence are complex.

Nasserism is a combination of practices, measures, and thoughts initiated through military coup by a group of young nationalist officers in the Egyptian army on the morning of July 23, 1952. The officer group, under the leadership of Lieutenant Colonel Jamal Abdul-Nasser, formed a secret organization within the Egyptian army that was known as the Free Officers. At the outset, it seemed that these officers had been driven to revolt by specific concerns; corruption and nepotism within army ranks and the scandals caused by the profiteering in transactions that supplied the army with unfit weaponry were thought to be the reasons that led to the creation of this movement. Soon after the military takeover, however, it became clear that the new leadership was motivated by much wider concerns. The slogans adopted by the Revolutionary Council and the purging of the old political cadre gave the movement a populist character. In its early stage, the movement set as its objectives the realization of the following six principles:

1. The destruction of imperialism and its stooges among Egyptian traitors.

2. The ending of feudalism.

3. The ending of monopoly and of the domination of capital over government.

Jacqueline Ismael, a doctoral candidate in the Department of Sociology at the University of Alberta, Edmonton, Alberta, Canada, is the author of this chapter.

78

4. Establishment of social justice.
5. Founding of a strong national army.
6. Establishment of a sound democratic life.

Even in their rudimentary form, these six principles revealed that the movement organized and led by the Free Officers had significantly altered the power structure of government and the social system. The system that existed under King Farouk—representing an alliance of feudalism, bourgeois mercantilism, and symbol of imperialism—had been qualitatively transformed. Seeking to implement their declared principles, the new leadership secured the withdrawal of British troops from Egypt, decreed on September 9, 1952, laws for agricultural reform, and undertook successive measures to curb monopolies and further the country's industrialization. The new leadership also attempted to organize and direct local capital, though with little articulate notion, theoretical or practical, as to the role required of the local bourgeoisie. When the latter, however, sought to envelop the movement, a series of measures and nationalizations were adopted in 1961 that dealt a heavy blow to large local capital and resulted in the founding of the public domain, consisting of state-run financial, industrial, and commercial enterprises. This action signaled the transformation of the national revolution into a social one. It is essential to remember that the change was not the result of calculated policies of social engineering, but the product of a long process of experimenting. The 1962 UAR Charter stated:

> The revolutionary vanguard that was responsible for the events of the eve of July 23rd was still not ready to assume the responsibility of the revolutionary change which it had prepared for.
> It opened the gate before the Revolution under the banner of the famous six principles, but these principles were only banners for the Revolution and not a technique for revolutionary action or a method to follow for the radical change.
> Things were exceedingly difficult especially in the context of the vast and far-reaching changes in the world.
> But, in its role as instructor, the Egyptian people, the creator of civilization, taught their vanguard the secrets of their great hopes and aspirations. They set in motion the six principles by means of trial and error towards a clearer vision and understanding, by which the planning of the new and aspired-to society could be made.[1]

1. *The Charter*, submitted by Jamal Abdul-Nasser on May 21, 1962, to the National Congress of Popular Forces (Cairo: Information Department), p. 32.

The passage above points clearly to the experimental nature of the
"July movement," and to the fact that the various measures adopted
by the new leadership were responses to the needs of development, or
measures aimed at safeguarding the revolution from the possible reaction of elements whose interests had been threatened. Working by trial
and error, and hampered by theoretical ambiguity and inability to
draw clear distinctions between friends and enemies, the leadership of
the July movement, nevertheless, managed to steer a general national
and anti-imperialist course. And it was able to realize significant accomplishments. As previously mentioned, these accomplishments
formed the basis of what later came to be known as "Nasserism," and
they allowed the flowering of a political movement that left a deep
national revolutionary impact on the Arab masses and on other Arab
political organizations.

The most pronounced effect of the July movement on the Arab
world was its ability through the leadership of Jamal Abdul-Nasser to
show by its actions the complementary nature in the Arab revolutionary movement of its national and social facets. Destroying the feudal
monarchical rule of Farouk, ridding Egypt of British colonialism, in-
stituting programs for agricultural reform, liberating the Suez Canal
from international monopolies, ending foreign control of Egyptian
banks and companies, nationalizing interests of large national capitalists, founding the public sector in the economy and public ownership
of the major means of production, and, finally, undertaking a large
movement for industrialization and the building of the Aswan Dam—
these were accomplishments that had profound impact on the consciousness, attitudes, and behavior of the Egyptian as well as the larger
Arab masses.

In the Arab world outside Egypt national liberation movements
concerned solely with liberation from foreign economic or political
control and the termination of military pacts with foreign powers were
inspired by Nasser's example to set social objectives for their movements. Thus, republican Iraq arose with the concomitant destruction
of the Baghdad pact and the adoption of extensive socialist measures;
Syria undertook an extensive nationalization program; the Sudan,
Libya, and South Yemen rid themselves of foreign occupation and reactionary regimes. A few of these countries launched policies that carried them far on the road to social progress. The new trend gave the
movement for Arab unity its present contours, not only as the aspiration of a people to realize its national unity, but also as one inextricably linked to questions of social liberation, progress, and socialism.

Nasser's thoughts and actions also affected Arab perceptions of the international scene. Nasser was able to discern the close relationship between the movement for Arab liberation and other national liberation movements of the Third World. Following the 1955 Bandung Conference, he assumed a leading role in Third World affairs and established links of communication between Egypt and socialist bloc countries. As a result, he was able to break the monopoly enjoyed by Western countries as the sole suppliers of arms to the Middle East, to obtain arms from the Soviet Union, to obtain long-term financial loans for the financing of heavy industry, to sign an agreement with the Soviet Union for building the Aswan Dam, to equip the Egyptian army with modern weaponry, and to enlist support for Egypt in its struggle against imperialism and Zionism.

This series of international and domestic accomplishments was responsible for Nasser's popularity with the Arab masses. Utilizing their support, Nasser was able, in turn, to popularize notions that the Arab masses had formerly viewed with caution and even hostility. Among these notions was that of socialism. Many Arab circles, influenced by tradition and religious sentiment, considered socialism to be a doctrine anti-religious and hostile to Arabism. Nasser, adopting the term "socialism," imparted several meanings to it. These meanings were at first ambiguous, then contradictory, but finally clear and forceful. Throughout, his manner of explaining the concept made it very popular among the Arab masses.

Nasserism, though it succeeded in becoming a popular and massive trend, failed to express itself in an organizational framework. Instead of creating an exclusive and unifying political party organization, Nasserism remains a conglomerate of institutions, hostile to political parties and to party life. This has been the most serious drawback in the thought and practice of Nasserism. Though Nasser was widely acclaimed as the most popular leader in the Arab world, his high-handed style prevented him from trusting mass-line organizations. This attitude was perhaps responsible for the continuous upheaval in the political organization that Nasser hoped to establish in Egypt and the Arab world. The political organization initiated by the Liberation Rally was soon disbanded and replaced by the National Union, which was replaced in turn by the Union of Active Popular Forces. It was not long before the latter organization was replaced by the Arab Socialist Union. Though the Arab Socialist Union remains the only officially acknowledged political party in Egypt, this union itself has been disbanded and reorganized several times. The basic changes introduced into the structure of this organization have failed to salvage it from its state of paralysis.

Endemic in these successive political organizations was the lack of party base initiative. Artificially imposed from above, these organizations have failed to strike any roots in society. Not surprisingly, therefore, it was this condition that led Jamal al-Atasi, Secretary-General of the Syrian Arab Socialist Union, to assess Nasserism after the death of Nasser in the following manner in the September 30, 1971, issue of the Lebanese daily *al-Nahar*:

> The masses are in constant need of a vanguard that would lead its struggle, and of a leadership more conscious and better disciplined than itself. The major drawback in Nasserism and in the practices of Abdul-Nasser was that he did not organize this vanguard into a revolutionary party, though he looked forward to doing that. Abdul-Nasser presented us with a formula for national unity . . . he called for a vanguard political organization . . . he called for a unified Arab liberation movement, but he did not march us far along on that road.
>
> It is for this reason that bewilderment, deep feelings of emptiness, and unfruitful attempts to continue the search of Abdul-Nasser remain with us even after the death of Abdul-Nasser.

Appealing to broad masses whose class origin and intellectual beliefs differ and are even, at times, contradictory, the Nasserites have fragmented, after Nasser, into a multiplicity of groups, collectivities, and organizations. These units often work at odds with each other under the wide banner of Nasserism. A review of the condition of Nasserite forces in some of the Arab countries helps illustrate the point.

After Nasser's death, a struggle for power in Egypt exploded among Nasser's closest associates who, in his lifetime, had been the deputies of Nasserite policy. The outcome of this struggle was decided when Anwar al-Sadat, the present President of the Arab Republic of Egypt, arrested his most prominent colleagues, including Ali Sabri, Shaw'rawi Jom'ah, Sami Sharaf, Muhammad Fawzi, and Muhammad Fa'iq. Sadat accused them of conspiracy against the state and his person. He disbanded the Arab Socialist Union and reorganized it along different lines.

In Syria, alongside the Nasserite Syrian Arab Socialist Union led by Jamal al-Atasi, exists an underground Nasserite political party known as the Revolutionary Action Party. This party, with branches in Lebanon and Iraq, is led by Ilyas Murqus and Yaseen al-Hafiz, among others. A few Nasserite groups formed from former Ba'athist members also exist.

In Lebanon there are a large number of Nasserite political organizations, among them the Union of Active Popular Forces, the Forces for Nasserite Action and the Nasserite Ideologues.[2] These groups often exchange verbal attacks and some of them have accused Anwar al-Sadat of being a "rightist revisionary" who is destroying the accomplishments of Jamal Abdul-Nasser. Others owe allegiance to the person of Anwar al-Sadat and conceive of him as the legitimate successor of Nasser. Still others remain loyal to Sami Sharaf, Ali Sabri, and their associates.

In an interview with the Lebanese daily *al-Nahar*, on September 30, 1971, Jamal al-Atasi, has described this state of affairs in the following manner: "In its existing frameworks, i.e., the forces and formation that are labeled as Nasserite, and especially in the Arab East, the Nasserite movement is subjected to conflicting cross currents and is ideologically divided among the right, left and center. It is affected by provincialist currents, despite the professed revolutionary and nationalist objectives; and by currents whose primary and fundamental feature is the transcending of provincialism."

It would seem from the various statements of Jamal al-Atasi carried in *al-Nahar* that the Arab Socialist Union in Syria now adds a new phenomenon to Nasserism. Following the death of Nasser, this political party publicly announced that it would not blindly adhere to Cairo's leadership; it criticized some of the policies pursued by Sadat and called for the further development of Nasserism. It emphasized the need for self-dependency and encouraged its membership to submit their own interpretation of Nasserism. To the Arab Socialist Union in Syria "not everyone who raises the banner of obedience to Abdul-Nasser or to the Egyptian regime is a Nasserite. The true Nasserite is the one with the proper conception of the historical experience of Abdul-Nasser's movement and the one inspired by it."

One other Nasserite organization, the Revolutionary Action Party,

2. Five Nasserite organizations in Lebanon—the Union of Nasirite Forces, the Organization of the Unity of the Nasirite Struggle, the Nasirite Socialist Union, the Nasirite Youth of al-Biqa', and the Unity of the Arab Struggle—announced the unification of their commands and their popular organizational cadres within a unitary Nasirite organization under the name of the Arab Socialist Union in January 1974. This was announced through the unified organization's paper, *al-Muharrir* (Beirut), January 28, 1974. Ten months later, however, the organization fragmented again, according to *al-Nahar* (Beirut), October 21, 1974.

shares some of the features displayed by the Arab Socialist Union in Syria. Through the writings of Ilyas Murqus and Yaseen al-Hafiz this party seeks to highlight the Marxist dimensions of Nasserism and to base its theoretical formulations on the premise that the thoughts and actions of Abdul-Nasser are of a Marxist nature. The party issues an underground paper called *al-Thawrah al-'Arabiyah* [The Arab Revolution], which criticizes Sadat's regime, condemning it as rightist. In its fifth issue, for instance, dated June 15, 1971, the paper had the following headline: "The attack against Nasserism in Egypt constitutes a strategic recession for the Arab revolution—the withdrawal of the Egyptian regime to the right and rear of the Nasserite experiment makes the issue of our alliance with it irrelevant."

In the same issue, the party gave its own interpretation to the arrest of Ali Sabri and his followers. It stated: "It was, in principle, not a question of struggle for power, though this struggle formed one aspect of the events. The basic issue which underlies the struggle is the survival of Nasserism. This was the basic issue from which all others sprang."

Despite the many shortcomings which Nasserism displayed—such as the vast increase in the secret service which led to the curtailment of democracy and some individual freedoms, the creation of a bureaucratic elite that directed the institutions of government and the economy and "imagined themselves to represent a new class that has replaced the old and has taken over its privileges"[3]—Nasserism achieved real gains for Egypt, the Arab World and the movement of national liberation. It represented a progressive stage in modern Arab history and violently awakened Arab countries to their future. Perhaps the most important lesson that Nasserism taught, however, was the need to merge the national revolution with the social revolution in the Arab world as well as in countries of the Third World.

NASSERISM AND ARAB UNITY

The first act of unity in the modern history of the Arabs was linked to the name of Abdul-Nasser and Nasserism. The declaration of union between Egypt and Syria in 1958 had an unprecedented welcome

3. *The Charter*, p. 87. Though Nasser cautioned in *The Charter* against this danger, he admitted in speeches following the defeat of June 1967 to the rise of such a situation in Egypt.

among the Arab people. During his historic leadership, Nasser was able to draw his country out of its self-centered isolation, restore to it its Arab identity, and reintroduce the question of Arab unity as a necessity that faces Egypt and the Arab countries. Such a task was formidable in view of the fact that Egypt, until the coming of Nasser, had seen itself as a Pharaonic—at best, African—country having only brotherly or neighborly relations with the rest of the Arab world.[4]

Although successful in bringing about unity, Nasserism, plagued by inner contradictions, failed to arrest the forces of counterinsurgency. Two of these contradictions offered fertile grounds for dissension and invited secession. First, Nasserism proposed itself as a movement capable of actualizing the aspirations of Arab masses but, concurrently, pursued an undemocratic policy which prohibited genuine mass-line political organizations from functioning in the new unified state. Second, the Nasserite leadership, eager to proceed with the integration of the two societies, did not give sufficient attention to the possible reaction of the Egyptian and Syrian bourgeoisie and to their incessant and dysfunctional competition within the unified state. There were others, of course, but these two main contradictions facilitated the engineering of a military coup in Syria and Syrian secession from the United Arab Republic.

For the second time, Nasser overcame the isolationist trend which gained momentum among Egyptian masses following the breakdown of unity. He set his country on a rejuvenated course of active participation in Arab affairs. During this new period, new notions of Arab unity appeared within the Nasserite movement. Basic to all was the association between Arab unity and socialism.

In the 1962 *Charter*, Nasser discussed the ill-fated experiment in unity. In a new assessment, he concluded that nineteenth-century European attempts at unity should not be emulated as models. Arab unity, he argued, must be premised on "peaceful appeal" and "unanimous approval" (p. 15). In the new formulation, Nasser explained the differences existing in the Arab world as local variations that attest to, rather than dispute, the unity of the Arabs. They originate in the process of struggle which the Arab world is undergoing. This process has polarized the Arab world into two camps: the popular progressive elements, on the one hand, and the forces of reaction, on the other.

4. Egyptian attitudes on the Arab world prior to Nasser are discussed by Dr. 'Abd al-'Azim Anis in his article "The Egyptian Revolution and the Question of Its Arab Identification," *al-Fikr al-mu'asir* 69 (Cairo, November 1970): 54–59.

Hence, Arab solidarity cannot be served by a meeting of Arab rulers, for those rulers lack a unity of objective. It is the broader masses, whom the social revolution has unified, that share a common objective. Their political revolution (their fight against imperialism) is now overshadowed by their social revolution (their fight against economic backwardness). Because Arab countries are at different levels of development, special efforts "to fill the economic and social gaps stemming from the difference in the stages of development of the various peoples of the Arab nation" (p. 94) must be made before political unity can be realized. Socio-economic differences allow elements opposed to unity to exploit and undermine any hurried attempts. Meanwhile, the UAR can provide the meeting grounds for all progressive nationalist movements.

The link between the political and social aspects of unity became even more distinct in Nasser's mind as he faced the recurrent dilemmas of Arab politics. Feudalism and exploitative capital were seen as the cornerstones of imperialism and monopoly and the enemies of unity. "A unified Arab society cannot be constructed except by freedom and socialism. Their victory will be crowned by unity."[5]

NASSERISM AND THE PALESTINE PROBLEM

From the outset, the July 23, 1952, movement was tied to the problem of Palestine. The loss of Palestine in 1948 and the scandals associated with that event had alienated the masses from the regime and were among the direct causes of the army revolt. Shortly after securing the reins of power, the movement came into confrontation with Israel. Continuous raids on Egyptian borders and the 1956 and 1967 large-scale wars in which Egypt found itself fighting for its survival have heightened the importance of the question of Palestine and made it into an Egyptian national question.

The Charter discussed the Palestine problem as a conspiracy directed against the Arab independence movement. It stated:

The aspiration for independence received severe blows.
The Arab states were divided among the imperialist states to satisfy their ambitions. Moreover, the imperialist statesmen coined

5. From a speech delivered by Abdul-Nasser on May 20, 1964, as quoted in *al-Tali'ah* (Cairo) 11 (November 1970): 135.

humiliating words such as Mandate and Trusteeship to cover up their crimes.

Part of the Arab territory was handed to an aggressive racial movement with neither historical nor natural justification, to be used by the imperialists as a whip in their hands to fight the struggling Arabs if one day they were able to overcome their humiliation and survive the crises.

The imperialists intended this territory to be a barrier dividing the Arab East from the Arab West, and a constant drain on the energy of the Arab nation, diverting it from positive construction.

All this was carried out in a provocative manner disregarding the existence of the Arab nation and its dignity.

It was the irony of fate that armies of the Arab Nation who entered Palestine to safeguard Arab rights, should be under the supreme command of one of the cheaply bought hirelings of imperialism. The military operations, were placed in the hands of a British officer who received his orders from the very statesman who gave the Zionist movement the Balfour Declaration on which the Jewish state in Palestine was based. (pp. 27–28)

Nasser's conviction that Israel served as a base for imperialism in the Middle East grew stronger. The Arab will to live is threatened, he said, and all the potentialities of this will must be channeled to challenge the Israeli danger.

After 1967, Nasser asserted that the June War unquestionably revealed the enemy's intention to expand in the area between the Nile and Euphrates.[6] The source of the Arab-Israeli conflict is the determination of imperialism not to allow the Arab nation to achieve its political and social freedoms. As to Palestinian resistance, he saw this movement as a landmark that qualitatively changed the nature of the Arab struggle. On various occasions, he asserted the movement's full right to operate without restrictions and to be free from outside interference.[7]

NASSERISM AND SOCIALISM

As mentioned earlier, Nasserism has made a significant contribution in popularizing the term "socialism" within wide sectors of the Arab

6. From a speech delivered by Abdul-Nasser at the opening session of the Palestinian National Council on January 1, 1969, as quoted in ibid., p. 73.

7. Ibid., p. 76.

population. The impact of Nasser's speeches and the effect of Egypt's economic accomplishments were the two prime media used to achieve this aim. The conceptions of socialism in Nasserite teachings, however, appeared in different forms and at different stages. Despite the revolutionary nature of some of the socialist measures adopted in Egypt, Nasserite socialism remains very different from Marxist-Leninist socialism.

It was not until 1957 that Nasser expressly used the term "socialism" and called for the establishment of a socialist order. Prior to that date, he had spoken of social justice, social revolution, and social equality. In *Philosophy of the Revolution,* Nasser alluded to the existence, within every human society, of two revolutions. The first is political, and the second is social. In the latter, a struggle among classes in society occurs and a new, more just order is established.[8] But on December 5, 1957, addressing members of the Cooperative Conference, Nasser expanded his visions of a democratic, socialist, and cooperative system in Egypt. The spirit of his address was directed against exploitation in society and for the need to draw classes nearer to each other. He referred to the need for planning, ascribed to the state the prime role of economic leadership, and placed no restrictions on local capital except that it should refrain from exploitation and should collaborate with the state in its development plans.[9]

Nasser embodied his notions of socialism in the 1962 *Charter.* This document remains the principal theoretical treatise summarizing the principles of Nasserism and contains its views on the social context of the Egyptian and Arab revolutions. It also included the general guidelines for the application of socialist measures in Egypt for the period 1962–70. In the *Charter,* Nasser for the first time labeled his concept of socialism "scientific socialism."

Whenever he used the term "scientific socialism" Nasser contrasted it with an "archaic socialism." The object of this distinction was evident. He hoped to impress on his audience that the socialist principles he advocated were based on an objective assessment of Egypt's social conditions and were not mere guesswork. The "trial and error" formula which had guided the leadership's course of action was being, by the early sixties, forsaken in favor of "objective scientific" laws. The shift,

8. Jamal Abdul-Nasser, *Philosophy of the Revolution* (Washington, D.C.: Public Affairs Press, 1955), pp. 39–40.

9. Anis, "The Egyptian Revolution and the Question of Its Arab Identification," *al-Fikr al-mu'asir* 69 (Cairo, November 1970): 43–45.

however, was not a wholesale adoption of any one brand of socialism. Nasserism diverged from Marxist-Leninist philosophy in four basic aspects. First, Nasserism rejected the materialist conceptions in Marxism which had led it to reject religion. As an institution, Nasserism asserted, religion can be exploited by reactionaries and made to serve the purposes of an economically dominant social class. In essence, however, religion has a progressive social message and it can assist and hasten the process of social change. Second, Nasserism spurned the validity of Lenin's "organized vanguard" theory and opted for a broad coalition of all active popular forces to lead society to socialism. Third, in the Nasserite conceptualization, a social order based on socialism is seen as a terminal stage. Nasserism did not subscribe to the Marxist notion of the inevitability of a communist society. Fourth, and finally, Nasserism did not maintain that private property is necessarily a social evil. Hence, private ownership of means of production is to be tolerated so long as it does not hamper state-set plans for national development.

Defining the basic features of Nasserite socialism is not an easy task. Nasser was not a political or economic theoretician. He did not work out a coherent or structured theoretical edifice to which one can turn for guidance. His thoughts on the questions of socialism have to be gathered from various sources—speeches, addresses, conversations, and the very few documents he wrote. It seems easier, rather, to point out what Nasser did not believe, or to demonstrate the manner in which he shifted his emphasis from one thing to the other without allowing himself to be bogged down with theoretical subtleties. Policy considerations, rather than mental blueprints, figured foremost in his actions. The following paragraphs will therefore merely outline his basic notions of socialism, in the hope that a fuller, more comprehensive study will yet appear.

A striking feature of Nasser's pronouncements on the subject was the manner in which he simplified rather complex and controversial notions. On various occasions, he asserted that socialism, notwithstanding all the interpretations, has one meaning and connotes one reality. Yet he would define the term differently at each occasion. It refers to a situation "where national income is common to citizens in the amount of each man's real effort in the making of this national income." It was also defined as "the ending of man's exploitation of man, the ending of exploitation in all its forms. At the same time it is the founding of an affluent society." On another occasion socialism was "a happy home for every family whose fit male and female members have jobs."[10] Underlying these definitions was Nasser's apparent assumption that socialism meant the ending of exploitation and the construction of a just system of distribution in society. It signified to him a condition in which individual self-seeking and selfishness are absent and social solidarity dominates.

By the early sixties Nasser believed that the application of the socialist solution to Egypt's problems was inevitable; contrary to earlier statements, he seemed to subscribe to the notion of historical determinism (see Appendix C). Throughout his leadership, however, he believed that the peaceful resolution of class conflicts was possible and that differences between classes could be made to narrow gradually until they became insignificant. Society would, nevertheless, always have classes.

To Nasser, the state in a socialist order should play the role of economic leadership. It should establish and direct a public domain that makes a national investment of the nation's assets. The overall production plans that it formulates also account for the free, but "supervised" private sector. Public ownership in the agricultural sector, however, did not figure in Nasser's schemes. He opposed such a measure and thought that the duty of the state should be the curtailment of land ownership. The purpose of such a policy would be to insure that feudalism should remain subverted and a more equitable system of land ownership should be established.

Finally, Nasser thought that decentralization and self-direction were necessary for the establishment of a socialist democracy in Egypt. Lacking the organized machinery to keep control, Nasser, ironically, helped in the greater bureaucratization and centralization of authority within Egyptian society.

NASSERISM AFTER NASSER

While Nasser lived, Nasserism meant most directly the leadership of Nasser. As an ideology, it remained incoherent, as a movement, unorganized. Most simply, it symbolized the force of Arab nationalism as embodied in Nasser. The movement, as such, was a conglomerate of

10. From speeches delivered by Abdul-Nasser on July 22, 1961 (ibid., p. 47); November 18, 1965 (ibid.), and March 18, 1967 (ibid., p. 48).

right, center, and left—with the only point of agreement being Nasser himself. What has happened to this conglomerate since Nasser's death?

As pointed out earlier, the Nasserite movement has fragmented into a plethora of contending organizations, each interpreting Nasserism differently. But this fragmentation does not herald the death of the Nasserite movement. Rather, it reflects first, Nasser's ability to bring such diverse political opinions together, albeit tenuously, and secondly, the universality of Nasserist ideology. As defined in *al-Tali'ah* ('Cairo), February 1975, by Nasser's close friend, confidant, and long-time editor of *al-Ahram*, Muhammad Haykal, Nasserism symbolizes "the direction of liberation, socialist transformation, the people's control of their own resources, and the democracy of the people's working forces." Every political movement in the Arab world today proceeds from these tenets. In this respect, they are all successors of Nasserism and bearers of the Nasserite tide.

◄◄ 6 ►►

THE POLITICAL AND ORGANIZATIONAL ROOTS
OF THE NEW ARAB LEFT

THE simplification of issues, problems, and solutions on the part of both radical nationalist regimes and parties, understandably enough, fell short of achieving the goals sought by those regimes and parties.[1] Major political developments in the area helped create and foster a new tide of frustration among the Arab masses in general, among the intelligentsia in particular, and among the rank and file of the radical nationalist parties.

It was during the period from late 1959 to early 1968 that the bases of the New Arab Left were laid down. This decade unfolded events that inevitably unmasked the naivete of both the programs and the practices of the radical Arab nationalist movement. These events included, first, the early disillusionment of the Ba'ath party with both the structures and process of the newly established United Arab Republic. The Ba'ath's consequent break with the other factions of radical Arab nationalism left a blemish on both the party and the movement toward union.[2] The drift to Nasserism among the Arab masses as well as among the rank and file of the Ba'ath itself greatly isolated and

1. To mention only two examples representative of both the Ba'ath and the ANM, respectively, see: Salahaldin al-Bitar, *al-Siyasah al-'Arabiyah Bayna al-Mabda' Wa al-Tatbiq* [The Arab Politics: Principle and Implementation] (Beirut: Dar al-Tali'ah, 1960). Also, Muhsin Ibrahim, *Fi al-thawrah Wa al-Dimuqratiyah wa al-tanzim al-Sha'bi* [On Revolution, Democracy and Popular Organization] (Beirut: Dar al-fajr al-jadid, 1962).

2. Salahaldin al-Bitar, *al-Thawrah Wa al-Thawrah al-'Arabiyah* [Revolution and Arab Revolution] (Beirut: Dar al-Fikr al-Arabi, 1967), pp. 43–53.

92

weakened the party. The Arab "masses had responded to President Abdul-Nasser, who emerged as the leader of Arab nationalism. And even the most brilliant among the party members were already making their ablutions for prayers at the new Arab mosque of Nasserism."[3] As a matter of fact, Abdullah al-Rimawi, the leader of the Ba'ath in Jordan, and his followers, split from the "National Command" of the party and declared their full support of Nasser.

The unexpected enmity of the originally Nasserite coup in Iraq on July 14, 1958,[4] as well as the failure of the "Shawef rebellion" in al-Mousel in 1959, paved the way for further frustration vis-à-vis Arab unity and had debilitating effects on the whole movement of radical Arab nationalism as evidenced by the bloody purges in Iraq of Arab military and civilian radicals, whether independents, members, and supporters of the Ba'ath or members and supporters of the Arab Nationalist Movement.[5]

The secession of Syria from the UAR on September 28, 1961, had far-reaching repercussions. It marked the beginning of a serious decline in the impetus of radical Arab nationalism.[6] For one thing, Nasser's charismatic image was shaken, though not shattered. The then conservative Arab regimes and rightist underground organizations and elites reached a new unexpected source of political oxygen that helped them recover from what appeared to be (before September 28, 1961), political suffocation. Moreover, "the break-up of the Union brought about a falling apart within the Ba'ath, which split up into separatists, anti-Nasserites, and unionists."[7]

By far the most important development, however, was the fact that the Palestinians, together with the influential Palestinian elements within the various Arab political parties, became the most disillusioned and frustrated among the Arab people. The secession of Syria delivered a strong blow to their long-cherished hopes of Arab unity as "the only bridge" to their homeland. To the Palestinians, participation in Arab

3. Salahaldin al-Bitar, "The Rise and Decline of the Ba'ath," Middle East International (London) (June 1971): 15.

4. Sabih Ali Ghalib, Qissat Thawrat 14 Tammuz Wa al-Dubbat al-Ahrar [The Story of the Revolution of July 14, and the Free Officers] (Beirut: Dar al-Tali'ah, 1968), pp. 40–46.

5. Khaldun Sati' al-Husari, Thawrat 14 Tammuz wa haqiqat al-shuyu'iyin fi al-'Iraq [The Revolution of July 14 and the Truth About Iraqi Communists] (Beirut: Dar al-Tali'ah, 1963), pp. 120–38.

6. Jihad Karam, al-Wihdah fi baramij al-Ahzab al-'Arabiyah [Unity in the Programs of Arab Parties] (Beirut: Dar al-Tali'ah, 1970), p. 36.

7. Salahaldin al-Bitar, "The Ba'ath Party," Middle East International (London) (July 1971): 14.

politics seemed to be, more than ever, an indulgence in a vicious circle
of politics. Rather than surrendering to pessimism, however, the Palestinians started looking for "other bridges."

The victory of the Algerian Revolution in 1961 taught the Arabs in
general and the Palestinians in particular to depend on themselves and
to initiate armed struggle. Moreover, the eruption of guerrilla warfare
against the British colonialists in Aden further reinforced the Palestinian desire for new alternatives. In consequence, and almost immediately, several exclusively Palestinian underground organizations
advocating armed struggle came into existence. The most important
among these were al-Fateh, the Organization of the Heroes of Repatriation "Abtal al-'Awda" (tacitly controlled by the Palestinian members of the Arab Nationalist Movement), and the Palestine Liberation
Front (better known as Ahmed Gibbreen's Group). Both the Arab
Nationalist Movement and the Ba'ath party had to adjust to the new
Palestinian pressures to establish special Palestinian units within their
wider pan-Arab organizations. This process of adjustment resulted in
the establishment of the Command of Palestinian Action—Qiyadat
al-'amal al-Filastini—with its military wing, Shabab al-Thair [the
Youth of Vengeance] in the Arab Nationalist Movement and the Palestinian Branch in the Ba'ath party.

Concomitant with the abovementioned Palestinian revival, a different kind of rejuvenation emerged within the pan-Arab parties (the
Ba'ath and the Arab Nationalist Movement). In this last development
one can more or less tangibly specify the organizational as well as the
ideological nuclei of the New Arab Left. The importance of the point
necessitates special examination. This is best delineated through the
several retrospective evaluations introduced by the various leaders of
the two parties mentioned above. In Bitar's words:

> The Ba'ath was more often content to set forth general principles,
> formulate abstract ideas and take refuge in theoretical concepts. It did
> not see fit to construct a clear theory of action or to work to acquire a
> scientific method, either for analysing situations or for anticipating
> events.
>
> In this way it evaded major concrete questions that it was soon to
> be faced with and which were to catch it off guard; such as Revolu-
> tion, State, party democracy and internal party democracy, pluralism
> or the one-party system, religion, agrarian reform, nationalisation of
> production, struggles on the local and Arab levels, and periods of
> transition.
>
> It should be noted here that the Ba'ath had no ideological [re-

view]. And so the Ba'ath was unable to be the melting-pot for unity of thought, the necessary basis for unity of strategy, action and organization.

In its place it handed out to its members hollow phrases and noisy slogans, and that is how revolutionary verbalism prevailed. All this was bound to have unfortunate repercussions on the organisation of the party and on its relations with the mass of the people. The members were not united in thought; and the leadership being divided—as was to be expected—there arose right and left-wing currents, factions and groups and verbal and personal quarrels.[8]

The general leadership of the Ba'ath took refuge in general ideas, abstract conceptions and declarations of intent. It did not take into sufficient consideration the great need of these outposts of the party in the matter of rational studies, analyses of concrete situations and satisfactory answers to questions arising from the development of events. It even lacked a scientific method for the analyses of these events and only offered the outposts words and slogans.

The result was eye-wash and bluff which gave rise to an absurd dogmatism and a self-satisfied sectarianism. The question of strategy and tactics, of which all parties are the instrument, was almost totally evaded and gave way to a revolutionary romanticism, to an irresponsible extremism, and soon to a childish leftism which was to remain the dominant feature of the Ba'ath and the essence of its chronic crisis.

Moreover, the party suffered from anaemia in its organisation. Its institutions were forsaken, the hierarchy scorned and "ultra-democratism" was developed to such an extent that the Ba'ath could be said to constitute a frame of mind rather than a so-called political party.

Soon, in face of these deficiencies, a reaction set in among the young militants in the fields of ideology and organisation. They started to feed on Marxist, Leninist and Maoist literature, not because they wanted to be converted to communism, but rather because of a need for ideological education. Advantage could be had from this literature only with a developed critical mind, which was exactly what these young men lacked, and this resulted in certain doctrinal deviations.[9]

In brief, and in the words of Dr. Muneef al-Razaz, onetime Secretary-General of the Ba'ath who succeeded the party's founder in that

8. Al-Bitar, "The Rise and Decline of the Ba'ath," *Middle East International* (London) (June 1971): 15.

9. Al-Bitar, "The Ba'ath Party," *Middle East International* (London) (July 1971). Also, Shibli al-'Aysami, *al-Wihdah al-'Arabiyah min khilal al-tajribah* [Arab Unity Through Experience] (Beirut: Arab Institute for Studies and Publications, 1971), p. 37. Also, ———, *Fi al-thawrah al-'Arabiyah* [On Arab Revolution] (Beirut: Arab Institute for Studies and Publications, 1971), pp. 17, 26.

position in 1965: "the Ba'ath . . . in its implementation and execution [of its goals] was neither up to the level of its doctrine not to the level of its aspirations."[10]

The continuous crisis of the Ba'ath resulted in fatal organizational disarray of the party. The confusion has been so comprehensive that it is very difficult to refer now to *a* unified Ba'ath party anywhere in the Arab world outside Iraq. To mention the most important splits, one is reminded of the emergence and secession of the Proletariat Group—Jama'at al-Kadihoon al-'Arab—from the Ba'ath party in Iraq in 1962. This was followed by the more serious split of Ali Saleh al-Sa'di and his followers in 1963 shortly after the Ba'ath coup d'etat on February 8, 1963. Once again the Iraqi branch of the party suffered additional splinters after its second coup in 1968. In Syria, the disintegration of the party was a continuous process; some of its leading members seceded between 1961 and March 8, 1963, the day on which the Ba'ath came to power through a military coup. Syria witnessed a series of coups by Ba'athist army officers against other Ba'athists. A military *putsch* led by Salah Jadeed's wing of the Ba'ath overthrew the national leadership of the party on February 25, 1966. This same group was overthrown by Hafiz al-Assad's military wing in 1971. This list, however, is by no means inclusive. Neither the "minor" splits and the several "military uprisings" in Syria, nor the repercussions of these coups on the other branches of the Ba'ath (particularly in Lebanon) are included. Finally, the fact that these coups were accompanied by all kinds of accusations among the fighting factions cannot be overemphasized. Epithets such as right-wingers, deviationists, opportunists, regionalists, and CIA agents, were harshly fired by one group against the other.[11]

The Arab Nationalist Movement, on the other hand, managed to keep close relations with the authorities of the United Arab Republic in general and with President Nasser in particular. This was possible because the movement, compared with the Nasserist forces and/or the Ba'ath, was a junior partner in the radical Arab nationalist alliance.

10. Munif al-Razzaz, *al-wihdah al-'Arabiyah: Hal laha min sabil?* [Arab Unity: Does It Have a Chance?] (Beirut: Arab Institute, 1973), 37.

11. For a detailed account of these events with the flood of accusations and counter-accusations among the various factions see: Michel Aflaq, *Niqtat al-bidayah* [The Starting Point] (Beirut: Arab Institute, 1971), pp. 185–205 and 207–54. Also, Ali Salih al-Sadi, *Minhaj Hizb al-'amal al-Ishtiraki* [The Program of the Socialist Action Party] (Beirut, 1964).

Moreover, the movement at that time and up to 1962 was not important in Syrian political life. Furthermore, the junior status of the movement was a function of both its relatively recent origin and the small size of its organized membership. 'Chiefly, however, it was the movement's low level of political and ideological sophistication that made it, for quite a long time, an easy prey for the UAR authorities.

The various developments through which the movement evolved between 1964 and 1969, however, were the sources from which the main organizational, political, and ideological structures and policies of the New Arab Left arose. That this origin is one of the most salient facts regarding the emergence of the new left explains the special examination of these developments intended in the following paragraphs.

As early as 1963, part of the leadership of the movement's branch in Lebanon, particularly those who constituted the Central Board of the movement's organ al-Hurriyah, made themselves the semi-official spokesmen for the mounting tide of frustration that then engulfed the various provincial leaderships of the whole organization.[12] This theorizing group of al-Hurriyah, together with the activist groups (the most eminent leaders of which were Dr. George Habash, Hani al-Hindi, and Dr. Wadi Haddad) who were busy leading the revolutionary work in other Arab countries, agreed, in the National Conference of the movement in the summer of 1963, on a new socialist program.[13] Nevertheless, the way in which al-Hurriyah group overpublicized the program planted the seeds of a crisis of confidence between the two groups. Such a crisis, in a movement where organizational and personal relations greatly overlapped and when a lack of a clear-cut ideology and constitution heightened friction, initiated the subsequent fragmentation of the movement.

The partial erosion of Nasser's charisma after 1961, particularly in 1965,[14] further caused the two nascent wings of the ANM to drift apart. Consequently, many articles (particularly by George Issa and Mohammed Kishly) criticizing certain UAR policies appeared in al-Hurriyah in 1965–66. This development was concomitant with the attempt by

12. Those were led by Muhsin Ibrahim, Muhammad Kishly and Nayif al-Hawatmeh; see Ilyas Murqus, 'Afawiyat al-nazariyah fi al-'amal al-fida'i' [The Spontaneity of Theory in (Palestinian) Commando Action] (Beirut: Dar al-Tali'ah, 1970), p. 12.

13. The Executive Committee of the ANM, The Report of the Executive Committee, unpublished monograph, 1964.

14. E. Hrair Dekmejian, Egypt Under Nasser: A Study in Political Dynamics (Albany: State University of New York Press, 1971), pp. 60–61, 238–40.

the movement's Egyptian members to infiltrate and organize themselves within the Arab Socialist Union, the only official party in the
UAR. It was little wonder that the attempt resulted in tense relations
between the movement on the one hand and Nasser and his colleagues
on the other. More important were the serious policy differences between the UAR and the ANM *vis-à-vis* both Yemen and the Southern
Yemen Liberation Movement; these eventually delivered a dangerous
blow to the relations of the two parties. The UAR's withdrawal of support from the National Liberation Front (NLF) in Southern Yemen
(organized and led by the Yemeni members of the ANM) and the subsequent extension of support to the conservative rival Front of Abd-
Allah al-Asnaj and Abdel-Qawi-Makkawi was the last blow to the already precarious alliance between Nasserism and the ANM. The
breakup, however, came as an aftermath of the June 1967 defeat.[15]

In the meantime, the crisis in confidence within the Arab Nationalist Movement was gathering momentum. The differences in policies
together with the deteriorating personal relations among the leaders
of the potential splinters of the ANM greatly weakened the movement
and initiated the process of its organizational disintegration. To deter-
mine the various stances and policies of the then-current two wings,
however, is next to impossible. The literature of the later splinters of
the movement and the author's personal interviews with the leading
participants, not only reveal confusing historical evaluations of that
period but also introduce contradictory ones. In order to avoid repeat-
ing the detailed discussion presented in Chapter 4 about the Arab Nationalist Movement, it is sufficient at this stage to discuss briefly the
various splinters which replaced the mother movement after 1967.[16]
These offshoots are:

1. Hizb al-'amal al-Ishtiraki al-Arabi [The Arab Socialist Action

15. For the details of these developments see the two conflicting evaluations in
Organizational Committee of the NFL, *Kayfa nafhamu tajribat al-Yaman al-
janubiyah al-sha'biyah* [How Do We Understand the Experience of the Peoples'
of Southern Yemen] (Beirut: Dar al-Tali'ah, 1969), pp. 57–62; Nayif al-
Hawatmeh, *Azmat al-Thawrah fi janub al-Yaman* [The Crisis of the Revolution in
Southern Yemen] (Beirut: Dar al-Tali'ah, 1968), pp. 38–42. In Egypt, the New
Left emerged as a literary movement during the Nasser era. In the aftermath of
the June 1967 defeat, however, it crystallized as spontaneous student protests and
violent demonstrations opposing the pro-Western orientation of the Sadat regime.
These protests culminated in a general student uprising in January 1972. Sadat
crushed the uprising brutally, in effect driving the New Left underground. *Al-
Intifadah al-Tullabiyah fi Misr January 1972*) [The Student Uprising in Egypt:
January 1972] (Beirut: Dar Ibn Khaldun, 1972).

16. For an account of the point of view of *al-Hurriyah* group, see Organization
of the Lebanese Socialists publication with an introduction by Muhsin Ibrahim,

Party] which was established in late 1969. Its inner core is composed of the various branches of the Arab Nationalist Movement which "succeeded in transforming themselves from the petty bourgeois orientations of the ANM into a new Marxist-Leninist orientation."[17] The slogan of the party is "Liberation, Socialism, Democracy and Arab Unity." Its organ is *Tariq al-Thawrah* [Path of the Revolution]. The party claims to have branches in Lebanon, Iraq, Syria, Jordan, Kuwait, and the Arabian Peninsula with various branches on the Arab Gulf. Due to organizational ties with the Popular Front for the Liberation of Palestine (PFLP), the party publishes much of its literature in the weekly *al-Hadaf* [The Goal]. The Secretary-General of the party is Dr. George Habash.

2. The Popular Front for the Liberation of Palestine (PFLP): This organization emerged in late 1967 as a merger of three Palestinian commando organizations, namely, Shabab al-tahrir [the Youth of Liberation], Abtal al-awdah [the Heroes of Repatriation], and the previously mentioned Gibbreen Group. The Youth of Vengeance (an early offshoot of the ANM) has dominated the PFLP since its very inception. The Jibreen Group, however, claim to have seceded from the PFLP in early 1969. The Secretary-General of the Popular Front is, again, Dr. Habash.

3. The Organization of Lebanese Socialists (OLS), established in early 1969. Its organ is the former ANM official newspaper, *al-Hurriyah* [The Freedom], published in Lebanon. The most eminent figures of this organization are Muhsin Ibrahim and Muhammad Kishly, both formerly on the editorial board of the ANM paper.

4. The Democratic Popular Front for the Liberation of Palestine (DPFLP), which emerged in February 1969 as a splinter of the PFLP. The official organ of the Democratic Popular Front is *al-Shararah* [The Spark], though its special relations with the OLS give it access to *al-Hurriyah*. Its leader is Nayif Hawatmeh.

The last two organizations claim to have various other offshoots.[18]

5. Al-Harakah al- ishtirakiyah al-'Arabiyah [the Socialist Arab Movement] in Iraq.

Limadha Munazzamat al-ishtirakiyin al-Lubnaniyin, Harakat al-qawmiyin al-'Arab min al-Fashiyah ila al-Nasiriyah [Why the Organization of the Lebanese Socialists? The Arab Nationalist Movement from Fascism to Nasserism] (Beirut: Dar al-Tali'ah, 1970); also for an account of Dr. Habash's followers see Popular Front for the Liberation of Palestine, *al-Jabhah wa qiyadat al-inshiqaq* [The Front and the Issue of Secession] (Beirut: al-hadaf, 1971).

17. George Habash, "The Trip of a Thousand Miles Begins with One Step," *Tariq al-Thawrah* I (1) (June 1970): 15–16; see also pp. 44–51.

18. Murqus, *The Spontaneity of Theory*, p. 12.

6. Al-Jabha al-sha'biyah al-dimuqratiyah li-tahrir Shubh al-Jazirah al-'Arabiyah [the Popular Democratic Front for the Liberation of the Arab Peninsula] in Saudi Arabia.

7. Al-Hizb al-dimuqrati al-thawri al-Yamani [the Yemeni Democratic Revolutionary Party] in the Arab Republic of Yemen.

8. The Leftist Wing of the NLF in the Republic of Southern Yemen.

9. The Popular Revolutionary Movement for Uman and the Arab Gulf in Bahrein and the Arab Gulf Sheikdom.

10. The Popular Front for the Liberation of the (Arab) Gulf.

11. The Revolutionary Popular Front for the Liberation of Palestine.

These splinters of the ANM constitute the bulk of the organizations of the New Arab Left. The disintegration of the Ba'ath party was also a fountainhead of some organizations that fall within the category of the new left as defined below. As a matter of fact, one can discern some leftist tendencies within the Ba'ath in the early sixties. The disillusionment with the coalition with Nasserism and the partial break with the movement in late 1959 not only resulted in pro-Nasserist and anti-Nasserist tendencies within the Ba'ath; it also engendered leftist uneasiness and factions as well. Some Ba'athists started questioning not only the party's policies toward Nasser, but also the whole body of policies advocated by the Ba'ath. The split of some Iraqi Ba'athists in 1962 and the consequent emergence of the Group of al-Kadihun al-'Arab has already been mentioned. A more or less similar and simultaneous development was taking place in the Lebanese branch of the Ba'ath. Some eminent Lebanese Ba'athists left the party to become either politically inactive or to limit their political activities to furthering their leftist ideological education. Of the latter, some went as far as establishing their own leftist organizations or (perhaps more exactly) their own political groups in the later stages. The most important among these groups was that organized and led by Fawwaz Tarabulsi, a well-known Lebanese intellectual. His group worked under the name of Lubnan El-Ishtiraki [Lebanon the Socialist]. Later, however, this group worked in close cooperation with one of the splinters of the ANM (the Organization of the Lebanese Socialists) during 1969–71. Finally, the two organizations merged to form the Organization of Communist Action in Lebanon (see Appendix E).[19]

19. "Munazzamat al-'amal al-shuyu'i fi Lubnan," *al-Hurriyah* (Beirut), No. 574-517/71, pp. 2–6 and 11.

The seizure of power by the Ba'ath party in Iraq and Syria on February 8, and March 8, 1963, respectively, marked the beginning of an era of more serious leftist splits within the Ba'ath. The Sixth Congress of the party witnessed the first serious split. In Bitar's words: "Certain leaders were accused of being 'right wingers' and were evicted from the leadership."[20] Aflaq and Bitar, the two founders of the Ba'ath, were among those. The new leftist leadership was led by the Syrian military officer Salah Jadeed and the triumvirate of medical doctors Yousuf Ze'ayen, Ibrahim Makhos, and Nour al-Din al-Atasi. The overthrow of this group in 1971 by the conservative wing of another military officer (Hafez al-Assad), put the former wing to what amounted to political death.

Finally, some of the Arab Communist parties were either threatened or shaken by neo-leftist tendencies. The most serious shakeup was that suffered by the Iraqi Communist Party. The Central Command of the Iraqi Communist Party, whose one-time most eminent figure was Aziz al-Haj, split from the mother Iraqi Communist Party—The Central Committee in 1968. Al-Haj, however, was evicted later by his own organization because of his "surrender" to the Iraqi Ba'athist regime (al-Haj in return, was rewarded with a diplomatic post as Iraqi representative to UNESCO in Paris).

FACTORS CONTRIBUTING TO THE EMERGENCE OF THE NEW ARAB LEFT

The New Arab Left emerged visibly during the months following the June 1967 War. This emergence was merely a *crystallization* of the political, ideological, and organizational unrest that the various existing political organizations had been experiencing since the early sixties. The whole spectrum of parties and intellectuals identify June 1967 as *the* most important turning point of Arab politics and thought in modern history. The varying responses generated by that significant event provide a key to understanding the crystallization of the New Arab Left.

To start with, the response of the classical liberal nationalist movement was more or less a reiteration of the old themes. Constantine Zurayk, one of the most eminent early proponents of liberal Arab

20. Bitar, *Rise and Decline of the Ba'ath Party*, p. 15.

nationalism, had almost nothing new to add in his post–1967 writings. The technological state of the Arabs, together with the "weak spirit of struggle" among the majority of them, constitute—according to Zurayk —the two faces of the new meaning of the 1967 catastrophe.[21]

The Founder-Leader of the Ba'ath party, on the other hand, called for a new starting point, "a return to the fountain of real strength . . . a return to the people." This, however, together with Aflaq's call for self-criticism, resulted in ideolization of his own party and defense of his position against the competing Ba'athist and non-Ba'athist factions and parties.[22] The analyses of other Ba'athist and former Ba'athist leaders made evident that basically they dwelled on the same old themes in the same old manner.[23] Shibli al-'Aysami, the Assistant Secretary-General of the National Leadership of the Ba'ath party that supports the regime in Iraq, made one step toward new left concepts in his analysis of the Arab revolution by rejecting the traditional Ba'ath view of socialism as social reform and by introducing clear socialist themes that were more radical than the older petty bourgeoisie themes. For example, he viewed Arab unity as the unity of the poor classes rather than the whole nation. Al-'Aysami's approach, however, fell short of placing his group in the category of the New Arab Left.[24]

One of the most interesting contributions to the emergence of the New Arab Left was the role played by some individual Arab intellectuals. These intellectuals, coming from different political origins and totally disillusioned with their political backgrounds, managed to leave their leftist intellectual imprint on New Arab Left thought. George Tarabishi, a Syrian former Ba'athist, focused his attention on translating several leftist studies into Arabic. In the process, Tarabishi demonstrated a mature conscious hesitation to copy or advocate ready-made solutions to the political and social problems confronting the Arabs. While Tarabishi classifies the Arab ideology as an "imported" one, he,

---

21. Constantine Zurayk, Ma'na al-nakbah mujaddadan [The Meaning of Catastrophe Once Again] (Beirut: Dar al-ilm lil-malayin, 1967), pp. 7–12 and 61–84.

22. Michel Aflaq, Niqtat al-bidayah [The Starting Point] (Beirut: Arab Institute for Studies and Publications, 1971), p. 41, 207–54.

23. See al-Razzaz, Arab Unity: Does It Have a Chance? pp. 38–44; also, Ilyas Farah, Tatawwur al-Aydyulujiyah al-'Arabiyah al-thawriyah [The Development of Arab Revolutionary Ideology] (Beirut: Arab Institute for Studies and Publications, 1971).

24. Shibli al-'Aysami, Fi al-thawrah al-'Arabiyah [On the Arab Revolution] (Beirut: Arab Institute for Studies and Publications, 1971), particularly pp. 129–38.

nevertheless, rejects the necessity of labeling it, as others have done, with any inherent metaphysical connotations or characteristics.[25] In an earlier publication, Tarabishi deliberately avoided committing himself or the Arabs to any final strategy. This attitude is due to his "deep feeling that the class strategy of the Arab revolution is still in the (early) process of construction, growth, and crystallization."[26] Another Syrian former Ba'athist intellectual showed a leftist awareness as early as 1965. Yasin al-Hafiz concluded that the petty bourgeois leadership of the Arab struggle was no longer qualified to lead the Arab masses to fulfill their aspirations: "Pushing the [Arab] unity struggle onto a leftist [path] means driving it forward. . . . This is the great lesson that the masses came to learn through their own direct experiences."[27] To al-Hafiz, Arab nationalism was not a product of the "capitalist market." It rather manifests international, democratic (anti-feudalist), socialist, anti-provincial and populist characteristics. The petty bourgeois class—according to al-Hafiz—should be categorically isolated from the leadership of the Arab masses and from its struggle. Moreover, the remnants of "socialist-nationalism" are to be eradicated and replaced by leftist mass ideologies. Finally, al-Hafiz calls for an "Arabization of Marxism" because without integrating the movement of the Arab masses with Marxist ideology, the Arabs, his rationale runs, will have no escape from their helplessness and miserable situation.[28] In brief, the writings of al-Hafiz in the late sixties were pioneering with regard to the emergence of new Arab leftist thought.

Another interesting intellectual phenomenon can be discerned in the experience of the Syrian Sadiq Jalal al-Azm. A professor of philosophy in the American University of Beirut, al-Azm was more or less isolated from active political life. It was the defeat of June 1967, however, that politically activated al-Azm and led him, in turn, to activate the New Arab Left thought. As a result he lost his position at AUB. In his *Self-Criticism After the Defeat*, al-Azm waged a violent campaign against Arab rightist and oscillating ideologies, concepts, traditions, and conservatism. Al-Azm's attack against almost all aspects of Arab social and political life was so comprehensive as

25. George Tarabishi, *al-Markisiyah wa al-Aydyulujiyah* [Marxism and Ideology] (Beirut: Dar al-Tali'ah, 1971), pp. 209–15.

26. George Tarabishi, *al-Istratijiyah al-tabaqiyah lil-thawrah* [The Class Strategy of the Revolution] (Beirut: Dar al-Tali'ah, 1970), p. 304.

27. Yasin al-Hafiz, *Hawla ba'd qadaya al-thawrah al-'Arabiyah* [On Some of the Issues of Arab Revolution] (Beirut: Dar al-Tali'ah, 1965), p. 8.

28. Ibid., pp. 13, 24–26, 33, 61, 271–79.

to cover almost all elites. The solution advocated by al-Azm was no less than the uncompromising achievement of the socialist revolution. In his own words:

> Without the emergence of new revolutionary forces which are ultimately committed to the [fulfillment] of the aspirations of the absolute majority of the Arab masses (namely, the very poor and the working class), the Arab world will have to wait for a long time [before it rids itself from the fetters of backwardness]. . . . Such forces are capable of shouldering the responsibility of transforming the [Palestinian] guerrilla action into a real populist and comprehensive liberation war. . . . [This war] will eventually accomplish total Arab liberation from the domination of the colonial economic interests and influences and will achieve comprehensive revolutionary changes in all aspects of Arab society.[29]

Al-Azm's Marxist-Leninist tendencies, however, became clearer in his later articles and publications. His Marxist-Leninist approach has been utilized as a cutting-knife ready to amputate rightist or semi-socialist concepts, ideas, and goals wherever and whenever they appear on the Arab political stage.[30] Nothing of all al-Azm's writings stirred debates, controversies, and emotions more than his *Criticism of Religious Thought*. The wrath that the book aroused among the old Arab establishments (especially Moslem religious leadership) led them to dramatically charge the author in the Lebanese courts with "instigating and arousing confessionalist hatred."[31]

Finally, no discussion is complete without referring to the writings of the Syrian critic Ilyas Murqus, and the Algerian writer, al-Afif al-Akhdar,[32] a former Communist who quit partisan membership in the

29. Sadiq Jalal al-Azm, *al-Naqd al-dhati ba'da al-hazimah* [Self-Criticism After the Defeat] (Beirut: Dar al-Tali'ah, 1969), pp. 127–28, 166.

30. Sadiq al-Azm, "The Arabs and the Marxist View of the Jewish Question," *Dirasat Arabiyah* 6 (3) (January 1970): 3–49; also, "Armed Resistance and Hykal's Stances," *Dirasat Arabiyah* 5 (10) (August 1969): 17–36; and, "A Reply to a Criticism," *Dirasat Arabiyah* 6 (1) (November 1969): 74–83.

31. Sadiq al-Azm, *Naqd al-fikr al-dini* [Criticism of Religious Thought] 2nd ed. (Beirut: Dar al-Tali'ah, 1969), pp. 233–45; also see al-Azm's *Dirasat Yasariyah: Hawla al-qadiyah al-Filastiniyah* [Leftist Studies on the Palestinian Issue] (Beirut: Dar al-Tali'ah, 1970).

32. Al-Afif al-Akhdar, "After the Massacre: What is to be Done?" *Dirasat Arabiyah* 7 (6) (April 1967): 47–66; also, "Notes on Resistance, Revolutionary War and the Present Situation," *Dirasat Arabiyah* 7 (9) (July 1971): 2–13; also, al-Akhdar and others, *Min Kumunat Baris ila majazir 'Amman* [From the Paris Commune to the Massacres of Amman] (Beirut: Dar al-Tali'ah, 1971).

late fifties. As an independent leftist, Murqus devoted his pen to criticizing and evaluating all leftist parties and factions including the Arab
Communist parties themselves. His analysis of the Arab Communist
movement is perhaps the best study written in Arabic. Murqus' prolific writings cover a wide spectrum of subjects. He has written exten-
sively about Arab nationalism and unity, socialism, Marxism, Leninism,
and the Palestine resistance movement.[33] Murqus' writings have had
great impact on the minds and thoughts of the new Arab Left.

   Al-Akhdar's writing reflects the frustrations of many independent
Arab leftists. He is in rebellion against existing ideologies. Though he
is ideologically leftist in the extremist sense of the term,[34] it is impossible to pinpoint his political partisanship or thought. An examination
of his political affiliations reveals his tendency to shift from one organization to another. Although he supported the Popular Front for the
Liberation of Palestine against al-Fateh in 1968, he turned against it
and aligned himself with the Popular Democratic Front for the Liberation of Palestine in 1969. In late 1970 and early 1971 he became very
critical of the latter organization. Although he is publicly viewed as a
Marxist-Leninist, he surprised many observers by once stating that he
is "Marxist BUT NOT LENINIST!"[35] In brief, it seems that he views

   33. Ilyas Murqus, *Tarikh al-ahzab al-shuyu'yah fi al-watan al-'Arabi* [The History of the Communist Parties in the Arab World] (Beirut: Dar al-Tali'ah, 1964);
also, *al-Markisiyah al-Lininiyah wa al-tatawwur al-' alami wa al'-Arabi fi barnamaj
al-Hizb al-shuyu'i al-Lubnani* [Marxism-Leninism and International and Arab
Developments in the Program of the Lebanese Communist Party] (Beirut: Dar
al-Haqiqah, 1970). Ilyas Murqus, M. Rodinson, and E. Tuma, *al-Ummah, al-mas'
alah al-qawmiyah, al-wihdah al-'Arabiyah wa al-Markisiyah* [The Nation, the
National Question, Arab Unity, and Marxism] (Beirut: Dar al-Haqiqah, 1971);
also, *Naqd al-fikr al-gawmi* [Criticism of National Thought] (Beirut: Dar al-
Tali'ah, 1966); also, *al-Markisiyah wa al-mas'alah al-qawmiyah* [Marxism and the
National Question] (Beirut: Dar al-Tali'ah, 1970); *al-Staliniyah wa al-mas'alah
al-qawmiyah* [Stalinism and the Nationalist Question] (Damascus: Dar Dimashq,
1963); *Mawdu'atila al-mu'tamar al-ishtiraki al-'Arabi* [Topics for an Arab Socialist
Conference] (Damascus: Dar Dimashq, 1963). Ilyas Murqus, *al-Markisiyah fi
'asrina* [Marxism in Our Time] (Beirut: Dar al-Tali'ah, 1965); *al Markisiyah wa
al-Sharq* [Marxism and the East] (Beirut: Dar al-Tali'ah, 1968); *Mafhum al-hizb
inda Linin wa al-mawqif al-rahin* [The Concept of the Party to Lenin and the
Contemporary Arab Stance] (Beirut: Dar al-Haqiqah, 1970); "Leninism," *Dirasat
'Arabiyah* 5 (6) (April 1969). Ilyas Murqus, *al-Muqawamah al-Filastiniyah wa
al-mawqif al-rahin* [The Palestine Resistance and the Present Stance] (Beirut:
Dar al-Haqiqah, April 1971); *'Afawiyat al-mazariyah fi al-'amal al-fidi'i* [The
Spontaniety of Theory in the Commando Action] (Beirut: Dar al-Haqiqah, 1970).
   34. See al-Afif al-Akhdar, "The Exit for the Resistance (Movement's) Crisis,"
al-Hurriyah (Beirut), October 20, 1969.
   35. See *Dirasat Arabiyah* 9 (July 1971): 13.

himself as the only leftist not only in the area, but, perhaps, in the whole world. His latest available article is in line with his tendency to attack every political group including the extreme leftist ones such as the Popular Front for the Liberation of Palestine. Finally, if some people think that al-Akhdar is anti-Soviet because he is a Maoist, they will be surprised by his attacks on China. In conclusion, it seems that al-Akhdar sees himself much (maybe very much) more leftist than either Brezhnev or Mao. The only leftists that have escaped al-Akhdar's criticisms, up till now at least, are the Viet Cong and the North Vietnamese.[36]

More important, perhaps, than any other development, was the impact of the June 1967 defeat on the Arab nationalist movement. The impact, indeed, was so great as to lead to the complete disintegration of the movement and the resulting birth of the New Arab Left as we know it now.

To conclude, the factors contributing to the emergence of the New Arab Left can be thus summarized:

1. The June 1967 defeat, as viewed in the Arab world, was not only due to the plot of neo-imperialism but also to the failure of the so-called Arab progressive regimes in mobilizing, organizing, preparing, and leading their masses on the path of the people's protracted war of liberation against imperialism. In a word, the disillusionment of the Arab masses with the Arab progressive regimes opened the door for a new political formula—the New Arab Left.[37]

2. Disappointment with the various programs of the old parties (including the Ba'ath and the Arab Nationalist Movement) was another reason for the emergence of the New Arab Left.[38] The ideologies, institutions, and programs of both the *traditional* left (the Arab Communist parties) and the petty bourgeois-oriented parties proved to be as effective as those of the petty bourgeois "progressive" regimes.

3. The strong support of the West, particularly of the USA, for Israel and the traditional Arab regimes resulted in anti-imperialist and anti-Western sentiments in the Arab world. These sentiments were

36. See ibid., 12 (October 1971): 100–31, 124–25.

37. The Executive Committee of Arab Nationalist Movement, "The Political Report of the Enlarged Executive Committee Meeting in July, 1967," as appeared in *al-Hurriyah* (Beirut), No. 577, September 4, 1967, pp. 12–13 and No. 378, September 11, 1967), pp. 11–13.

38. Muhammad Kishly "Tajribat Jabhat al-ahzabal-taqaddumiyah" [The Experience of the Front of the Progressive Parties], *al-Hurriyah* (Beirut), No. 387, November 13, 1967, pp. 8–9.

strengthened by the support extended to the Arabs by the socialist camp, especially by the support of the Soviet Union, and to a lesser degree by that of the People's Republic of China. Against this background of alienation from the West and support from the socialist camp, socialist ideas became more accessible and acceptable.[39]

4. Finally, other international cultural influences paved the way for the emergence of new political forces advocating struggle after the example set by the Vietnamese and other revolutionaries in the developing countries. It is to be remembered, however, that the above-mentioned influences were facilitated by the earlier and more intimate influences of the Arab liberation wars in Algeria and Southern Yemen.

39. David P. Forsythe, "The Soviets and the Arab-Israeli Conflict," *Middle East Forum* (Beirut: Alumni Association of the American University of Beirut) 46 (4) (1970). About China see John Cooley, "Israel and the Communist Bloc," *The Middle East Newsletter* (Beirut: AJME) 5 (6) (October–November, 1971): 7–8.

✦❪ 7 ❫✦

THE IDEOLOGICAL, POLITICAL, AND ORGANIZATIONAL STRATEGIES OF THE NEW ARAB LEFT

THE usual difficulties one encounters in drawing a line between leftist, non-leftist, and rightist organizations in the developing countries are more complicated in the context of Arab politics. The emergence of the new political organizations (especially in the Palestinian case) is usually confused with the emergence of the new left. It should be remembered that by no means are all new political organizations part of the New Arab Left. Moreover, the problem is further accentuated by some subjective claims put forward by some of these new organizations. To be sure, all new organizations, in one way or another, claim to be an integral part of the New Arab Left. As a matter of fact, al-Fateh claims that it is the New Left. Abu-Iyad, one of the most important members of al-Fateh's Central Committee, considers his organization to be "related to progressive thought more than those who merely declare their support for [Marxist-Leninist] thought."[1] Furthermore, the problem of defining which is and which is not a part of the New Arab Left is complicated by the fact that all traditional Communist parties in the area claim that there is no New Left.[2] The only leftist

1. A dialogue between Abu-Iyad and Lutfi al-Khuli, editor-in-chief of the Egyptian monthly magazine *al-Tali'ah*, June 1969, issue as cited in Leila S. Kadi, ed., *Basic Political Documents of the Armed Palestinian Resistance Movement* (Beirut: Research Center, 1969), pp. 68–69.

2. Majid Abd al-Rida, "On the Party and Revolution: A Purposive Discussion with the Arab Nationalist Movement," *al-Tariq* [The Path] (Beirut) 2 (1971): 11–12.

organizations—the rationale runs—are the Communist parties themselves. In certain cases some of the New Left organizations are looked upon by the Communists as nothing but "parasitic groups of opportunists." Was it not Comrade Lenin who once said—the Arab Communist parties argue—that "if two 'Communist' parties exist in one place at the same time this automatically means that one of them is opportunist?"

In brief, and to free the discussion from the abovementioned confusing conditions, it is maintained here that only those new parties and/or organizations that *publicly* and *unequivocally* declare adherence to Marxism-Leninism, are the ones that fit the definition of the New Arab Left. Bearing this in mind limits the organizations and groups of the New Arab Left to the following members:

1. In Palestinian politics the Popular Front for the Liberation of Palestine (PFLP) and the Democratic Front (PDFLP) are the only two neo-leftist commando organizations.

2. In non-Palestinian Arab politics, the Arab Socialist Action Party, the Organization of Communist Action in Lebanon, and the liberation fronts in the Gulf area mentioned earlier are members of the New Left.

3. The independent Arab intellectuals mentioned earlier can be considered members of the New Left.

We can now proceed to briefly discuss the ideological, political and organizational strategies of the New Arab Left. To start with, one should make it very clear that there is nothing more frustrating than reading the prolific publications of the organizations of the New Arab Left. The frustration is not due to the abundance of the material but rather to the sometimes unnecessary ideological and political wars waged among the various factions of the New Arab Left on the one hand and between every group of the new left and the other political groups whether rightists, non-leftists or traditional leftists.[3] As to the

3. For an excellent, though incomplete, description of the detailed ideological, political lines and particularly the differences of the various leftist groups see *The Official Proceedings of the Arab Intellectual Meeting in Khartoom—the Sudan between 5–12 March 1970*, as appeared in *al-Hurriyah* (Beirut), April, 1970, Nos. 509, 510, 511, and 512 in pp. 11–12, 14–15, 12–13, and 13–14, respectively. It should be remembered, however, that the proceedings mentioned above were subjected to conflicts and differences. For this consult the PFLP's *al-Hadaf* of April 1970. Moreover, for an exposition of the detailed different stances of the various political parties and groupings consult Talal Salman's "The Left and the Regime(s): Who Rejects Who and Why?," *al-Sayyad* weekly (Beirut), Year 28, No. 1402, July 29–August 5, 1971), pp. 21–27. Also see Muhammad Kishly, "A Con-

detailed ideological and political conflicts no justice could be done without reading the all too many daily, weekly, or monthly publications of the competing and, in many cases, conflicting parties. Reading the PFLP's *al-Hadaf,* the PDFLP's *al-Shararah,* the Organization of Communist Action's *al-Hurriyah,* the Arab Socialist Action Party's *Tariq al-thawrah,* and the more or less leftist intellectuals' *Dirasat Arabiyah* is essential, though even so it does not present the whole picture. The Egyptian semi-official monthly *al-Tali'ah,* the Lebanese Communist Party's organ *al-Tariq,* the independent monthly *Mawaqif,* and the independent Kuwaiti weekly *al-Tali'ah* all help in clarifying the basic and minor strategies and tactics of the New Arab Left. The various publications (books and pamphlets) are essential for anyone who seeks information about the abovementioned fronts and parties. Because of the limited space in this discussion such an ambitious exposition of the major and minor stances of the New Left groups is not possible. A brief discussion of the major ideological, political, and organizational strategies of the New Arab Left organizations will be attempted instead.

Before we embark on delineating the ideological, political, and organizational positions of the New Arab Left, one major fact should be clearly stated: Whether for good or ill, it was the transformation which the Arab Nationalist Movement had undergone after June 1967 that gave birth to both neo-leftist political thought and organizations. In other words, the credit for the emergence of the New Arab Left or, perhaps, the blame—as some would like to assert—should be laid at the doors of the Arab Nationalist Movement. Notwithstanding the fact that the roots of the abovementioned transformation can be traced back to the early sixties, it was the "Report of the Executive Committee of the Arab Nationalist Movement," published after its meeting in July 1967, that drew attention to the movement's great critical review of the old programs of all Arab active revolutionary forces, including its own programs. This report put an end to the period of political and ideological confusion through which the movement was living, particularly in the month following the 1967 defeat. A clear manifestation of the confusion referred to is best reflected in the articles written by

tribution to the Discussion About the Palestinian Democratic State," *al-Hurriyah* (Beirut), No. 506, March 16, 1970, pp. 10–13, and (Beirut), No. 507, March 23, 1970), pp. 8–10. Also, Aziz E. Jasim, "The Idealism of the Ba'ath and the Childish Leftist Realism," *al-Ahrar* (Beirut); Murqus, "A Parasitic Intellectualism Grows on the Margin of the Marxist Tendencies," *al-Hurriyah* (Beirut), No. 533, September 21, 1970, pp. 12–14.

Muhsin Ibrahim, the then philosopher of the movement in its weekly organ *al-Hurriyah*.[4]

The Popular Front for the Liberation of Palestine, which was the Palestinian phase of the post–June 1967 Arab Nationalist Movement, took the lead in introducing neo-leftist thought to the area.[5] In its conference of August 1968, the Popular Front for the Liberation of Palestine agreed on what came to be known as "the Basic Political Report of the Popular Front for the Liberation of Palestine" or "the Report of August 1968" (see Appendix D). This report signaled official emergence of the New Arab Left.[6]

THE NEW ARAB LEFT AND THE IMPERATIVE OF POLITICAL THOUGHT

The frustration of the old Arab national movement with its lack of theory or ideology to guide its revolutionary action was the starting point for a new intellectual venture. Political theory to the New Arab Left, "is not an abstract idea hanging in a vacuum, or a mental luxury, or an intellectual hobby for the educated." New revolutionary political thought, the New Arab Left asserts, is not a readymade rigid dogma but rather "a clear vision of the battle." Carrying arms and fighting, the New Arab Left argues, is not a guarantee against failure. "A clear perspective of things and of the real forces taking part in the struggle leads to success, while impetuosity and spontaneity lead to failure." Political thought is not an end but rather a means to an end. Its function is to make the masses "able to understand their enemy, his points of weakness or strength and the forces which support and ally them-

4. Muhsin Ibrahim, "No, Neither the Arabs nor Nasser Have Been Defeated," *al-Hurriyah* (Beirut), June 12, 19, and 26, 1967.

5. In August 1968 the Congress of the Popular Front for the Liberation of Palestine was held in Jordan (near Jarash). Two wings appeared. However, the whole congress, through various compromises, agreed on what came to be the "August Report" of the Popular Front for the Liberation of Palestine. Later when the Nayif Hawatmeh group split, they claimed that the report was theirs but the others did not believe in it. This, as was remarked later, was a subjective claim on the part of Hawatmeh's group.

6. The Popular Front for the Liberation of Palestine, *al-taqrir al-siyasi al-'asai lil-jabhah al-sha'biyah li-tahrir Filastin* [The Basic Political Report of the Popular Front for the Liberation of Palestine] (August 1968; neither the place nor the exact date of publication is mentioned).

selves to the enemy. Likewise the masses should understand their own forces, the forces of revolution, how to mobilize, how to overcome the enemy's points of strength and take advantage of the weaknesses of the enemy, and through what organization, mobilization and political and military programs they can escalate their forces until they can crush the enemy and achieve victory." Moreover, revolutionary political thought should be scientific, specific and "within the reach of the masses."[7] Finally, the first step in the course of national salvation, the New Arab Left maintains, lies in the "adoption of a revolutionary scientific ideology. . . . [For] the national salvation course starts with arming the people with revolutionary ideas."[8]

THE IDEOLOGY OF THE NEW ARAB LEFT

The "August 1968 Report" of the Popular Front for the Liberation of Palestine, contrary to its enthusiastic advocation of courageous, explicit, and vivid ideological and political theory, partly fell short of meeting the goals it urged. Though the Report advocated a "revolutionary scientific theory," a "scientific ideology," "the ideology of the proletariat" or, in other cases, the "ideas of the revolutionary classes . . . the workers and poor peasants," it never went so far as declaring its clear unequivocal adoption of Marxism-Leninism.[9] Nevertheless, a clear adoption of Marxism-Leninism by both the mother Front (the Popular Front for the Liberation of Palestine) and the splinter (the Popular Democratic Front for the Liberation of Palestine) was to come soon. In its February 1969 conference the Popular Front for the Liberation of Palestine declared: "Within this context the Popular Front adopts Marxist-Leninist theory as a basic strategic line for the building of the revolutionary party on a solid theoretical basis which will unify its thinking and view of the battle and will enable it to mobilize the masses to exert their efforts in one direction, which will make of them a solid force capable of achieving victory."[10]

7. The Popular Front for the Liberation of Palestine, *A Strategy for the Liberation of Palestine* (Amman: Information Department of the Popular Front for the Liberation of Palestine, 1969), pp. 4, 5, 6.

8. See Appendix D.

9. See Appendix D. Also see the Popular Front for the Liberation of Palestine, *The Basic Political Report,* pp. 2–16.

10. The Popular Front for the Liberation of Palestine, *A Strategy for the Libera-*

In the same manner, the Popular Democratic Front stated that the solution to the problems facing the national liberation movement in backward societies such as the Arab world lies in "adopting the programme of laborers and poor peasants and the [adherence] to the ideology of the proletariat—Marxism-Leninism under the leadership of the revolutionary dictatorship of the proletariat as represented by its organized political vanguard—the revolutionary Marxist-Leninist Party."[11]

Moreover, and as early as September 1969, Nayif Hawatmeh, on behalf of the Popular Democratic Front for the Liberation of Palestine, wrote: "The Arab and Palestinian national liberation movement have to choose between the reactionary bourgeoisie ideology which led to both failure and defeats all through this century or adopt the ideology of the proletariat, the theory of the working class for national democratic revolution and the national liberation war."[12]

Furthermore, the Arab Socialist Action Party made a clear commitment to Marxism-Leninism. In the words of its Secretary-General: "Not all the lines of Revolutionary Action can be implemented except with a revolutionary party, committed to a revolutionary theory— namely, Marxism-Leninism."[13]

---

tion of Palestine, p. 98; also the Popular Front for the Liberation of Palestine, al-Sitratijiyah al-Siyasiyah wa al-tanzimiyah [The Political and Organizational Strategy] (Ed. No. 1), (neither the place nor the date of publication is mentioned), p. 73; also ibid., (Amman: The Central Information Department of the Popular Front for the Liberation of Palestine, 1970), p. 140; Finally, see the Popular Front for the Liberation of Palestine, 'Ala tariq al-thawrah al-Filastiniyah (Beirut: Dar al-Tali'ah, 1970), p. 104.

11. The Popular Democratic Front for the Liberation of Palestine with an introduction by Nayif Hawatmeh, Hawla azmat harakat al-muqawamah al-Filastiniyah [On the Crisis of the Palestine Resistance Movement], 2nd ed. (Beirut: Dar al-Tali'ah, 1970), p. 32; Also see al-Hurriyah (Beirut), No. 498, 1911/1970, pp. 9, 15.

12. The Popular Democratic Front for the Liberation of Palestine with an introduction by Nayif Hawatmeh, Harakat al-muqawamah fi wad 'iha al-rahin drasah naqdiyah [The Palestinian Resistance Movement As It Stands Now—A Critical Study], 2nd ed. (Beirut: Dar al-Tali'ah, 1970), p. 9.

13. The Arab Socialist Action Party, Tariq al-thawrah [The Path of Revolution] Year 1 (1) (June 1970): 14; Also see anonymous, " 'al-Maham al-hizbiyah al-lati yanbaghi injazuha" [The Party's Duties That Need Fulfillment], Tariq al-thawrah, Year 1 (2) (1971): 2–6; Also "Hal yumkin lil-ahzab al-thawriyah al-burjuwaziyah al-saghirah al-mithaliyah 'an tatahawwal ila ahzab brulitariyah Markisiyah Lininiyah?" [Can Revolutionary Petty-Bourgeois Idealistic Parties Transform Themselves Into Marxist-Leninist Proletariat Parties?"], ibid.: 13.

Finally, and in the same manner, the Organization of Communist Action in Lebanon, in its first conference in Beirut in May 1971, concluded:

> The Organization of Communist Action in Lebanon is a political revolutionary organization enlightened in its struggle by the general principles of Marxism-Leninism which constitute the theory that inspires the struggle of the working class and the poor masses rallied around its leadership [in the struggle] against its class and national enemies. The organization works to utilize Marxism-Leninism in its struggle in order to understand the existing conditions and consequently change them. In doing so [the Organization] makes use of the theoretical and practical experiences of the revolutionary movements. . . . [The Organization] also struggles against any trend of revisionism in Marxism-Leninism or any infiltration of bourgeoisie ideology to it, and struggles to develop [Marxism-Leninism] in the light of experience and necessity.[14]

The question that emerges, then, is this: In what way does the New Arab Left differ from traditional Arab communist parties? Two major points are emphasized by the New Arab Left in this regard. First, notwithstanding the fact that its ideological source is Marxism-Leninism, the New Arab Left stresses the non-dogmatic aspect of the doctrine. To the New Arab Left, Marxism-Leninism is a "tool of analysis" and a "directory for actions" rather than a ready-made dogma. Marxism-Leninism, according to the neo-leftist Arabs, is an indispensable means for comprehending the forces of revolutions on the one hand, and perceiving the forces of counterrevolution in these societies and outside, on the other. The Popular Front for the Liberation of Palestine, for instance, maintains:

> The essence of Marxism is the method which it represents in viewing and analyzing things and in determining the direction of this motion. Consequently, the revolutionary understanding of Marxism is the understanding of it as a working guide and not as a fixed, rigid, doctrine. Lenin and Mao Tse-Tung, and before them Marx and Engels, have recorded on more than one occasion the need for the Marxist view as a working guide and not as a rigid doctrine.[15]

14. The Organization of Communist Action in Lebanon, "The Communiqué of Establishing the Organization of Communist Action in Lebanon," *al-Hurriyah* (Beirut), No. 574-51/1971, p. 11.

15. Popular Front for the Liberation of Palestine, *A Strategy for the Liberation of Palestine,* p. 93.

Moreover, the Popular Front continues:

> Theory in Marxist concept is constantly in continuous dialectical relation with reality and action. The fact that it is a dialectical relation with action means that it is in a state of growth, progress and modification and not in a fixed state.
>
> The most dangerous thing that confronts us in our adherence to Marxist theory is understanding it in a mechanical, idealistic manner which deprives it of its ability to explain the living reality. (pp. 94–95)

In a more direct statement, the Popular Front for the Liberation of Palestine defines the issues on which it views itself as different from the old left as follows:

> By the application of Marxism-Leninism to our actual circumstances and the battle which we are fighting—our adherence to Marxist-Leninist theory becomes meaningful and capable of being translated into results. It would be a gross error to imagine that our mere declaration of adherence to Marxism-Leninism is a fairy wand which will open before us the road to victory. If there are examples of what Marxism-Leninism has represented in respect to certain revolutions, such as those of China and Vietnam, there are corresponding examples where adherence to Marxism-Leninism has not led to anything. The Arab communist parties which are formally and verbally committed to Marxism-Leninism have not been able to lead the revolution in our homeland because this commitment has been verbal, or because they have understood the theory in a rigid and fossilized manner, or because they have not been able to apply this theoretical weapon to our actual living circumstances in such a way as to deduce from it a clear view of the battle and a sound strategy for its leadership. (pp. 95–96)

A more specific enunciation of criticisms against the Arab communists is provided once again by the Popular Front for the Liberation of Palestine: "Moreover, the failure of the communist parties and their attitude toward the issues of the masses, such as those of [Arab] unity, Arab nationalism and Israel, has produced in the minds of the masses a confusion between Marxist thought and these attitudes" (p. 97).

The leadership of the Popular Democratic Front for the Liberation of Palestine, who leveled almost the same criticisms against the Communists, went one step further and considered the Communist parties as nothing but part of the "revolutionary progressive wing of the petty bourgeoisie." Moreover, the stances of the communists after June 1967 were a target for more criticisms from the Democratic Front. According to the Popular Democratic Front for the Liberation of Palestine:

> The communists implemented a rightist and backward program in the two banks [of the River Jordan]. This contributed to [the emergence] of a forged and ignorant program of revolutionary national action. . . . The program under which the communists waged their national struggle in the two banks stemmed from a mistaken understanding of the nature of the class forces and the political and national role that might be played by the big bourgeoisie and the political feudalists at this stage. The Stalinist conceptions persisted in controlling the program of the communist party.[16]

In consequence, the Popular Democratic Front for the Liberation of Palestine argues, the Communists gave new life to the big bourgeoisie leaderships and participated in implementing a program that ultimately served the rightist interests rather than the leftist ones. Furthermore, the rationale maintains that the Communists reinforced their original "mistaken rightist" analysis of the Israeli questions and enhanced their "revisionist" stance vis-à-vis the Arab "progressive" regimes whose leadership had already fallen and whose policies had been condemned as bankrupt.

The stand that the Arab Socialist Action Party took with regard to the communists is most interesting. Notwithstanding the fact that the Arab Socialist Action Party and the Popular Front for the Liberation of Palestine have the same Secretary General and consider themselves to be one party, the early Arab Socialist Action Party's publications showed a political rather than an ideological stance. The attitude of the Arab Socialist Action Party toward the Communists, more or less apologetic and flirting, is quite clear. In the party's words:

> There might be differences between us and the Arab communist parties, yet any animosity towards [these parties] and [any confrontation] with them, under any name or slogan or title whatsoever, not only harms the Arab liberation movement but it also makes those who advocate that [animosity], consciously or not, enemies of the working class and

16. Popular Democratic Front for the Liberation of Palestine, *On the Crisis of the Palestinian Resistance Movement*, pp. 109, 140.

servants to both the big and the petty bourgeoisie if not [servants] to reactionary and imperialist forces.[17]

In a perhaps even more perplexing statement, the Arab Socialist Action Party asserted:

We declare our party a group, among the other groups of the Arab working class, standing with awareness and responsibility beside the communist parties. Despite the party's autonomous existence, it does not constitute, in our eyes, a substitute for the communist parties which, for the last forty long years, led the struggle of the glorified Arab working class and for which [the Arab communist parties] paid huge sacrifices that history will record [for the communists] with honor and esteem. (pp. 50–51)

The honeymoon mentioned above did not, however, last very long. Once the Arab Socialist Action Party was criticized by both the Iraqi and the Lebanese communist parties, it quickly though in a "comradely" manner introduced a list of fatal criticisms against the Arab communists. The list included the famous "indirect" assistance of these parties to the establishment of Israel, the Arab communists' call for the recognition of Israel, the Iraqi communists' mistaken stance after the 1958 revolution in Iraq, the hesitation to support cost of the Palestine resistance movement, and the doubt of the Arab Communists (particularly the Jordanian Communist Party) as well as other issues such as Arab unity and relations with the two socialist camps.[18]

Finally, the Organization of Communist Action in Lebanon directed the bitterest attacks against the Arab communists. This organization maintains that the Arab communist parties developed a "rightist opportunist" position. In fact, the organization goes so far as to deny the right of the Lebanese Communist Party to call itself "Communist" because it does not deserve that title.[19] It should be mentioned here, however, that the Lebanese Communist Party has retaliated against

17. Anonymous, *Tariq al-thawrah* 1 (June 1970): 47.

18. The Editorial Board, "On the Party and the Revolution," *Tariq al-thawrah* 1 (2) (1971): 148–60.

19. The Organization of the Communist Action in Lebanon, "The Communiqué of Establishing the Organization of the Communist Action in Lebanon," *al-Hurriyah* (Beirut), 574, pp. 2, 6.

the attacks of *al-Hurriyah* with relentless enthusiasm and that the war goes on.[20]

The second major area in which the New Arab Left finds itself different from the Arab communist parties can be summarized in the following: The New Arab Left's adherence to Marxism-Leninism is by no means an adherence to the remnants of Stalinism in international relations. The Arab neo-leftists reject any relations with the Soviet Union or Communist China that would reduce them to mere satellites for this or that Communist camp. While they recognize the two communist camps, as well as other socialist regimes and liberation movements, as their natural allies, the New Arab Left is hypersensitive to any relationship that would fetter their freedom for independent actions.[21]

Finally, it should be remembered that despite the ideological and political wars between the organizations of the New Arab Left on the one hand and the Arab communist parties on the other, all leftist groups (old and new) occasionally support each other against their common enemies. The clearest and most recent example of this was the solid stand that all the factions of the New Arab Left took in support of the Sudanese Communist Party in its crisis of July 1971.[22]

THE POLITICAL THOUGHT OF THE NEW ARAB LEFT

The New Arab Left has given much attention to discerning and categorizing political allies and enemies. The efforts of the Popular Front for the Liberation of Palestine in this regard were particularly conscientious. The other neo-leftist factions do not differ in their analyses

20. Anonymous with an introduction by Karim Murwah, *al-Yasar al-haqiqi wa al 'yasar al-mughamir* [The True Left and the Adventurous Left] (Beirut: Dar al-Farabi, 1970).

21. The Editorial Board, "On the Party and the Revolution," *Tariq al-thawrah* 1 (2) (1971): 160; also see an interview with Dr. Habash, Secretary-General of the Popular Front for the Liberation of Palestine and the Arab Socialist Action Party conducted by Abdullah Schleifer, "Enemy Brothers of the Palestinian Front Speak Out," *Jeune Afrique* (Tunis) (March 1969): 52–53; finally, see Mohammed Kishly, *Hawla al-nizam al-Ra 'smali wa al-yasar fi Lubnan* [On the Capitalist System and the Left in Lebanon] (Beirut: Dar al-Tali'ah, 1967), pp. 110–11.

22. For the stand of the Organization of the Communist Action in Lebanon see *al-Hurriyah* (Beirut), No. 577-(26/7/1971), p. 2; The Arab Socialist Action Party in *El-Rayah* (Beirut), No. 356 (28) (2/8/1971), p. 4.

in this regard from the Popular Front for the Liberation of Palestine. We can assume, therefore, that what is said in the pages to follow about the Popular Front for the Liberation of Palestine applies as well to all other factions; when differences arise, special attention will be given to clarify them.

In a very systematic way, the Popular Front for the Liberation of Palestine outlined both the *potential* and the *actual* political forces expected to be active and operational in the Palestinian and Arab struggle. These forces were divided into two major camps, one for the revolution and one against it. Each of these two camps, however, was divided into three levels: the Palestinian level, the Arab level and the international level. An elaboration of this view will eventually provide us with the political map as drawn by the New Arab Left.

THE ENEMY CAMP

On the local Palestinian-Arab level Israel stands as the primary enemy: "In our battle for the liberation we first face Israel as a political, military and economic entity which is trying to effect the maximum military mobilization of its two and a half million nationals to defend its aggressive expansionist racial structure and prevent us from regaining our land, our freedom and our rights."[23]

On the Palestinian level still, there are other potential forces of counter-revolution that the New Arab Left does not fail to recognize. The PFLP, together with all other neo-leftist groups, rejects the conciliatory slogans which advocate such notions as "We are all commandos" or, "The Palestinian people with *all* its classes is taking part in the armed struggle." In more specific words, the Palestinian bourgeoisie, living in the occupied territories or outside, are "not among the forces of the revolution." This is because the

Palestine bourgeoisie is essentially a business and banking bourgeoisie whose interests are interconnected among its members and are linked with the business and banking interests of imperialism. The wealth of this class is derived from brokerage transactions in foreign goods, insurance operations, and banking business. Therefore, in the strategic field, this class is against the revolution which aims at putting an end to the existence of imperialism and its interests in our homeland, which

23. PFLP Information Department, *A Strategy for the Liberation of Palestine,* p. 8.

means the destruction of its sources of wealth. Since our battle against Israel is at the same time a battle against imperialism, this class will stand by its own interests, that is, with imperialism against the revolution.[24]

It needs no emphasis that the PFLP, as well as other factions of the New Arab Left, are aware of the fact that "*certain* sectors of this bourgeoisie may be an exception to this rule and that, by virtue of the special character of the Palestinian question, they may remain on the side of the revolution and abstain from working against it."[25]

On the Arab world level, the Arab millionaires (merchants, bankers, feudal lords, owners of large estates, kings, emirs, and sheikhs), the Arab neo-leftists maintain, are closely connected with world capitalism. In consequence their interests automatically lie with world imperialism. "This means that . . . Arab reaction cannot but be on the side of its own interests, the continuation of which depends on the persistence of imperialism, and consequently cannot side with the masses."[26]

On the international level, the list of enemies provided by the Popular Front for the Liberation of Palestine includes the World Zionist Movement. This is due to the Arab New Left's belief that "Israel is in reality an integral part of the World Zionist movement; indeed, it is an offshoot of this movement."[27] Zionism, the New Arab Left argues, provides Israel not only with moral support but with "material support which includes providing Israel with more people, more money, more arms, more technical knowhow . . . in addition to its support through publicity and propaganda in every part of the world."[28]

Finally, perhaps the most dangerous enemy of both the New Arab Left and Arab revolutionary aspirations is world imperialism in general and United States imperialism in particular:

Here also we want to stress that the addition of imperialism to our image of the enemy camp should not be regarded as an addition of

24. Ibid., p. 35–36.

25. Ibid., p. 36.

26. Ibid., p. 14.

27. Ibid., p. 9; also see PFLP's *al-Jabhah al-sha' biyah wa al-'amaliyat al-kharijiyah* [The Popular Front and the Foreign Operations] (Beirut: al-Hadaf Series No. 2, n.d.), pp. 9–19.

28. PFLP, A *Strategy For*, p. 9; also see ASAP *Tariq al-thawrah* 1, p. 11. Again Nayif Hawatmeh, introd., *On the Crisis of the Palestine Resistance Movement*, pp. 40–41.

mere words to our definition of the enemy, for it enters into the concrete picture we have of the enemy against whom we are waging this battle. Imperialism here means more arms, more support and more money for Israel. It means Phantom jets, atomic bomb secrets, and the building of an economy capable of facing the permanent blockade and state of war which we try to impose.[29]

THE REVOLUTIONARY CAMP

The forces of revolution on the Palestinian level, according to both the PFLP and the New Arab Left, are the classes of workers and peasants who constitute "the majority of the Palestinian people and physically fill all camps, villages and poor urban districts." But why restrict it to these classes? Because, the PFLP answers, "it is these classes which are daily suffering the oppressive exploitation process exercised by world imperialism and its allies in our homeland. . . . Here lie the forces of revolution—the forces of change [who are ready] to fight and die because the difference between death and life . . . is not much."[30] This same analysis is projected on the wider Arab level where again the "workers and peasants are the mainstay of the revolution, its basic class material and its leadership."[31]

The New Arab Left's stand *vis-à-vis* both the petty bourgeois class *and* regimes merits special attention. It was the analysis of the role of this particular issue that aroused fierce and hot debates and flooded the Arab intellectual market with articles and books. Notwithstanding the fact that the role of the petty bourgeoisie was discussed before 1967 in some pioneering studies, such as that of Yasin al-Hafiz, it was not until after June 1967 that the issue fell within the focus of Arab intellectual inquiry, debate, and struggle.[32]

29. PFLP, A *Strategy For*, pp. 12–13; also see *Tariq al-thawrah* 1, p. 107; finally see Hawatmeh, introd., *The Palestinian Resistance Movement as It Stands Now*, p. 120.

30. PFLP, A *Strategy For*, pp. 24–25. Also see George Habash, *al-Thawrah wa al-'ummal* [The Revolution and the Workers] (Amman: PFLP Central Information Department, 1970), pp. 7–28.

31. PFLP, A *Strategy For*, pp. 24, 33, and 37; also see Tariq al-thawrah 1, (2) (1971): 6; also see Hawatmeh, introd., *On the Crisis of the Palestine Resistance Movement*, p. 9.

32. Yasin al-Hafiz, *On Some Issues of the Arab Revolution*. Nayif Mawatmeh, *The Crisis of the Revolution in Southern Yaman, 1965 and 1968* and The Organi-

As to the petty bourgeois *class* in general the New Arab Left basically agrees with the conclusions of the PFLP. The latter maintains

> Unlike the working class, the petty bourgeoisie does not live within specific class conditions, and here lies the reason for its vacillation and its habit of shifting from one position to another according to the progress of the revolution and the particular stage it has reached. However, it is possible for us to say in general that, during the stage of democratic national liberation, this class *may* be an ally to the force of the revolution and to its basic material represented by the workers and peasants, but alliance with this class must be *so* alert as to prevent it from infiltrating into the position of command because that would expose the revolution to vacillation and deviation or slackness.[33]

While the New Arab Left recognizes the historical and contemporary antagonism of the Arab petty bourgeoisie *regimes* to imperialism, Zionism, Israel, and Arab reactionary establishments (and despite the achievements of these regimes "on the road to national democratic revolution"), the New Arab Left believes that "these regimes are no longer capable . . . of pursuing their march on the road of revolution" effectively. In consequence, "On the basis of the fact that these regimes oppose colonialism and Israel on the one hand, and the fact that they put forward [petty bourgeois] compromising programs for confronting the enemy on the other, the relationship with these regimes should be one of *alliance and conflict at the same time.* Alliance with them because they are opposed to imperialism and Israel, and conflict with them because of their [petty bourgeois] strategy in confronting the enemy."[34]

Finally, and to complete the map of political alliances as drawn by the New Arab Left, a picture of the forces of the revolution on the international level should be presented. In this regard it is interesting to notice the cool attitude toward the Eastern Socialist Bloc in general and the Soviet Union in particular.[35] In contrast, a leftist group like the PFLP showed more or less excessive enthusiasm and admiration of the

zation Committee of the NLF, *How Do We Understand The Experience of the Southern Yemen,* 1969 and the OLS; *Why the Organization of Lebanese Socialists?,* 1970.

33. PFLP, *A Strategy For,* p. 28; also see Hawatmeh, introd., *On The Crisis,* pp. 25–29.

34. See Appendix D.

35. See *Tariq al-thawrah* (2): 54 and 160.

"great People's Republic of China" because of the "strategic congru-
ence" is has with the Arab revolutionary leftist aspirations. Moreover,
the list of allies includes "the enslaved peoples . . . of Africa, Asia and
Latin America . . . the liberation movement in Vietnam, the revolu-
toinary forces in Cuba and the Democratic People's Republic of Korea
and the national liberation movements"[36] in the third world. In brief,
it is easy to discern that the alliances envisaged by the New Arab Left
on the local, Arab and international levels are conditioned by their
beliefs in an armed people's protracted war which rejects any solutions
(such as the Security Council resolution of November 22, 1967,[37] or
the Rogers Plan) that fall short of achieving a "free democratic state in
Palestine," which is an integral part of a free progressive Arab society
where Jews, Christians, and Moslems live together without any discrimination whatsoever in duties or right.[38]

THE ORGANIZATIONAL STRATEGY OF
THE NEW ARAB LEFT

In order to confront and defeat the very strong enemy camp, the New
Arab Left maintains, the Palestinian and Arab national progressive
movements need a strong revolutionary party. The major characteristics of such a party are these:

1. A revolutionary theory, for without it no revolution is possible.
In more specific terms, a revolutionary theory (Marxism-Leninism) is
a condition *sine qua non* for any solid revolutionary party.

2. A class strategy whereby the classes of city workers, peasants,
and revolutionary intellectuals constitute the rank and file of the party.
The leadership, however, should be kept in the hands of those who
demonstrate "deep understanding of and commitment to scientific
socialism."[39]

3. A mass-oriented party that believes in and works for the masses
without arrogant, seclusive, isolationist or elitist attitudes. In brief, "the

36. PFLP, A *Strategy For,* pp. 67–68.

37. Appendix D. Hawatmeh, introd., *On the Crisis of the Palestine,* pp. 100–
101; and Information Department of the PFLP, *Rihlat al-Istislam min qarar Majlis
al-amn ila Mashru' Rogers* [The Trip of Capitulation: From the Security Council
Decision to Rogers' Plan] (Place of publication not mentioned, 1970), pp. 37–53.

38. PFLP Information Department, *Filastin: Nahwa hallin Dimuqrati* [Palestine:
Toward a Democratic Solution] (1971).

39. PFLP Information Department, A *Strategy For,* pp. 91–98, 99–103.

relationship between the party and the masses is a dialectical one. It teaches them and is taught by them, affects them and is affected by them."[40]

4. No armed struggle can be waged and gained without a combatant party. While the party should have a military wing, its political organization, nevertheless, must have both a military structure and training. Briefly, "the motto which says 'every combatant is a party member and every party member is a combatant' traces before us a basic strategic line for the building of the fighting party in conformity with our view of the Palestinian national movement and of the liberation struggle."[41]

5. The basic relations within the revolutionary party are governed by the principle of "Democratic Centralism." The latter principle is composed of two major elements

    (i) Democracy
        a. The right of every member to know, discuss and criticize in a responsible manner any issues relating to the party's programs and actions.
        b. Collective leadership
        c. The members' right to criticize and even change leadership whenever necessary; and
    (ii) Centralism
        a. The duty of all members to adhere to the programs and policies that have already been designated by the defined organizational channels.
        b. The submission of subsidiary leadership units to the higher ones.
        c. The "leadership's absolute power during execution . . . of what the party has democratically decided."[42]

6. Finally, no revolutionary party can proceed with its struggle toward victory without practicing the principle of "criticism and self-criticism." Adherence to this principle is necessary because "no party or individual can avoid mistakes in work." Moreover, "Stopping to evaluate our work from time to time, placing the party and its policies and activities on the dissection table once in a while is a necessity for success."[43]

40. Ibid., p. 111 and 104–11.
41. Ibid., p. 116 and 112–16.
42. Ibid., p. 123 and 117–24.
43. Ibid., p. 125.

EPILOGUE

As to the future of the New Arab Left, it should be emphasized that any attempt to foresee and predict what will be is, at this stage, nothing more than mere speculation. Nevertheless, one can introduce some general hypotheses as to the future trends on the basis that these assumptions are more probable than others. In this regard, it seems sound to assume that the future of the New Arab Left is conditioned and consequently dependent on the same factors that initially gave birth to and subsequently reinforced this leftist trend.

To begin with, the stalemate in the Arab-Israeli conflict eventually contributed to the consolidation of the new leftist positions and undermined the positions and policies of the "moderate" Arabs, whether those were regimes or parties.

Secondly, the continued existence of obsolete traditional regimes in the area has fostered the policies advocated by the revolutionary leftists. Any effort by these traditional elites to ameliorate the deteriorated situations in their countries will help to limit the programs and activities of the new leftist forces inasmuch as misery, poverty, and oppression constitute the seedbed necessary for the survival and for the multiplication of leftist ideas in the area.

Third, the continuation of United States support for Israel against the Arabs will serve as a direct catalyst in the growth of the Arab leftist forces in the area. Moreover, the partisan policies of the United States will, indirectly, promote the influence of communist states, a condition which will buttress the position of both the old and new Arab left.

To conclude, it is difficult for us to accept the more or less hasty conclusions adopted by some students of the Middle East who, particularly after the fatal blow rendered to the Palestinian commandos in Jordan in September 1970, suggested that the New Arab Left, if not already dead, would never manage to stand on its feet again. It is our belief that the New Arab Left will exist along with other extremist movements in the area as long as the reasons that created it and fostered its existence continue. In a word, if the sufferings of the Arab masses are not alleviated and if the basic aspirations of these masses are not considered, it is to be expected that the extremist violent politics, including those of the New Arab Left, will sustain, flourish, and perhaps, dominate the politics of the area.

THE CONSTITUTION OF THE BA'ATH PARTY, 1947

BASIC PRINCIPLES

I. Unity and Freedom of the Arab Nation

The Arabs are one nation which has a natural right to live in one state and
be free in directing its destinies.

Therefore the Arab Ba'ath Socialist Party considers that:—

(1) The Arab homeland is an indivisible political and economic unity,
and that it is impossible for any one of the Arab countries fully to
realize the requirements of its life in isolation from any other Arab
country.

(2) The Arab nation is a cultural unity, and all the differences existing
between its sons are accidental and spurious and will pass away
with the awakening of Arab consciousness.

(3) The Arab homeland is for the Arabs and they alone have the right
to manage its affairs, dispose of its wealth, and direct its destinies.

II. The Personality of the Arab Nation

The Arab nation is characterized by certain qualities clearly seen in its successive revivals: a fertile vitality and creativeness, and a capacity for renewal and resurgence—a resurgence which is always related to the growth of
individual freedom and the extent to which the evolution of the individual
is in harmony with the national interest.

Therefore the Arab Ba'ath Socialist Party considers that:—

(1) Freedom of speech, assembly, belief, and art is sacred and not to
be diminished by any authority.

(2) The value of the citizens—after they have been granted equal opportunities—is to be assessed according to their contribution in work towards the progress and prosperity of the Arab nation, without regard to any other consideration.

III. The Mission of the Arab Nation

The Arab nation has an eternal mission which appears in renewed and complementary forms in the different stages of history and aims at revitalizing human values, stimulating the progress of mankind, and furthering harmony and cooperation between the nations.

Therefore the Arab Ba'ath Socialist Party considers that:—

(1) Colonization and all that pertains to it are a criminal enterprise against which the Arabs struggle with all possible means endeavoring, up to the limit of their material and moral capabilities, to help all peoples struggling for their freedom.

(2) Humanity is an entity held together by common interests and sharing the same values and civilization. The Arabs are nourished by world civilization and in their turn nourish it; they stretch the hand of brotherhood to other nations and cooperate with them in creating just institutions guaranteeing to all peoples welfare, peace, and moral and spiritual advance.

GENERAL PRINCIPLES

Article 1.

The Arab Ba'ath Socialist Party is a comprehensive Party with branches in the other Arab countries; it does not concern itself with regional policy except from the point of view of overall Arab interests.

Article 2.

The party's headquarters is at present in Damascus, but may be transferred to any other Arab city if the national interest requires it.

Article 3.

The Arab Ba'ath Socialist Party is nationalist and believes that nationhood is a living and deathless fact and that the feeling of nationalism which closely binds the individual to his nation is a sacred feeling, charged with creative power, impelling to sacrifice, inspiring a sense of responsibility, directing the humanity of the individual along a practical and fruitful course. The nationalist idea preached by the party is the will of the Arab people to become free and united, to have the opportunity of realizing the Arab personality in history and to cooperate with other nations in all that ensures for humanity its advance along the right path to welfare and prosperity.

Article 4.

The Arab Ba'ath Socialist Party believes that socialism is a necessity springing from the very heart of Arab nationalism because it is the ideal social order through which the Arab people may realize its potentialities and achieve the fullest flowering of its genius, and which therefore will guarantee for the nation continuous growth in its moral and material production and ensure the closest brotherly ties between its members.

Article 5.

The Arab Ba'ath Socialist Party is a popular party believing that sovereignty belongs to the people which alone is the source of all authority and leadership, and that the value of the state results from its derivation from the will of the masses and its sanctity depends on the extent of their freedom in choosing it. For the accomplishment of its mission, therefore, the party relies on the people and seeks to be in close contact with it and strives to raise its intellectual, moral, economic, and health standards, so that it can be aware of its identity and be able to exercise its rights both in individual and national life.

Article 6.

The Arab Ba'ath Socialist Party is a revolutionary party believing that its principal aims—resurrecting Arab nationalism and building socialism—cannot be realized except by revolution and struggle, and that reliance on slow evolution and contentment with superficial and partial reforms threaten these aims with failure and extinction.

Therefore the Party resolves upon:—

(1) The struggle against foreign imperialism for the complete and absolute liberation of the Arab homeland.

(2) The struggle to bring together all Arabs in a single Arab state.
(3) The overthrow of the existing corrupt order by a revolution that shall embrace all aspects of life—intellectual, economic, social, and political.

Article 7.

The Arab homeland is that area of the globe which is inhabited by the Arab nation and which stretches between the Taurus Mountains, hte Pocht-i-Kouh Mountains, the Gulf of Basra, the Arabian Sea, the Mountains of Ethiopia, the Great Sahara, the Atlantic Ocean, and the Mediterranean Sea.

Article 8.

The official language of the state and the recognized language of the citizens in writing and teaching is the Arabic language.

Article 9.

The flag of the Arab state is the flag of the Arab Revolt which broke out in 1916 to free the Arab nation and unify it.

Article 10.

An Arab is one whose language is Arabic, who has lived in the Arab land or aspired to live in it, and who believes in his belonging to the Arab nation.

Article 11.

Anyone who has preached or joined a racial grouping against the Arabs shall be removed from the Arab homeland, as also shall be anyone who emigrates to the Arab homeland for imperialistic purposes.

Article 12.

The Arab woman shall enjoy the full rights of a citizen and the party is struggling to raise her level, so that she may deserve to enjoy these rights.

Article 13.

The party seeks to realize the principle of equality of opportunity in education and economic life in order that, in all the fields of human activity, the citizens may be able to reveal their abilities in their true form and to the maximum degree.

THE WAY

The Party's Internal Policy

Article 14.

The system of government in the Arab state will be a constitutional representative system, and the executive power will be responsible to the legislative power, which will be directly elected by the people.

Article 15.

The national bond will be the only bond existing in the Arab state—a bond that guarantees harmony between the citizens and their fusion in one nation and that combats other and factious forms of solidarity such as the religious, the sectarian, the tribal, the racial, and the provincial.

Article 16.

The system of administration in the Arab state will be a decentralized one.

Article 17.

The party strives to spread the popular spirit (government by the people) and make it a living reality in the life of the individual; it seeks to draw up a constitution for the state that will guarantee to Arab citizens absolute equality before the law, the expression of their will with complete freedom, and the choosing of their representatives truly, thereby preparing for them a free life within the framework of the law.

Article 18.

A unified code of laws will be enacted for the Arab state in complete freedom; it will be in harmony with the spirit of the present age and take account of the past experiences of the Arab nation.

Article 19.

The judicial power will be independent of, and safeguarded from, interference by any other power. It will enjoy absolute immunity.

Article 20.

Full rights of citizenship will be granted to every citizen who has lived on Arab soil, been loyal to the Arab motherland, and detached himself from any racial grouping.

Article 21.

Military service will be compulsory in the Arab state.

The Party's Foreign Policy

Article 22.

The foreign policy of the Arab state will derive its inspiration from Arab national interest and from the eternal mission of the Arabs whose aim is to participate with other nations in bringing into existence a harmonious, free, and safe world that will forever march from progress to progress.

Article 23.

The Arabs will struggle with all their strength to destroy the bulwarks of colonialism, occupation, and all foreign political influence in their country.

Article 24.

Since the Arab people alone is the source of all authority, therefore all treaties, agreements, or bonds concluded by governments in infringement of the Arabs' complete sovereignty will be abrogated.

Article 25.

Arab foreign policy will aim to give a true picture of the Arabs' will to live as free men and of their sincere desire to see all nations enjoy freedom like them.

The Party's Economic Policy

Article 26.

The Arab Ba'ath Party is socialist, believing that the economic wealth of the homeland belongs to the nation.

Article 27.

The present distribution of wealth in the Arab homeland is unjust. It will therefore be reviewed and distributed among the citizens in a just manner.

Article 28.

All citizens are equal in their human value. The party therefore will forbid the exploitation of the work of others.

Article 29.

Public utility institutions, major natural resources, the principal means of production and transport are the property of the nation and will be administered by the state directly. Companies and foreign concessions will be abolished.

Article 30.

Agricultural property will be fixed in proportion to the owner's ability to exploit it fully without exploiting the effort of others, under the supervision of the state and in accordance with its general economic program.

Article 31.

Small industrial property will be fixed proportionately to the economic standards enjoyed by other citizens in the state.

Article 32.

Workers will participate in the management of the factory and will be granted, in addition to their wages which will be fixed by the state, a share of the profits of the factory in a proportion to be fixed by the State.

Article 33.

Ownership of built-up landed property is allowed to all citizens, but they will not be entitled to let and exploit it at the expense of others, and the state will guarantee a minimum of ownership to all citizens.

Article 34.

Acquisition of property and inheritance are natural rights and will be safeguarded within the limits of the national interest.

Article 35.

Usury between citizens will be forbidden and a single government bank will be founded which will issue the currency, guaranteed by the national production. This bank will finance necessary agricultural and industrial projects.

Article 36.

The state will directly supervise internal and foreign trade in order to abolish exploitation between consumer and producer, and in order to protect trade and national production from foreign competition and ensure a balance between exports and imports.

Article 37.

A comprehensive program will be drawn up in the light of the most recent experience and economic theories for industrializing the Arab homeland, expanding the national production toward new horizons, and directing the industrial economy in each country in accordance with its possibilities and the availability of raw materials in it.

The Party's Social Policy

Article 38.

Family, Offspring, and Marriage:—
    (1) The family is the basic cell of the nation, and the state is responsible for protecting it, developing it, and ensuring for it the conditions of happiness.
    (2) Offspring is a trust given to the family first, and secondary to the state. Together they must strive to increase it and to care for its health and upbringing.
    (3) Marriage is a national duty and the state must encourage, facilitate, and supervise it.

Article 39.

The Health of the Community
    The state will establish at its expense the institutions of preventive medicine, sanatoria, and hospitals that are necessary to meet the full needs of all citizens and to guarantee them free treatment.

Article 40.

(1) Work is compulsory for anyone who is able to do it, and the state must guarantee mental or manual work to every citizen.

(2) Earnings from work must insure for the worker—as a minimum—a decent standard of living.

(3) The state must guarantee the livelihood of all those who are unable to work.

(4) A law just to the workers will be enacted, fixing the daily hours of work, granting the worker paid weekly and annual holidays, safeguarding his rights and ensuring social security for old age and indemnity for partial or total unemployment.

(5) Free unions will be formed for workers and peasants and will be encouraged to become a good instrument for defending the workers' and peasants' rights, raising their standards of living, improving their ability, increasing the opportunities offered to them, creating a spirit of solidarity among them, and representing them in the higher labor tribunals.

(6) Special labor tribunals will be formed, on which the state and the unions of the workers and peasants will be represented, to settle disputes that may arise between them and between the managers of industry and the representatives of the state.

Article 41.

The Culture of the Community

(1) The party seeks to create a common culture for the Arab homeland; a culture that will be Arab, free, progressive, comprehensive, deep, and humanist in its aims. This culture the party seeks to spread through all strata of society.

(2) The state will be responsible for safeguarding freedom of speech, publication, assembly and protest, and freedom of the press, within the limits of the overall national interest on the Arabs. All the means necessary to realize these freedoms will be provided by the state.

(3) Intellectual work is one of the most sacred kinds of work and it is for the state to protect thinkers and scientists.

(4) Scope will be given within the limits of the Arab national idea for the founding of clubs and the formation of societies, parties, and youth organizations, and tourist organizations. Use will be made of the cinema, broadcasting, television, and all the means of mod-

ern civilization to spread national culture and to promote the welfare of the people.

Article 42.

The party aims at abolishing class differences and privileges, which derive from a corrupt social setup. The party therefore struggles on the side of the toiling and the oppressed classes of society and will continue to do so until these differences and privileges have ceased to exist and all citizens have regained their full human value and a new life is offered to them under a just social order in which no citizen shall enjoy any distinction over another save that based on intellectual ability and manual skill.

Article 43.

Nomadism is a primitive social condition which weakens national production and makes of a large section of the nation a paralyzed organ and an obstacle to its growth and advance.

The party therefore strives to settle the Bedouin and grant them lands, and to abolish tribal customs and apply the laws of the state to the tribes.

The Party's Educational Policy

The party's educational policy aims at creating a new Arab generation believing in the unity and eternal mission of its nation, taking to scientific thinking, freed from the bonds of superstition and reactionary traditions, infused with the spirit of optimism, struggle, and national solidarity among all citizens in realizing the total Arab revolution and serving the cause of human progress. The party therefore resolves:—

Article 44.

That all intellectual, economic, political, architectural, and artistic manifestations of life be stamped with a national Arab character which will restore the nation's links with its glorious past and urge it forward to a future still more glorious and exemplary.

Article 45.

Education is one of the exclusive functions of the state. Foreign and private educational institutions will therefore be abolished.

Article 46.

Education in all its stages will be free to all citizens. In its primary and secondary stages it will be compulsory.

Article 47.

Vocational schools with the most up-to-date equipment will be established and training in them will be free.

Article 48.

The teaching profession as well as all that pertains to education will be confined to Arab citizens, except for higher education.

AMENDMENT OF THE CONSTITUTION

The basic and general principles may not be amended. Other parts of the constitution may be amended by a two-thirds majority of the party's council on a proposal put forward by the executive committee, or by a quarter of the members of the council or by a tenth of the general assembly.

THE POLITICAL MANIFESTO OF
THE TENTH NATIONAL CONFERENCE
OF THE SOCIALIST ARAB BA'ATH PARTY

(March 1–10, 1970)

The Resolution passed by the Tenth National Convention of the Arab Ba'ath
Socialist Party, which convened in Baghdad during the first half of March,
were announced on April 13, 1970. The Political Manifesto of the convention was broadcast by Comrade Shibli al-'Aysami, Assistant Secretary-General of the party, over the Broadcasting Station of Baghdad, the Broadcasting Station of the Armed Forces, and the Baghdad Television Station. Following is the text of the Manifesto:

"Masses of our struggling Arab nation!

"The national conventions of the Arab Ba'ath Socialist Party have been,
across the party's advance of struggle, major stop-stations where experiences
of revolutionary work gather, the incentives of the ideological, political, and
social development of the Arab Revolution come forward and the features
become clear of the scientific visibility of Arab realities and of the laws of
their fundamental development within the framework of the progressive
revolution of national liberation in the Third World and the socialist revolution as a whole. It was in the light of that consideration that the Tenth National Convention of the Party convened in Baghdad between March 1 and
10. The convention stressed the necessity of solving the Kurdish issue in
northern Iraq in a manner conforming with the humane dimension of the
Ba'ath party's nationalist credo as well as with the requirements of the unity
of struggle of the Arab and Kurdish masses for the achievement of their nationalist goals of liberation that place them in one line against the imperialist-Zionist conspiracy coalition.

"The Tenth National Convention has demarcated the nature of the current stage of Arab conditions in the light of a comprehensive analysis of the

political and class conditions in the Arab world. As a result, the convention came to produce a strategy for party, political, and commando work.

"It was quite natural for the convention to embark upon its work by addressing greetings to the party strugglers in the territory of Iraq who, between the Ninth National Convention held in February 1968 and the Tenth National Convention, succeeded in detonating the July 17 revolution and achieving important victories to Iraq and to the Arab nation. Coming at the top of these victories was the recognition of the German Democratic Republic and the Revolutionary Government of South Vietnam; the crushing of spies and conspiratorial attempts; heroic steadfastness in the face of imperialistic and reactionary pressures and inroads; resistance in the face of the Iranian invasion schemes and imperialistic influence in the Arab Gulf; promptness in supporting the two revolutions of Libya and the Sudan; committing the Iraqi armed forces to serve the interests of commando work, offering constant and growing support to it, and protecting it against attempts to encircle or impair it; offering material and moral support to the progressive Arab governments and to national liberation movements; bolstering national liberation movements in all three continents; pursuing a courageous national policy in the fields of the national exploitation of sulphur in cooperation with the friendly Soviet Union; pursuing similar steps in the fields of popular work, agrarian reform, and social security for workers; maintaining openings to other nationalities and creativing positive climates for the settlement of the Kurdish issue. The Tenth National Convention had also to greet the spirit of heroic endurance with which the Arab masses faced the outcome of the nationalist ordeal of June 5 and by which they broke all encirclement attempts.

FIRSTLY—ON RELATIONS BETWEEN IDEOLOGY, STRATEGY, AND TACTICS

"The convention stemmed from the premise of defining this relationship, and established distinction between the party's long-term strategy which involves the building of the united democratic socialist Arab society (i.e. the achievement of the goals of unity, liberty, and socialism) and the transitional strategies dealing with nationalist issues of destiny which demand actual and direct attitudes within the streamline of the general objectives of the Arab revolution. Among the issues covered in this category is the Palestine issue, the settler-invasion in the Arab Gulf, the creation of set forms of unitary work and the liquidation of the residues of feudalism, bourgeoisie, and backwardness within the framework of the dialectical comprehension of relationships between the nationalist factor and the socialist factor. The convention pointedly stressed that the party's political strategy cannot be but an application of its ideology in a phased-out plan marked with set and definitive conditions related to both time and place and taking into consideration the obtaining forms of external and internal strifes and the real weights of the political and social forces.

SECONDLY—THE NECESSITIES OF THE CURRENT STAGE

"The convention defined the present stage as one of confrontation with encountered challenges and of preparation for the coming battle with the Zionist-imperialistic aggression. The present stage was also considered a transitional one leading to a new plane of thought, action, planning, and implementation characterized with revolutionary maturity and complete cohesion between nationalist liberation strife and class socialist strife. The convention also affirmed that the stage of catastrophe has made of the rejection of regional fragmentation and of proceeding from the starting point of unity in the strategic sense, an objective need meeting the minimum of the requirements of Arab struggle against the Zionist-imperialistic-reactionary alignment. Further, it was made clear that the present stage is among the most revolutionary in the contemporary life of the Arabs; consequently, it is the stage of doctrinal strategic work and the stage characterized by the presence of revolutionary instruments capable of absorbing the defeat and of making theoretical planning and practical preparations for the battle in a manner assuring definite victory.

"The convention, while analyzing the contemporary Arab struggle, also emphasized that the nationalist liberation aspect and the class social aspect are two sides of one fact which the Arab Revolution is seeking out. The convention came to the conclusion that the class analysis of the development of Arab revolutionary work in the pre-1967 catastrophe period has borne out the political analysis and the analysis of ideological and doctrinal currents marking that stage. The net result of the analysis in question was that the 5th of June [1967] spelled out the end of the era of the petit-bourgeoisie's leadership and marked the beginning of the era of the leadership of the revolutionary masses. This is the era of organized and planned strategic cohesion between these masses believing as they are in the Arab revolutionary ideology and the vanguard revolutionary forces, coherent in their composition and qualified to play, through the nationalist front conceived on a pan-Arab level, the leading role in the Arab struggle.

"The convention further proved that the existing Arab political institutions have no way of gaining the confidence of the Arab masses unless these institutions brought themselves to measure up to the new level dictated by the obtaining revolutionary stage and managed to rid themselves of the passive streaks of the preceding era. These streaks are summed up by resignation to the state of fragmentation; the predominance of regional mentality and bureaucratic usages; opposition to the revolutionary party setup;

settling down to outward support of armed struggle without affording it the real opportunity to develop into a true war of national liberation; stopping by the limits of mere verbal support of the working class without assuring to its struggle the conditions of growth and effective participation in leadership and using the scientific rejection of international formulas smacking of capitulation as a veneer to cover up their defeatist attitudes.

"The convention also stressed that the predominance of the nationalist mentality and nationalist contents over the regional mentality together with the achievement of the strategy of unity, both represent the main goal of the Arab struggle—this being in addition to party work receptive of frontal formulas and practices; the release of the energies of the toiling masses; the support of commando action and armed struggle; and the rejection of all settlements seeking the liquidation of the Palestine issue. The convention further stressed that the creation of objective conditions for facing up to the imperialistic-Zionist challenge presupposes the realization of the progressive nationalist front on a pan-Arab level. This is because Arab revolutionary forces will be impotent to lead the masses and ready them for the battle as long as they remain in their present splintered situation and if they fail to achieve concert between the objective and the subjective within the framework of the current stage.

"The convention further came to the conclusion that the answer to the regional impulse arising from the state of fragmentation and to the non-unity conditions lies in a revolutionary unity where the nationalist factor becomes welded to its socialist democratic contents—not in a unity with an individualistic character or in a state of domineering or in a unity fraught with contradictions.

"The answer to the absence of strategy lies in strategic planning, not in settling down to tactics. Likewise, the answer to domineering impulses lies in a state of interaction between the revolutionary authorities and the masses and in practicing popular democracy as distinct from proforma democracy given to serving the interests of the non-revolutionary classes. In the same vein, the answer to auctioneering lies not in biddings but rather in discovering the right equations.

"On this basis of analytical processes and definition of the nature of the obtaining stage, the Tenth Nationalist Convention proceeded to lay down the broadlines of the strategy of the stage."

THIRDLY:

"On the party level, the convention passed resolutions on the following:

1. "Developing the struggle and class edifice of the party in a manner answering the exigencies of the current revolutionary stage and making of

commando action and armed struggle the main axis of the life of its members.

2. "Deepening and consolidating self-criticism for transition to a new level of party work, revolutionary outlook, and attention to party education with the intent of delivering it from the ideological, political, and organizational errors that marked the preceding stage.

3. "Devoting serious attention to party upbringing and to the achievement of the conditions of developing party work in both theory and practice with the object of realising the oneness of the party personality and enhancing its struggle and ethical character marked with a comprehensive scientific outlook.

4. "Defining the party's position on any regime it might come to have in any given country by striking a balance between the independent character of the party on the one hand and taking into consideration the circumstances of such a regime, on the other, with due care to protecting it against conspiracies."

FOURTHLY:

"On the pan-Arab (nationalist) level, the convention passed resolutions on the following:

1. "Achieving full ties between the political strategy on the one hand and the ideological framework on the Arab revolution on the other and opposing all endeavors to deviate or drop below this level.

2. "Reckoning with the achievement of unity as the effective factor for transition to the stage of serious confrontation with the Zionist-imperialistic aggression. Such unity must, in addition to unifying political, economic, and cultural institutions, take care to unify the forces of Arab revolution within a nationalist frontal framework capable of leading the Arab masses in accordance with a political program defining the requirements of confronting on all levels.

3. "Going back to the people and putting them in the picture about the difficulties that might confront the advance of the struggle for unity and frontal work so that the Arab masses could place their weight behind the party.

4. "Focusing the party's endeavors on the Palestine issue and commando action side by side with drawing attention to other problems such as the imperialistic-reactionary schemings in the Arab Gulf. Every effort should be made in the fields of ideology, politics, information, and popular work to accentuate those schemings and awaken Arab masses, everywhere in the Arab homeland to this menacing danger side by side with getting ready to encounter and overcome it and prompt the Gulf states and principalities to

achieve real unity which answers the minimum of the requirements of confronting the danger in question.

5. "Mobilizing the party's entire energies on a nationalist (pan-Arab) level for shoring up the party's rule in Iraq and deepening and enriching its experiment."

FIFTHLY:

"On the political level, the convention passed resolutions on the following:

1. "Undertaking serious and speedy work to change the features of Arab realities with the object of achieving objective conditions necessary for confronting the Zionist-imperialistic alliance. This is to be had by tireless endeavours for the realization of unity in its progressive substance. The view on the edifice of Arab conditions is to be totally revised along with creating mental and psychological preparedness to link up the Arab life fully with the necessities of long-term confrontation. Economy, politics, and everyday life should all be converted into supporting media with the object of directing Arab struggle in the way of the battlefield.

2. "Lay emphasis on the adoption of the strategy of the national liberation war previously endorsed at the Ninth National Convention. The requirements of that strategy (including the creation of the policy of confrontation, the economy of confrontation, the school of confrontation) should be considered as the natural key to the realization of a full-fledged, drastic, and deep revolution in the contemporary Arab life, all in a manner totally removing fragmentation, backwardness, and class exploitation.

3. "Creating objective conditions for uniting Arab revolutionary forces around a comprehensive program of revolutionary work helpful to releasing the effectiveness of the Arab masses and to placing the reins of the battle in their hands. This is to be achieved by creating the progressive nationalist front on pan-Arab levels.

4. "Arab masses are considered the instruments as well as the objective of the revolution and the quarter which has a real stake in liberation. Consequently, the advance should always be in the direction of the masses and of mobilizing them for waging the battle, all the more so after the formulas coming down from above have proved their impotence and their utter failure to attain to the minimum levels required for the confrontation and for joint Arab action."

SIXTHLY:

"On the Palestine issue and commando action, the convention passed resolutions on the following:

1. "Reckoning with the Palestine Revolution as the main center of gravity to the Arab Revolution and doing away with all deviationist tendencies arising from local concepts or opportunistic stances aiming at cracking the dialectical unity of the Arab Revolution and the Palestine Revolution.

2. "Endeavoring to carry out the strategy of the war of national liberation and armed struggle by bolstering the Palestine commando work and popular resistance in the occupied territories and assuring to them all political, material and moral necessities.

3. "Fostering relations between the party and commando organizations through the Unified Palestine Leadership and on the bias of comradeship in struggle between Arab revolutionary forces.

4. "Backing up all endeavors that seek the realization of the slogan of the unity of commando action under the leadership of revolutionary ideology.

5. "Turning down all advocacies smacking of capitulation and resisting all attempts to struggle and contain the Palestine Revolution and liquidate the Palestine issue.

6. "Disseminating comprehension of the nature of the battle fought in Palestine, uncovering the organic association between imperialism and Zionism and fostering the ties of friendship between the Palestine Revolution and progressive movements of liberation the world over."

SEVENTHLY: ON THE IRAQI TERRITORY

"The convention has drawn up the broadlines of the advance of the regime in the territory of Iraq in the following manner (with the object of attaining to the new required pattern in the post–June 5 era–i.e., by coverting the territory of Iraq into a revolutionary Arab force and committing the country's possibilities to serving nationalist strategy):

1. "Solving the territory's problems in the light of the strategy of confronting the Zionist-imperialistic-reactionary alliance. The convention stressed that the proclamation of a peaceful, democratic settlement to the Kurdish issue on the basis of self-rule within the framework of Iraqi unity and in a manner assuring best conditions of cooperation and solidarity between the Arab and Kurdish nationalities, should be in the forefront of the party's accomplishments so as to release its armed forces and its economic and human energies for confronting the Zionist danger and undercutting imperialistic and reactionary conspiracies in the region.

2. "Achieving deep revolutionary accomplishments leading to drastic transformations in production relationships along with the necessary conditions for embarking upon the socialist transformation stage.

3. "Considering the Palestine Revolution as the center of gravity for the policy of the territory of Iraq and getting the strategy of unity and of popular and regular armed struggle (both in conscience and in practice) to enter

every home, factory, school, and barrack and shape up the life of the individual, the family, the village, and the city in the light of the requirement of confrontation.

4. "Viewing struggle for unity as setting the road to liberation and looking upon struggle waged across Palestine as the right way to a type of unity correcting all the consequences of the preceding experiment. This is because the road of unity and the road of liberation are inseparable the one from the other.

5. "Building the progressive national front on both the regional and nationalist levels (local and pan-Arab levels).

6. "Bringing about an information, cultural, and social revolution disburdening Arab life of all residues of fragmentation and prejudices against the human nationalist associations and of all ideas and traditions disruptive to a scientific and revolutionary confrontation with the enemy.

7. "Ever taking initiatives on both official and popular levels for creating climates accommodating to unitary work.

8. "Inviting Arab institutions and Arab popular organizations to a program of action reviving the hopes of the Arab masses and creating among them confidence in victory once all revolutionary Arab possibilities are pooled under its banner. Such a program of action would also provide a sharp revolutionary yardstick of criticism.

9. "Backing up every Arab revolutionary uprising and using all possibilities to protect it against encirclement and assault.

10. "Uncovering the dangers converging on specific areas, the scenes of imperialistic conspiratorial activities such as the Arab Gulf and northern and Southern Yemen and endeavoring to give them every boost side by side with laying down a strategy for protecting the Gulf against imperialistic conspiracies."

ON THE INTERNATIONAL LEVEL

"On the international level the role of the party is defined by the courageous, decisive, and intelligent confrontation of world attempts to liquidate the Palestine issue under the pretext of resolving the crises emanating from the June 5 war, with a view to realizing the political objectives at this stage, namely:

1. "Foiling the attempts which would destroy the future of the issue and constitute a form of international compromise at the expense of the interest and destiny of the Arab Nation.

2. "Taking the initiative to establish the closest ties with the socialist community.

3. "Creating an understanding public opinion capable of perceiving the reality of the Arab revolutionary attitude, in defense of the Arab survival

and destiny, and in defying a serious danger threatening the destiny of humanity.

4. "Calling attention to the schemes of the Zionist-imperialistic-reactionary alliance, as well as to the real dimensions of conspiring against the Arab homeland and to the nature of the strategic alliance between the U.S. and Israel.

5. "Acquiring real friends for Arab Revolution capable of comprehending its objectives and appreciating the significance of the role undertaken in the field of world revolution.

6. "Deepening the impact of Arab resistance on the Palestinian territories, and expanding the framework of international backing and assistance both on the popular and official levels.

7. "Reducing the impact of the Zionist propaganda influence and the scope of the Zionist scheming on world public opinion.

8. "Supporting the national liberation movements in Asia, Africa, and Latin America and establishing objective ties therewith.

9. "Establishing extensive and organized assimilation of the socialist experiences in the world, interacting with them and utilizing such experiences and know-how, especially those who have undergone similar conditions as those of the Arab nation.

10. "Emphasizing the presence of the party, on official and popular levels, at the international domain, by means of expanding and deepening contacts with all progressive forces and regimes, and devoting serious attention to the establishment of organized ties therewith, and also displaying keeness to attend conferences, conduct visits, extend invitations, and take the initiative to prepare for the convention of progressive forces.

11. "Embarking on dialogues with the socialist parties in the socialist countries, with a view to explain the party opinion and the objectives of the Arab Revolution, and bringing about an atmosphere of mutual understanding of the outlook to the Arab question, through the openness which has become characteristic of the attitudes of the Soviet Union and other socialist countries toward the party after the July 17 Revolution in Iraq.

12. "Devoting attention to the world progressive public opinion, and establishing friendly and acquaintance ties with the progressive parties and organizations in the West, so as to render such relations an auxiliary instrument for exposing imperialist attitudes of the pro-Zionist governments in the West, before their peoples; exposing Zionist groundless propaganda, and for explaining the Arab right and the dimensions of the Arab issue; curbing the influence of Zionist propaganda on world public opinion in the West; bringing about a positive atmosphere dominated by the objective and human outlook over the passive sentimental attitudes created by the Zionist schemes to serve as an insulator between public opinion in the West on the one hand and the issues of Arab Revolution on the other.

13. "Consolidating ties among the Arab vocational labor unions as well as the international organizations, as such ties constitute a significant factor

for foiling the Zionist propaganda, and help bring about a mutual understanding of the revolutionary issues the world over, and develop the constructive critical feeling required for dealing with the fallacies and ailments which penetrate into the Arab revolutionary action, before they become too acute.

14. "Emphasizing that the policy and attitudes of the party depend at the current stage on a definite and clear-cut criterion, namely the attitudes of others *vis-à-vis* the Arab Palestine Issue."

STRUGGLING MASSES OF THE ARAB NATION

The Tenth National Convention has adopted several resolutions and recommendations on the fulfillment of the strategy of the party and political action embodied in this declaration and also on matters related to organization in a manner that would guarantee the development of the organizational instrument, with a view to raising it to the level that would qualify it for undertaking the burdens of the stage and to implement the required strategy. The convention also resulted in the election of a new national leadership, and concluded its activities to let the party proceed in its struggle through its resolutions and recommendations, and in the light of the strategy it has adopted.

The Arab Ba'ath Socialist Party, which has spent 30 years in the fields stand fast before the conspiracies and sabotage woven against it, does assure of struggle, and which has managed to bypass its mistakes and setbacks, to the masses of the Arab nation that it will stay with them on the thoroughfare of stern and everlasting struggle until unity, liberty, and socialism are realized.

ON THE INEVITABILITY OF
THE SOCIALIST SOLUTION

Socialism is the way to social freedom.

Social freedom cannot be realized except through an equal opportunity for every citizen to obtain a fair share of the national wealth.

This is not confined to the mere redistribution of the national wealth among the citizens, but foremost and above all it requires expanding the base of this national wealth, so as to achieve to the lawful rights of the working people.

This means that socialism, with its two supports, sufficiency and justice, is the way to social freedom.

The socialist solution to the problem of economic and social under development in Egypt—to achieve progress in a revolutionary way—was never a question of free choice. The socialist solution was a historical inevitability imposed by reality, the broad aspirations of the people and the changing nature of the world in the second part of the 20th century.

The capitalist experiments to achieve progress correlated with imperialism. The countries of the capitalist world reached the period of economic takeoff on the basis of investments they made in their colonies. The wealth of India, of which British imperialism seized the largest share, was the beginning of the formation of the British savings used to develop agriculture and industry in Britain.

If Britain reached its period of takeoff, depending on the Lancashire textile industry, the transformation of Egypt into a large field for cotton-growing pumped the blood through the artery of the British economy, leaving the Egyptian peasant starved.

Gone are the ages of imperialist piracy, when the people's wealth was looted to serve the interests of others with neither legal nor moral control.

From *The Charter* (Cairo: Information Dept.), pp. 49–59.

We should stamp out the remaining traces of those ages, especially in Africa.

Moreover, other experiments of progress realized their objectives at the expense of increasing the misery of the working people, either to serve the interests of capital or under pressure of ideological application which went to the extent of sacrificing whole living generations for the sake of others still unborn.

The nature of the age no longer allows such things.

Progress through looting or through the forced labor system is no longer tolerable according to the new human values.

These human values ended colonialism and ended the forced labor system. Not only did they achieve this but they also expressed positively the spirit and the ideals of the age when, through science, those values introduced other means and methods of work to attain progress.

* * * * * * * * * *

Scientific socialism is the suitable style for finding the right method leading to progress.

No other method can definitely achieve the desired progress.

Those who call for freedom of capital imagining that to be the road to progress are gravely mistaken.

In countries forced to remain underdeveloped, capital in its natural development is no longer able to lead the economic drive at a time when the great capitalist monopolies in the advanced countries grew, thanks to the exploitation of the sources of wealth in the colonies.

The huge development of world monopolies allows only two ways for local capitalism in countries aspiring to progress:

First—Local capitalism is no longer capable of competition without the protective tariff paid for by the people.

Second—The only hope left for local capitalism to develop is to relate itself to the movements of world monopolies, following in their footsteps, thus turning into a mere appendage and dragging the country to doom.

On the other hand, the wide gap of underdevelopment which separates the advanced states and those trying to catch up no longer allows the method of progress to be left to desultory individual efforts motivated by mere selfish profits.

These individual efforts are no longer capable of facing the challenge. Facing the challenge calls for three conditions:

(1) Assembling the national savings;

(2) Channeling all resources of modern science into the exploitation of national savings;

(3) Drafting a complete plan for production.

These are concerned with increasing the product. On the other hand, fair distribution calls for planning programs for social action, programs that enable that working people to reap the benefits of economic action and create the welfare society to which they aspire and which they struggle to promote.

Work to expand the base of national wealth can never be left to the haphazard ways of exploiting private capital with its unruly tendencies.

The redistribution of the surplus national work on the basis of justice can never be accomplished through voluntary efforts based on good intentions, however sincere they may be.

This places a definite conclusion before the will of the national revolution, without the acceptance of which it cannot realize its objectives. This conclusion is the necessity for the people's control over all means of production and for the direction of the surplus according to a definite plan.

This socialist solution is the only route for economic and social progress. It is the way to democracy in all its social and political forms.

The people's control over all the means of production does not necessitate the nationalization of all means of production or the abolition of private ownership, nor does it violate the legitimate right of inheritance. Such control can be achieved in two ways:

First—The creation of a capable public sector that would lead progress in all domains and bear the main responsibility of the development plan.

Second—The existence of a private sector that would, without exploitation, participate in the development within the framework of the overall plan provided that the people's control is exercised over both sectors.

This socialist solution is the only path where all elements participating in the process of production can meet, according to scientific rules, capable of supplying society with all the energies to rebuild its life on the basis of a carefully studied and comprehensive plan.

✳ ✳ ✳ ✳ ✳ ✳ ✳ ✳ ✳ ✳

Efficient socialist planning is the sole method which guarantees the use of all national resources, be they material, natural or human, in a practical, scientific and humane way to realize the common good of the people, and ensure a life of prosperity for them.

Efficient socialist planning is the guarantee for sound exploitation of actually existing resources or those which are latent or potential. At the same time, it is a guarantee of the continued distribution of fundamental services. It is also a guarantee of raising the standard of the services already offered. It is a guarantee of extending those services to the areas which have fallen victim to negligence and inefficiency, the outcome of long deprivation imposed by the selfishness of the ruling classes who looked down upon the struggling people.

It follows, then, that planning must be a scientifically organized creative process that would meet the challenges facing our society. It is not a mere process of working out the possible; it is a process of achieving hope. Hence, planning in our society is required to find a solution to a difficult problem. In the solution of that difficult problem lies the material and human success of the national action.

How can we increase production?

At the same time how can we increase the consumption of goods and use of services?

And this, besides the constant increase of savings for the sake of new investments.

This difficult solution, with its three vital branches, requires the existence of a highly efficient organization capable of mobilizing forces of production, raising their material and intellectual efficiency, relating them to the production proces.

Such an organization must be aware that the aim of production is to widen the scope of service and that services, in turn, are a driving force turning the wheels of production.

The relation between services and production and their rapid, smooth-running movement creates a sound national blood circle vital to the life of the people as a whole and individually.

This organization must depend on centralization in planning and on decentralization in implementation, which insures placing the planning programs in the hands of all the people.

*   *   *   *   *   *   *   *   *   *

Consequently, the major part of the plan should be shouldered by the public sector owned by the people as a whole.

This not only insures the sound development of the production process along the set path of productivity, but is also fair, considering that the public sector belongs to the people as a whole.

The national struggle of the people has provided the nucleus of the public sector, through the people's determination to retrieve and nationalize the foreign monopolies, and restore them to their natural and legitimate place, namely to their ownership by the whole people.

Even during the military fight against imperialism, that same national struggle added to the public sector all the British and French capital in Egypt—that capital was seized from the people at the time of foreign privileges and at a time when national wealth was subjected to looting by foreign adventurers.

Moreover, in seeking social freedom and penetrating into the strongholds of class exploitation, that national struggle was able to add to the public sector the major part of production equipment through the July 1961 laws and their deep revolutionary impact reflecting the will of overall change in Egypt.

Those gigantic steps which allowed the private sector to undertake the initial role leading to progress, traced clear-cut lines imposed by national reality and a thorough study of the nation's circumstances, potentialities, and aims.

Those lines and principles can be summed up in the following:

First—In the field of production in general:

The major skeleton of the production operation, such as the railways, roads, ports, airports, the potentialities of the driving force, such as the dams, means of sea, land and air transportation, and other public services should be within the framework of public ownership.

Second—In the field of industry:

The greater part of the heavy, medium, and mining industries should be part of public ownership. Although it is possible to allow private ownership in this domain, such private ownership should be controlled by the public sector owned by the people.

Light industries must always be beyond monopoly. Though this field is open to private ownership, the public sector must have a role enabling it to guide that industry in the people's interests.

Third—In the field of trade:

Foreign trade must be under the people's control. Here, all import trade must be within the framework of the public sector. Though it is incumbent upon private capital to participate in export trade, the public sector must have the main share in that field to preclude all possible fraud. If a percentage could be defined in that field, the public sector must be in charge of three quarters of exports, while encouraging the private sector to shoulder the responsibility of the remaining share.

The public sector must have a role in internal trade. The public sector should, within the coming eight years—the remaining period of the first overall development plan for doubling national income in ten years—be in charge of at least one-quarter of the internal trade to prevent monopoly and expand the range of internal trade before private and cooperative activities. It should be understood, of course, that internal trade is service and distribution at a reasonable profit which, under no circumstances, should reach the extent of exploitation.

Fourth—In the field of finance:

Banks should be within the framework of public ownership. The role of capital is a national one and should not be left to speculation and adventure. In addition, insurance companies should be within the same framework of public ownership for the protection of a major part of national saving and to insure its sound orientation.

Fifth—In the domain of land:

There should be a clear distinction between two kinds of private ownership: private ownership which opens the gates to exploitation, and non-exploiting private ownership which does its share in the service of national economy while serving the interests of the owners themselves.

In ownership of rural land, the agrarian reform laws have limited individual ownership to one hundred feddans. Yet the spirit of the law implies that this limitation should cover the whole family—father, mother, and children under age—to avoid clustering together maximum ownerships allowing some form of feudalism. This spirit can be made to rule within the coming eight years provided the families affected by that law sell for cash to the agricultural cooperative societies or to others, the land in excess of those limits.

Regarding ownership of buildings, the laws of progressive taxation of buildings, the laws limiting rents, and those defining levies, place ownership of buildings beyond exploitation. Yet constant supervision is imperative, although the increase in the public and cooperative housing will contribute in a practical manner to combat all attempts to exploit this field.

* * * * * * * * * *

Through the accomplishment of their great socialist achievement, the July 1961 laws are the greatest triumph of the revolutionary drive in the economic field.

These laws, an extension of other preliminaries, formed a bridge that led to the change to socialism with unprecedented success.

That decisive revolutionary phase could not have been completed with such efficiency and in such a peaceful spirit had it not been for the deep faith and consciousness of the people, the pooling of their efforts to make a firm stand against the reactionary elements invading their strongholds, and the assertion of the people's mastery of the country's wealth. The glorious laws of July and the decisive manner of their implementation, as well as all the successful and brave efforts in the delicate period following, of hundreds of thousands of nationals working at the organizations whose ownership passed to the people under those laws, have insured the preservation and consolidation, of productivity in those firms.

All this, while asserting the people's determination to control their resources, shows the people's ability to direct those resources and their readiness, through sincere elements, to shoulder the most difficult and delicate responsibilities.

Undoubtedly the measures adopted in the wake of the July socialist laws have successfully realized a liquidation that was incumbent and imperative.

Following a reactionary atempt to attack the social revolution, a drastic move was effected to wipe out the vestiges of the era of feudalism, reaction, and domination.

❖ ❖ ❖ ❖ ❖ ❖ ❖ ❖ ❖ ❖

These measures asserted that the people are unflinchingly determined to reject every form of exploitation whether it be the consequence of class inheritance or of parasitic opportunism.

However, we should bear in mind that reaction has not been eliminated forever. Reaction is still in possession of material and intellectual influences that may tempt it to stand in the way of the sweeping revolutionary current, particularly when it relies on the remnants of the reaction in the Arab world backed by forces of imperialism.

The revolutionary vigilance is, in all circumstances, capable of crushing every reactionary infiltration, whatever its methods and whatever the supporting powers.

It is of prime importance that our outlook toward nationalization be freed from the stigmas that private interests have tried to attach to it.

Nationalization is but the transfer of the means of production from the sphere of private ownership to that of public ownership.

This is not a blow to individual initiative, as alleged by the enemies of socialism, but rather a guarantee of and an expansion of the range of general interest in cases urged by the socialist change effected for the benefit of the people.

Nationalization does not lead to a decrease in production.

Experience has proven the ability of the public sector to shoulder the greatest responsibilities with maximum efficiency, whether in achieving production targets or in raising the standard of quality. Although some mistakes may occur during this great evolution, we must recall that the new hands that have assumed the responsibility are in need of training to undertake such responsibility. At any rate it was inevitable that the major national interests should be handed over to the people even at the cost of facing temporary difficulties.

Nationalization is not, as suggested by some opportunist elements, a punishment inflicted upon private capital when it deviates and consequently is not applied as a punishment.

The transfer of a means of production from the sphere of private ownership to that of public ownership is more significant than mere punishment.

The great importance attached to the role of the public sector, however, cannot do away with the existence of the private sector.

The private sector has its effective role in the development plan. It must be protected to fulfill that part.

The private sector is now required to renovate itself and strike a new path of creative effort not dependent, as in the past, on parasitic exploitation.

The crisis which befell private capital before the revolution actually stemmed from the fact that it was the heir of the era of the foreign adventurers, who, in the 19th century, helped transfer abroad the wealth of Egypt.

Private capital was accustomed to live under a protective trade policy which gave it benefits at the expense of the people. It was also accustomed to dominating the government with the aim of pursuing a policy of exploitation.

It was futile that the people should bear the cost of the protective trade policy to enhance the profits of a group of capitalists who mostly were no more than local façades for foreign interests wishing to carry on their exploitation from behind the scenes.

Therefore, the people could not forever remain indifferent before the maneuvers to direct the government in favor of the minority controlling the wealth, and to guarantee the maintenance of their privileged position at the expense of the people's interests.

In this event, the returns would go to a small minority of the people who have so much money in excess that they squander it on various forms of wasteful luxury, ignoring the deprivation of the majority.

This sharpens the edge of the class strife and wipes out every hope for democratic evolution.

But the socialist path, providing opportunities for a peaceful settlement of the class strife and affording possibilities for dissolving class distinctions, leads to the distribution of the returns among all the people according to the principle of equality of opportunity for all.

The socialist path thereby paves the way for an inevitable political development leading to liberation from the rule of the feudalist dictatorship allied with capitalism and the establishment of the rule of democracy representing the rights and aspirations of the working people.

The political liberation of man cannot be achieved unless an end is put to every shackle of exploitation limiting his freedom.

Socialism and democracy form the wings of freedom with which socialism can soar to the distant horizons aspired to by the people.

THE POLITICAL REPORT OF THE POPULAR FRONT FOR THE LIBERATION OF PALESTINE

The national Palestinian question cannot be separated, all through history, from the circumstances which involve Palestine and international struggles. A scientific historical review of the Middle East situation reveals that there is a dialectical relationship between the development of the Palestine situation and that of the Middle East in general and the immediate area surrounding Palestine in particular. The totality of these developments has decided, and is still deciding, the future of Palestine and its struggling people.

The modern history of Palestine ultimately proves the validity of this historical truth. The weakness of the Ottoman regime which was based on religious feudalism, in the face of European capitalism, prompted imperialism to covet the inheritance of the Ottoman Empire and to divide the "sick man of Europe." At the same time Zionism, led by Jewish capitalism, began to envisage the seizure of Palestine under the pretext of religion, in order to establish a Zionist racist movement encompassing Jewish groupings in different countries of the world. As a result of their common interests, the colonial-imperial powers and Zionism, which opposed the liberation movement of the Palestinians and the Arabs, formed one bloc in the face of the Ottoman Empire.

Following World War I, two of the imperialist countries—Britain and France—annexed the Arab East. (In 1917 Britain had published the Balfour Declaration which gave Zionism a national right for the Jews in Palestine.) The British attitude was not accidental, or an error on the part of its foreign minister, but was an objective result of its imperialist policy in the Arab East. The aim was to implant in the Arab world an armed human stronghold for imperialism which would resist the Arab nationalist liberation movement whose success would threaten imperialist bases and interests in their entirety in this strategic area of the world. In addition, the attitude adopted by

The August Program and a Democratic Solution (np, nd).

Britain was in compliance with Zionist aspirations to settlement, which agreed with colonial-imperial plans, and opposed Palestinian-Arab national liberation aspirations.

The Arab feudal regimes in Palestine and the other Arab states provided imperialism and Zionism with good opportunities to execute their plans for Palestine in particular, and for the other Arab states in general. Since their establishment the Arab feudal regimes—especially bourgeois—have associated themselves with the colonialist-imperialist powers, i.e., the counterrevolutionary bloc, against the Palestinian and Arab national liberation movements. The common interests of imperialism and the Arab feudal regimes have led to an alliance between them. Such an alliance is best exemplified in the protection accorded by imperialism to the Arab feudal regimes and the exploiting class, in addition to the protection it has given to its own imperialist exploiting interests. Furthermore, the Arab regimes protected the interests of imperialism since neither of them could exist in the area without the help of the other.

As a result of the dependence on imperialism of the Arab feudal, bourgeois regimes, they remained handicapped *vis-à-vis* Zionist aspirations, and the promises made by imperialism regarding the judaization of Palestine. These regimes were satisfied by merely calling on the "ally" Britain to understand the rights of the people of Palestine.

It is natural that the reactionary Arab regimes took such a defeatist attitude toward the judaizing of Palestine because, as a result of their feudal-bourgeois setup, they could not confront the plans of imperialism and Zionism with the force of arms and popular national revolutions. Reactionary regimes, at all times and places—and this applies to the Arab states—fear the masses more than they fear imperialism. The confrontation of imperialist and Zionist plans requires arming and organizing the people, and this is specifically what the reactionary regimes refuse to do, as they oppose national liberation in the Arab states and in the underdeveloped countries of Asia, Africa, and Latin America. Furthermore, the interests and existence of these regimes, by the very nature of their feudal-bourgeois structure, are intrinsically connected with the interests of traditional imperialism and neo-imperialism in the Arab world.

Thus since the beginning of the modern history of Palestine, it has become clear that the destiny of Palestine will be decided by the struggle of a national movement. This will be essentially a class struggle between the national liberation bloc on the Palestinian and Arab land and the enemies of the liberation movement, such as imperialism. Arab reactionary regimes in alliance with imperialism, and world Zionism.

Since the comprador, feudal-bourgeois classes, by their control over the suppressive, police-like agencies of the government, were able to dominate the leadership of the national movement, the destiny of Palestine was predictable. In spite of all the slogans put out by the governing classes, they adopted a cooperative and defeatist stand *vis-à-vis* the judaizing of Palestine.

Instead of defying imperialism and opening a national front against it—but this is not in the nature of the reactionary ruling classes—these classes undertook, throughout the history of the Palestinian and Arab liberation movement, a policy of suppression and siege *vis-à-vis* revolutionary national forces. At the same time the ruling classes continued to cooperate with imperialism and protect their interests in the Arab world, foremost among which is the exploitation of Arab oil.

If one analyzes the history of Palestine, it becomes clear that the history and destiny of Palestine is decided by the totality of the circumstances involving Palestine and international policies and struggles. The modern history of Palestine is a proof of the truth of such an argument. The 1948 defeat came at the hands of religious feudal Palestinian leaders such as Hajj Amin al-Husseini, the bourgeoisie, such as the Independence Party and the Defence Party, etc., and the Arab feudal regimes exemplified in the Arab kings and presidents. This defeat gave direct evidence of the dialectic connection between the actual state existing in Palestine, the Arab world, and the international setup. The disaster of Palestine and the creation of the "state of Israel" is the result of the Palestine-Arab dialectic.

✿　✿　✿　✿　✿　✿　✿　✿　✿　✿

This condensed introduction is necessary in the present decisive circumstances through which the Palestine question is passing in order to point out the inevitable connection between developments in the Arab world and the destiny of the Palestine question. The developments which took place, and are still taking place, in the Arab world and throughout the history of Palestine touch, in one way or another, on the situation and destiny of Palestine. Any attempt to ignore such a question is suspicious; it is a reactionary, imperialist, or Zionist attempt.

At the present stage the national Palestinian question is passing through its most difficult phase. To be more specific, since the June 1967 defeat, proposals have been made, and are still being made, by some Palestinian and Arab rightists calling for the isolation of the Palestine struggle movement from all the happenings and developments in the Arab area under the slogan of "non-interference in the internal affairs of the Arab countries." In the final analysis this slogan, at the hands of the Palestine resistance movement, has been transformed into "non-interference in Palestinian affairs," since what happened, and is happening, in the Arab land is dialectically connected with the Palestine question, and the lessons of 1936, 1948, and the 1967 defeat are still fresh and before our eyes. After June 1967 the Arab regimes did not isolate themselves from the Palestine question and whatever happens inside their countries touches on the Palestine question.

The reactionary Palestinian, who is partnered by the Arab reactionary rightist in his call for a separation between the Palestinian question and the Arab regimes, implants the beginning of a new political or military defeat. This defeat will lead to the liquidation of the Palestine question in accordance with the political settlement proposed by the Security Council on November 22, 1967. Such a call on the part of the reactionary Palestinian rightists aims at ignoring historical facts and obliterating the contradiction between the existing Arab regimes, which were responsible for the 1948 disaster and the 1967 defeat, and the question of liberating Palestine. With regard to the imperialist-colonialist-Zionist attack of June 1967, the Arab reactionary and defeatist regimes have issued suspicious statements concerning the dimensions of the national liberation movement within their countries. Similar statements have been made about the lessons and results of the 1948 disaster and the 1967 defeat, the responsibility for which falls on the existing regimes. At the same time these regimes continue to handle the Palestine problem on the basis of the Security Council resolution. Thus, the Palestine resistance movement should judge the Arab regimes on the basis of their actual stand *vis-à-vis* the Palestinian national problem. Otherwise, the Palestinian resistance movement will lose its Palestinian identity and will be transformed into a "quantitative addition" to the present circumstances and to the existing Arab regimes responsible for the failure of the 1936 revolution, the 1948 disaster, and the 1967 defeat. Any public examination of the Palestinian national question cannot be isolated from the examination and criticism of the circumstances of the Arabs responsible for the "historical dilemma" which now faces the Palestine problem after the June defeat. The existing Arab regimes, and the Palestinian and Arab liberation movements, are faced with two basic alternatives *vis-à-vis* the Palestine problem. The destiny of Palestine depends on one of these alternatives: the liquidation of the problem or the adoption of a popular liberation plan. Any judgment to be passed on these alternatives is not isolated from the work plans of the existing Arab regimes and the national Palestinian and Arab liberation movements. The formulated plans, manifested in daily interpretations from the June 1967 defeat until the present day, will decide which of choice does not depend on the will or intentions or emotional and demaalternative will be adopted, liquidation or national liberation. The question gogic slogans, but on the daily work programs which the existing Arab regimes and the national Palestinian and Arab liberation movements adopt and practice. To make claims contrary to the actual facts and adopt demagogic slogans is an expression of rightist reactionary behavior whose result will be another political defeat or a military defeat which will be crowned by a political defeat.

LESSONS FROM THE JUNE 1967 DEFEAT

The June defeat was not only a military one, but also a defeat for the totality of the class, economic, military, and ideological setup of the national Palestinian and Arab liberation movements (official and popular). The feudal-bourgeois Arab regimes were not responsible for the June War and defeat because those regimes had already revealed, in 1948, the utter bankruptcy of their policies. However, the June defeat was not only a military defeat. In 1948 the disaster had been a defeat to the feudal-bourgeois regimes and all the class, political, and reactionary practices that they represented. These regimes were responsible for the underdeveloped economy of Palestine and the Arab world, which was at the mercy of international capitalism. Furthermore, those regimes, because of their feudal-bourgeois structure, failed to solve the dilemmas of the national Palestinian and Arab liberation movements, by achieving their countries' economic and political independence from international capitalism, colonialism, and imperialism. On the contrary they collaborated with the colonial powers to protect their class privileges in the economic and political fields. It was these regimes who sided with colonialism against the national Palestinian and Arab liberation movements. Throughout their modern history they have followed a policy of encirclement and suppression toward the national Palestinian and Arab liberation movements (e.g., the 1919 revolution in Egypt, the 1939 revolution in Palestine, and the 1941 revolution in Iraq).

As a result of the nature of those regimes which are underdeveloped, feudal, bourgeois, weak, and in alliance with colonialism and imperialism, they could not form modern national armies capable of protecting their countries and confronting the imperialist and Zionist policies in Palestine and the other Arab countries. Thus, those regimes entered the 1948 war with weak armies and only attempted military and political action within the geographical limit of the partition resolution.

The disaster and the creation of the "State of Israel" came as a result of Palestinian and Arab conditions which were dominated by feudal, bourgeois, and underdeveloped regimes, in alliance with colonialism. Such results also indicate that the elimination of the state of Israel and the "liberation of Palestine" depend on the rejection of feudalism, colonialism, and the bourgeoisie, the basic causes of the disaster. This is what the lessons of 1948 offered to the national Palestinian and Arab liberation movement. President Nasser was right when he said to his comrades that "the defeat was not decided in the battlefield, but here in Cairo," and "the liberation of Cairo from the feudal-bourgeois regime of King Farouk, in alliance with colonialism and Arab reaction, constitutes the basic requirement in the national work plan for the liberation of Palestine."

Thus, the basic point in the program of the national Palestinian and Arab liberation movement became the liquidation of the feudal-bourgeois regmies responsible for the 1948 disaster. The liquidation of these regimes has paved the way for the national liberation movement to overcome the dilemmas of the national Palestinian and Arab liberation movements. Such liberation required the destruction of the underdeveloped feudal-bourgeois economy, linked, as it was, with international capitalism, and the setting-up of a modern national economy (through industrialization and agrarian reform) independent of international capitalism. It is impossible to build regular or popular armies capable of taking part in a long-term war against counterrevolutionary forces on the soil of Palestine and the Arab countries (Israel plus colonialism plus reactionary Arab regimes in alliance with colonialism) without building a solid economic base free of pressures exerted on it by international capitalism and colonialism.

Since the 1948 disaster the national Palestinian and Arab revolutionary movement has entered a new phase with regard to class, ideology, and politics. In the light of the bankruptcy of the feudal-bourgeois regimes and leadership, which wholly allied themselves with the counterrevolutionary forces after the disaster, the national resistance movement began to adopt new class, ideological, and political definitions. The basic features of such definitions could be traced back to World War II. The emerging petit bourgeois class, which perceived the bankruptcy of the feudal-bourgeois class with regard to the solution of national liberation dilemmas, adopted an active nationalist policy hostile to colonialism, imperialism, and Zionism.

The new leadership proposed the establishment of an alliance between workers, peasants, the poor, and the military. Thus, the petit bourgeoisie began to play the role of the leading class as their ideology became dominant.

This national struggle, which is basically a class struggle, was expressed in the changing class, economic, and political programs—officially represented in the United Arab Republic, Syria, Algeria, and to an extent in Iraq—which aimed at disrupting the alliance between feudalism, capitalism, and imperialism. This leadership also attempted to solve the dilemmas of national liberation and the democratic national revolution. It broke up the feudal economy which was bourgeois and compradoric in nature, and established an economy which depends in the first place on light industrialization. It attempted to solve the problems of the agricultural sector of the economy in favor of the wage-earning peasants and the poor. All this was done to establish an economic base, independent of world capitalism; and a national political and social base, hostile to colonialism, imperialism, and Zionism; and to build modern, organized, national armies with which to protect the homeland and liberate Palestine. In face of the fierce national-class struggle, the forces of counterrevolution did not wait long. They began to plan the 1956 Anglo-French-Zionist aggression to liquidate the regime which was hostile to imperialism, reaction, and Zionism, and which threatened the interests and basis of the counterrevolutionary forces in Palestine and the Arab world. After the 1956 aggression, neo-colonialism—headed by the United States of America—attempted to patronize the Arab national liberation movement. But the national regimes resisted this encirclement and continued to fight their national battle against traditional colonialism and neo-imperialism. This continued in accordance with their hesitant petit bourgeois class nature. Eventually the Americans were convinced of the failure of their policy of peaceful encirclement to break the Arab national liberation movement, to liquidate the Palestine problem in the interest of Israel, and to rearrange the class and political map of the Arab world for the benefit of the bourgeois-feudal regimes, which act as the material and political base for imperialism in the area and guarantee the security of the state of Israel.

Thus it was not the Arab reactionary regimes, but the nationalist regimes and the whole Palestinian and Arab national liberation movements, who were responsible for the June War. Why did they fail? And with what work program did they face the June defeat?

Theoreticians of the Palestinian and Arab petit bourgeoisie, reaction, and the bourgeoisie proper gave explanations and analyses of the defeat which were limited to the educational, technical, and cultural superiority of Israel and American imperialism which protects it. The Arab countries are underdeveloped and small and cannot "confront and fight" American imperialism, which is far superior technically to any underdeveloped country in Asia, Africa, and Latin America. This group of analysts concluded that to be able to defeat Israel we should become superior to it in education and technology.

Another group of petit bourgeois and feudal intellectuals attempted to explain the defeat in terms of technical military faults committed by this army or that, such as their unpreparedness in the face of the devastating surprise attack on the Arab air forces.

The Palestinian and Arab petit bourgeois and reactionary theoreticians and analysts deliberately neglect the facts of modern history in their analysis of the Arab defeat in June. They ignore the basic reasons for the acceptance of the six-day defeat, in spite of the heated slogans prior to june 5, such as "inch by inch," "popular liberation war," "the policy of the scorched earth." These slogans formed the material objective antecedents to the following result: the June defeat. If the educational and technical superiority of Israel and imperialism is the main cause of the defeat, what is the explanation for the ability of the North Vietnamese people to confront half a million American soldiers in addition to half a million soldiers of the Saigon government? If we did not have the ability as a weak and underdeveloped country to resist and fight the United States, how can the ability of the Vietnamese and Cubans fight against American imperialism be explained? And if the defeat was a result of a vast number of technical military faults, how can one explain the acceptance of this defeat and the disappearance of the above-mentioned slogans, particularly at a time when Vietnam is conducting its popular revolutionary war "inch by inch," both in word and deed, and its war is not devoid of setbacks and defeats?

If the people of Palestine and the peoples of the Arab world accept the analyses of the reactionary and petit bourgeois theoreticians, it will need more than a century to catch up with the Zionist-imperialist educational and technical superiority, and overcome the wide cultural gap between the underdeveloped agrarian countries of the Arabs and modern industrialized Israel, supported by American imperialism.

The facts of the modern revolutionary history of the underdeveloped nations expose and falsify the claims of reactionary and petit bourgeois theoreticians. They also disclose the basic cause for the Arab defeat in June, as well as the resistance of the small Vietnamese nation (30 million), and of the Cuban nation (7 million) in the face of American imperialism.

There are in Vietnam and Cuba national regimes composed of the proletariat and poor peasants, which use the material, cultural, and moral potentialities of their countries to solve the dilemmas of national liberation, and the democratic national revolution. This is achieved by liquidating all the material and moral class concessions (feudal and bourgeois) and by the establishment of the solid material base for economic and political independence through heavy industrialization and agrarian reform. In society, the revolutionary classes head the alliance of classes and political forces which oppose feudalism, capitalism, and imperialism. Such a national economic and political program can mobilize and arm all the revolutionary classes to solve the dilemmas of national liberation and foster the struggle against imperialism and neo-colonialism. Under such circumstances the slogan of popular liberation acquires its practical connotations where the working and poor masses are organized into a popular militia force, partisan phalanges, and the regular national army in order to defeat imperialism and the local forces in alliance with it.

In the Arab world the problem is different: the circumstances and composition of the Palestinian Arab national liberation movement were responsible for the June war, and it is that movement which must be responsible for the reversal of the June defeat. The petit bourgeois class occupies the leading role in the Palestinian and Arab national liberation movements and this class has led the entire range of the class, political, economic, and military changes within the ideological, class, and political structure of the petit bourgeoisie. In June 1967, this program was the one which was defeated. The economy that was set up by the petit bourgeoisie could not resist the Zionist-imperialist attack because it was a consumer economy based on light industrialization and agrarian reforms (the redistribution of land to raise self-sufficient production). Such an economy—following the closure of the Suez Canal—was forced to retreat and ask for assistance from the reactionary oil-producing countries, to be able to sustain itself.

As for the political and ideological relationship, this class remained at the head of the social-political pyramid and translated the alliance of the popular working forces into an alliance which put it at the top of this pyramid and the masses—workers, peasants, the poor, soldiers—at its base. Therefore the petit bourgeoisie remains in control of the totality of changes that are taking place in the Arab homeland and in the Palestinian and Arab national liberation movements.

Because of the nature of the petit bourgeois class—which fears the popular masses as much as it fears the feudal-capital concentration—it could not through its ideological, political, and class program "build a national war economy" independent of world capitalism. As a result the petit bourgeoisie could not break all its connections with neo-colonialism and world imperialism in general, and American imperialism in particular.

The petit bourgeoisie has gambled with the necessity of protecting the country and preparing it (economically, politically, and militarily) for the liberation of Palestine. It gambled on the regular armies, refusing to arm the people and train and organize them into popular militia forces, thereby putting the slogan of "popular liberation war," which they had superficially adopted, into practice.

Under such circumstances, and with this national program, the petit bourgeois regimes entered the June War, only to prove that such a program cannot resist neo-imperialism and Zionism. The moment the defeat of the regular armies became known, these regimes asked for (or accepted) a cease-fire, and all their revolutionary slogans—"fighting inch by inch," "the popular liberation war," and "the policy of the scorched earth"—evaporated.

The petit bourgeois regimes had to choose between two alternatives. The first alternative was to follow the Vietnamese and Cuban experience by drastically changing the national work program of their countries. This could be accomplished by mobilizing the material, human, and moral capabilities of society and the national Palestinian and Arab liberation movements, and by arming the masses and waging a revolutionary popular liberation war. This war should be directed against all the interests and bases of colonialism, Zionism, and reaction in alliance with colonialism; and should apply the slogan "fighting Israel and those supporting Israel" by resisting all the counterrevolutionary forces which support Israel or which interact with those who support Israel. By doing so the balance of power would start to shift to the side of the national Palestinian and Arab liberation movements, and the possibility of antagonizing the United States would become practical. Moreover, Arab human superiority—waves of fighting people—would overcome the Israeli-American technical superiority as happens daily in Vietnam and Cuba.

The second alternative was to stick to the positions and programs which prevailed before June 1967 and which resulted in the June defeat. This would mean that the national Palestinian and Arab liberation movements would be forced to retreat continuously in the interest of Israel, imperialism, and Arab reactionary forces in alliance with both neo- and traditional colonialism. This is what actually took place and it was not by accident. The feudal-bourgeois regimes cannot wage a war on colonialism and imperialism since they have formed alliances with imperialism against their people and the national liberation movements. Since 1948 they have proved that they cannot protect the homeland and liberate Palestine and they have allied themselves wholly to the counterrevolutionary camp. Moreover, the national regimes which are hostile to colonialism and Zionism are incapable—because of the nature of their petit bourgeois ideological class structure—of drawing up and executing programs for a "popular liberation war" since this would necessarily require them to give up all of their material, political, and moral concessions in favor of the economic, political, and military program of the "popular revolution" against Israel and neo-imperialism. In the course of history no class has worked in a manner harmful to its interests, and given up voluntarily its interests and concessions to save its country from disintegration.

The Vietnamese-Cuban course of action is the only course leading to victory for underdeveloped countries against the educational and technical superiority of imperialism and neo-colonialism. The rejection of this course necessarily means the adoption of a policy of retreat in the face of Zionism and neo-colonialism, led by the United States of America, enemy number one of the underdeveloped countries throughout Asia, Africa, and Latin America.

The progressive and reactionary Arab regimes, for the last fifteen months, have adopted the same positions and programs which were adopted prior to June and which resulted in the defeat. They have adopted the policy of continuous retreat. First they declared that the Security Council resolution was rejected, then they considered it insufficient, then ambiguous and demanded that certain clauses (especially passage through the Suez Canal) should be linked to the whole Palestine problem, and lastly they accepted the Security Council resolution as a whole without any conditions coupled with statements of reassurance to Israel considering it one of the facts of the Middle East.

Any objective look at the Security Council resolution of November 22, 1967, proves that its acceptance and execution means the beginning of the liquidation of the Palestine problem. The Security Council resolution is in itself an imperialist plot for the liquidation of the Palestine problem. The resolution stipulates:

—The right of each state in the Middle East to live within "secure boundaries."

—Recognition by each state in the Middle East of the right of others to live.

—The right of "innocent" passage through waterways for all the states of the area without exception.

—Finding a "just" solution for the refugees.

Thus the Security Council resolution places the Palestine problem in a critical historical situation which necessarily and ultimately leads to the liquidation of the Palestine problem.

The demand put forward to the present Arab regimes and the national Palestinian and Arab liberation movements is not to embark on a discourse on the Security Council resolution and what it offers the Arabs and Israel. Nor is it a discussion of the nature of the stand to be adopted by the Arabs. The question we put concerns the nature of the economic, political, military, and ideological program which the Arab regimes and the national Palestinian and Arab liberation movements will adopt. Will this program lead to the liquidation of the consequences of the June aggression, namely the liberation of Sinai, the West Bank, and the Golan Heights, as a step in the direction of a long-term war for the liberation of Palestine and the liquidation of the Israeli-racist-aggressive entity?

The presentation of the question in its proper context is a national need. It must be done in order to circumvent the Palestinian reactionary rightist intellectuals who call for the isolation of the Palestinian resistance movement from the development of the Arab region.

These same reactionary intellectuals, together with those of the petit bourgeois class, at times present their attitude toward the Security Council resolution as a tactical step. At other times they assert that it is an unavoidable necessity because Arabs cannot fight the United States with its educational and technical superiority. What applies to the United States also applies to Israel. Thus they argue that the acceptance of the Security Council resolution is a necessity.

Even those who reject the resolution are requested to link this rejection with the need to establish a war economy and a military program of a different calibre from that which existed prior to the defeat. If not, their attitude of rejection becomes a demagogic false attitude of no value whatsoever; similar to the demagogic revolutionary slogans which were put forward before the June War and not applied.

THE ARAB SITUATION AND THE PALESTINE PROBLEM

Fifteen months have elapsed since the June defeat and it has become clear, through direct analysis, that the Arab regimes and the national Palestinian and Arab liberation movements have been incapable of judging critically the events which led to, and the results which came from, the June defeat. Further, they have been incapable of the crystalization of this judgment in a national revolutionary work program, which would be able to effect a series of changes in the Arab situation and capacities to prepare the area for a "popular liberation war" against counterrevolution (Israel plus Arab reactionary forces in alliance with neo- and traditional imperialism). It is natural that this should be so because the Arab regimes and the national Palestinian and Arab liberation movements are not prepared under their present conditions (class, ideological, and political) to put into practice deep-rooted policies which would prepare the Palestinian and Arab masses to resist the forces of counterrevolution. Instead, the Arab and Palestinian masses have remained, and are forced to remain, observers awaiting a miracle in an age when miracles do not happen. Furthermore, asking the present regimes to adopt a policy of "popular liberation war" is basically a fallacious request. These regimes will not harbor their antithesis, which could only ultimately clash with their nature, interests, and local and international relationships.

Instead of adopting a "popular liberation war" program, such as the Vietnamese-Cuban one, and resisting and struggling against the imperialist-Zionist attack, the Arab regimes have maintained the same program and premises which prevailed until June 1967 and resulted in the defeat.

This is what has made these regimes, whatever their class and whatever their policies, retreat continuously since June to the advantage of Israel and imperialism. The Arab regimes have not waged an ideological, political, revolutionary campaign throughout the Arab lands to start an armed and unarmed popular action to destroy the interests and strategic bases of imperialism, headed by the United States, which has outrageously supported and protected Israel since 1948. Instead the regimes retreated and started courting the United States by protecting all of its imperialist interests. It is a well-known fact that breaking Israel will come about by breaking American imperialism throughout the Arab land.

Instead of rejecting the liquidationist Security Council resolution, the Arab regimes ended up by accepting it and calling on the four Great Powers to guarantee it internationally and to force Israel to accept it.

Instead of immediately, without any hesitation, adopting plans for a long-term war by drawing up plans for a war economy, arming the people, organizing people's militia units in addition to the arming of the regular armies, the Arab regimes adopted the policy of depending on the regular armies which had collapsed in the face of Israeli-imperialist educational and technological superiority in the June War. (Regular war is not to the advantage of the Arabs or of any underdeveloped country involved in a national liberation struggle against forces superior in the field of education and technology.) This—at a time when it has become clear that national liberation wars in underdeveloped countries require numerical superiority to overcome imperialist technical superiority.

THE PALESTINIAN RESISTANCE MOVEMENT AND THE NATIONAL PALESTINIAN QUESTION

Following the June defeat the Palestinian and Arab masses put their faith in the Palestinian resistance movement to pave the way for a new course of action to promote the liberation of Palestine, in particular, and the Arab liberation movement, in general.

Has the resistance movement paved this way?

A critical analysis of the development and activities of the Palestinian resistance movement during the last fifteen months will give the answer to such a question.

(1) WITH THE SPHERE OF ARAB RELATIONS: All groups of the resistance movement put forward the slogan "non-interference in the internal affairs of the Arab countries." How did the movement translate this slogan? It is clear that the Palestinian resistance movement is not required to take the place of the national liberation movement of each Arab state in its struggle to solve the dilemmas of national liberation and national democratic revolution. But it is also clear that the slogan "non-interference in the internal affairs of the Arab countries" is a double-edged weapon. In addition to meaning that the Palestinian resistance movement should not take the place of the Arab liberation movement, it should also mean that the former should interfere with whatever effects the Palestine problem in the policies adopted by the Arab regimes. Otherwise the slogan, in the final analysis, will mean "non-interference on the part of the Palestinian resistance movement in Palestine affairs." The Palestinian problem cannot be separated from the developments taking place in the world. Such a step is a suspicious attempt to overlook ancient, medieval, and modern historical facts. Following June 1967 the Arab regimes—in an attempt to face the imperialist-Zionist aggression—adopted the policy of finding "a political solution to the Palestine problem" through the liquidationist Security Council resolution. Thus a new relationship between "Arab affairs" the "the Palestine problem" has been established.

Reactionary Palestinians who, following the June defeat, put forward the slogan "non-interference in the internal affairs of the Arab countries" arbitrarily separated Arab affairs from developments in the Palestine problem. When it attempts to imitate the Algerian experience, the slogan forgets, or pretends to have forgotten, that the subjective and objective characteristics that connect the Palestine problem with developments in the Arab world and the policies of imperialism in the Middle East, radically differ from those of Algeria. Moreover, these reactionaries have previously determined to neglect the particularities of Israel and its difference from all other kinds of neo- and traditional imperialism.

Israel represents the spearhead and base for neo- and traditional imperialism in the Arab countries and the Middle East. Israel is supported by imperialism which gives it the freedom—according to imperialist plans— to participate in quelling the national Arab liberation movement which threatens the interests of imperialism in the Arab world. An observer should notice the link between the "promise to judaize Palestine" and the imperialist invasion of Palestine and the Arab countries. Furthermore, he should watch the role Israel and Zionism have played since the defeat in responding to the imperialist plans drawn up for the Middle East to liquidate the nationalist regimes and the nationalist liberation movements in the area for the benefit of counterrevolutionary forces.

Israel represents a dynamic society which has expansionist aims in the area in addition to Palestine. As a society it is superior to the underdeveloped Arab countries in the educational and technical fields. This makes its expansionist policy easier. The relationship between Israel and American imperialism necessitates the amalgamation of the national Palestinian and Arab liberation movements. In addition, Palestine is a part of the Arab world and its future is related to that of the Arab countries.

In spite of all this, reactionary Palestinians neglect the facts of history and put forward the slogan "non-interference in the internal affairs of the Arab countries." This has quietly overlooked defeatist Arab stands with regard to the problem of Palestine. All groups of the resistance movement, including the Popular Front for the Liberation of Palestine, went along with this reactionary demagogic slogan which was interpreted as "non-interference in the Arab stand *vis-à-vis* the Palestine problem." Not one of the resistance groups has passed a critical judgment on the June defeat or on Arab responsibility for this defeat after twenty years of preparation for the liberation of Palestine. Because of the principle of "non-interference in the internal affairs of the Arab countries," not one group has openly condemned the stands taken *vis-à-vis* the Palestine problem and the Security Council resolution. It is ridiculous to find Hajj Amin al-Husseini, who sold the 1936 revolution, openly criticize certain Arab leaders' statements regarding the Security Council's resolution in *Le Monde,* in May 1968, while all the groups in the resistance movement, including the Popular Front, kept quiet about these developments in the Palestine problem.

The Popular Front openly condemns this slogan in the context in which it has been practiced for the last fifteen months. The resistance movement is not expected to substitute for the national liberation movements in the Arab countries, but it is expected openly to criticize the stands adopted by the Arab governments toward the Palestine problem and put the blame on those responsible for the defeat. If the resistance movement keeps quiet about the Arab governments with regard to decisions pertaining to the Palestine problem, then it will be plotting against Palestine.

(2) THE QUESTION OF PALESTINIAN NATIONAL UNITY: All groups of the resistance movement, including the Popular Front, have committed a basic error toward the question of Palestinian national unity, both on the theoretical and the practical level. This has come about through the leadership of the Palestinian right and its ideology and theories.

The resistance movement has neglected the modern history of Palestine in its understanding and application of the problems of "national unity." The policies adopted toward the question of national unity were reactionary and wrong. This has led to placing the reactionary classes at the head of the resistance movement. This leadership is the same one which has led the national Palestinian liberation movement and the national revolution to its failure throughout the modern history of Palestine. At a time when the sons of the revolutionary classes of poor workers and peasants and revolutionary intellectuals fight for the liberation of the homeland and rejection of the Zionist occupation, the military leadership of the resistance movement has placed political leadership in the hands of rich feudal capitalist groups which have had nothing to do with the armed struggle throughout the modern history of Palestine. The resistance movement has understood the slogan of "national unity" in an inverted manner. Thus the concept of national unity was formulated under the leadership of feudal elements, bankers, big merchants, and reactionary Palestinians. The starting point was participation in the "Jordanian national front," which was composed of Palestinian and Jordanian reactionary elements under whose hands the people have suffered many hardships. The final point was the creation of the National Palestinian Congress which is composed of reactionary Palestinian elements headed by bankers and big contractors whose condition for joining the Congress was that they should be given its leadership, while the Popular Front and al-Fateh should form its left and right arms.

The problem before us is not how to choose between acceptance or refusal of the slogan "national unity." The problem is putting this thesis in its proper perspective, nationally and politically.

We have already pointed out the treachery and failure of the feudal and bourgeois classes. This review also brings out one of the basic laws of national liberation movements, namely, that the anti-imperialist and anti-Zionist classes which are capable of leading the national liberation movement and of carrying arms in the period following June 1967 are the same classes which fought against British imperialism and the plots to judaize Palestine. These are the revolutionary classes in Palestinian society. They will lose nothing if they carry arms and fight until death; on the contrary they will gain everything—their land and their homes. This has been reasserted after June 1967. Those who carried arms were the sons of the poor workers and wage-earning peasants, while the sons of the feudal landowners and capitalists disappeared from the scene of armed struggle. In spite of all the experience of the national Palestinian movement and its basic lessons, the Palestinian right has been able to penetrate the leadership of the resistance movement and take over its political leadership for fifteen months since June 5, under the slogan "Palestinian national unity" and the pretense that "the liberation question concerns everybody," at a time when historical facts, both before and after 1948, disprove these claims.

Palestinian unity is a political necessity. But what sort of national unity? The sort of national unity which accomplishes liberation. It leads the resistance movement on the road to victory by mobilizing and arming the Arab masses. It awakens their basic and collective capabilities in the long struggle of resistance. This resistance will depend upon violence in the face of an enemy whose strategy is to deliver rapid blows and accomplish swift victories.

This unity is the unity of all classes and political forces under the leadership of the revolutionary patriotic classes which have carried arms throughout the modern history of Palestine. It is the sons of these classes who have answered the call to arms since June 1967. The modern history of the people of Palestine, and that of popular liberation wars in all underdeveloped countries, proves that the workers and peasant classes are the ones who are prepared to carry arms and fight a long-term war against the enemies of national liberation, namely, imperialism and its agents.

National Palestinian unity should be based on the unity of the revolutionary fighting forces, under whose leadership all the class and political forces will be organized in an all-embracing national liberation front, committed to a national political and military work program for solving the dilemmas of national liberation and democratic national revolution.

Thus the Popular Front openly declares its condemnation of the slogan "national unity" in its present context and application. Furthermore, it condemns and openly criticizes its previous practices starting with its participation in the Jordanian national front and finally in the National Palestinian Congress.

The Popular Front puts the slogan "national unity" in its proper perspective, namely, as a unity whose vanguard and leadership are the revolutionary fighting forces. This slogan has to be exemplified in a radical national work program, the aim of which is the organization of a national liberation front to include all the class and political forces hostile to Zionism and world imperialism in general, and American imperialism in particular, and all the forces which collaborate with and are agents of imperialism.

THE PALESTINIAN RESISTANCE MOVEMENT AT THE PRESENT STAGE

The nature of the practices of the resistance movement (Palestinian and Arab) during the period following the June defeat have led to political results which in their totality form a relapse as far as the ideological, class, and political lessons of 5 June 1967 are concerned. These results also form a relapse as far as the modern history of the national Palestinian popular liberation movement is concerned.

The resistance movement has come to the following basic conclusions:

(1) On the theoretical and practical level all groups of the resistance movement (including the Popular Front) have become captives of the ideology of the reactionary Palestinian and Arab right. They have actively participated in obliterating Palestinian and Arab class ideological and political contradictions. This has led to the defeat of the Palestinian and Arab peoples at the hands of the ruling regimes. These regimes have kept the masses, and the more radical and revolutionary classes, away from any

responsibility forces to play the role of observers by limiting the concept of liberation to mean combat between the armies.

Consequently, the resistance movement has fallen victim to a series of demagogic slogans (such as "non-interference in the internal affairs of the Arab countries," "Palestinian national unity," "no right and left in the national liberation stage"). These slogans are used as a cover for the reactionary forces of the right and the Arab regimes, which have led to the defeat of the Arabs. Moreover, the resistance movement has applied these slogans within a context which has served the interests of the forces and regimes of defeat and not those of the Palestinian and Arab liberation forces. By doing this it has completely failed to expose and condemn the reasons—intellectual, class, and political—which led to the 1948 disaster and the 1967 defeat. In fact the resistance movement has assisted in hiding the existing contradictions which have resulted in the defeat. It has also defended the Arab regimes that caused the defeat, and those Arab countries which are in alliance with imperialism and therefore against the liberation and progress of their people. This will ultimately lead to the failure of the Palestinian and Arab liberation movements.

(2) Through its dependence for arms on the Arab regimes, the resistance movement has allowed itself to be transformed into a tactical weapon of pressure in the hands of the regimes—pressure to be used to keep the Arab masses as observers awaiting relief from afar. All this is taking place in the name of the Palestinian resistance movement. This alternative has been put forward instead of arming and organizing the people in popular militia uints, and preparing them ideologically, politically, and economically for a long-term war of popular liberation against Israel, and those who are behind Israel, throughout the Palestinian and Arab homeland.

In addition, the resistance movement is being used as a tactical means of bringing pressure on imperialism and Israel in order to attain a political settlement of the Palestine problem. It is hoped that the concessions demanded by Israel and imperialism as a price for the application of the Security Council resolution concerning withdrawal from the occupied territories will be minimized as a result of this pressure.

(3) In the light of such wrong policies and demagogic slogans of the resistance movement, the Palestinian and Arab masses have remained ideologically, politically, and materially disarmed. They cannot protect and develop the resistance movement in the face of the possibilities of a "political solution," the basis of which would be "liquidating the resistance movement."

The resistance movement, by keeping quiet about the lessons of 1948 and 1967 and by its refusal to take a critical national stand towards the Palestinian and Arab situation (both subjective and objective) which resulted in the defeat, have disarmed the masses of the intellectual and political weapons through which the resistance movement could be protected. Furthermore, the resistance movement, by keeping quiet and not putting forward to the masses a program for a war of popular liberation, has assisted in opening the way for demagogic slogans. Thus, when the possibilities of a "political settlement" are put forward, the resistance movement will find the masses are not armed and are not equipped with an ideological, political, only superficial and limited support from the masses. This will be so because and national consciousness.

THE DILEMMA OF EXISTING RESISTANCE MOVEMENTS

All groups of the Palestinian resistance movement are a part of the Arab national liberation movement because of their subjective constitution (ideological, class, and political) and because of the objective circumstances which find their expression in the daily dialectical relationship between the dilemmas of national liberation and the responsibilities of the democratic revolution—Palestinian and Arab.

The dilemma of the Palestinian and Arab liberation movements is specifically the dilemma of the petit bourgeois class which has occupied the position of leadership since the Second World War. This class, because of its education and interests, which are anti-feudal and anti-imperialist, has recognized the failure of feudalism and the bourgeois class to solve the problems of national liberation and of attaining economic and political independence. It has also understood the dependence of the feudalist-bourgeois regimes on colonialism and imperialism.

Since the 1948 disaster the role and ideology of the petit bourgeois class has dominated the scene, thus enabling this class to lead the Palestinian and Arab national movements. The petit bourgeoisie put forward a work program, based on its class and ideological structure, to solve the dilemmas of national liberation as a step on the road to mobilizing the material and human capabilities of the masses to liberate Palestine. The main part of the program was based on the need to foil the alliance between feudalism, capitalism, and colonialism (in other words, the counterrevolutionary camp) and to establish an alliance between the petit bourgeoisie, workers, and poor peasants.

The June defeat put the programs of the petit bourgeois class and its leadership to the test. As was pointed out in the course of this report, the defeat proved their failure to withstand the imperialist-Zionist attack, and to solve the dilemmas of national liberation in an underdeveloped country in this age—the age of colonialism and imperialism.

Thus the petit bourgeois class was confronted with two alternatives: either to adopt the Vietnamese-Cuban course of action to face the consequences of the June War; or to retreat continuously before the forces of counterrevolution and accept the liquidationist UN Security Council resolution of 22 November. The petit bourgeois class has chosen what best serves its interests and its class-ideological and political considerations, i.e., the Security Council resolution; the Vietnamese course of action has its own price, namely the totality of its class and political concessions. Of course the regimes of the 1948 disaster, the regimes of feudalism and the bourgeois class, blessed this choice and cooperated with it.

The Palestinian national liberation movement is of the same ideological, class, and political structure as that of the Arab national liberation movement led by the petit bourgeois class. At the same time it represents one of the weakest groups in the national liberation movements in the area. This is the case because of a number of subjective and objective characteristics, headed by the contradictions of the Palestine problem and the large number of nonproductive human beings among the dispersed Palestinian people.

From here we can touch on a basic characteristic of the Palestinian liberation movement. The petit bourgeois class, the leader of the Arab liberation movement, was able to eliminate the forces of feudalism and the bourgeois class from a leading position within the national movement, and was able to expose the alliance of these forces with colonialism and imperialism. Yet the Palestinian petit bourgeois class failed to remove this incapacitated bourgeois class from playing a national role. Thus the petit bourgeois class was able continuously to infiltrate the leadership of the national liberation movement and make it serve its ideological, political, and class interests. Consequently—and following June 1967—the Palestinian right supported by the Arab right was able to dominate the resistance movement through demagogic slogans and lead it within the scope of its theoretical and political beliefs. These beliefs serve the interests of the bourgeoisie and those of Arab reaction and destroy the means by which the Palestinian and Arab national movements can save themselves from imperialist-Israeli occupation. In the final analysis, these policies do not serve the resistance movement. They tend to transform it into a tactical means of bringing pressure to bear. This pressure aims, first, at containing the national revolutionary uprising of the Arab masses. Secondly, it aims at minimizing the concessions to be made by Arabs in order to ensure the implementation of the Security Council resolution, which threatens the Palestine question, in its entirety, with liquidation. The leadership of the petit bourgeois class has failed to salvage itself and the leaders of the resistance movement. The reasons for this failure are: its adoption of hesitant ideological and political policies; its faliure to comprehend the basis of a nationalist policy; and the domination of the ideology of the reactionary right over important sectors of it.

In spite of the belief that a popular war of liberation is the course of action to be adopted in order to achieve the liberation of Palestine and in spite of the high morale among the Palestinian people in the Arab nation, the leadership of the resistance movement, namely, the bourgeoisie and petit bourgeoisie, has put the resistance movement in a critical historical situation which has transformed it into a means of pressure.

THE COURSE OF NATIONAL SALVATION

The concept of armed struggle will necessarily result in an ideological and political dialectic among the members of the resistance movement and those outside it. Through this dialectic the more revolutionary and progressive elements will stress the necessity to overcome the present critical period by looking forward to the development of a more radical resistance movement. This will interact openly and responsibly with the masses, and refrain from the adoption of demagogic slogans.

The resistance movement will critically examine the experiment of the Palestinian and Arab national liberation movements in order to point out the basic laws of failure and success. It will also draw up a program for national salvation. This will reject all proposals that aim at reinstating the pre-5 June programs—"reliance on regular armed forces and a swift regular war; a consumer economy dependent on capitalism; holding back the struggle against those who are behind Israel; and limitation of the war to the areas occupied after 5 June 1967." The resistance movement considers the acceptance of the Security Council resolution of 22 November to be the logical conclusion of the programs which resulted in the June 1967 defeat.

The experience of the national liberation movement in our countries (Palestine and the Arab countries) is similar to that of the underdeveloped countries of Asia, Africa, and Latin America. It clearly shows that the road to national salvation and liberation of the homeland, together with the solution of the problems of national liberation, requires forces armed with revolutionary arms. These will be capable, in underdeveloped countries, of defeating the advanced imperialist powers in the fields of military effort and skill.

These experiences teach us—especially the experience of fifty years of failure of the Palestinian national liberation movement and the successful experience of Vietnam and Cuba—that the course of national salvation starts with and depends on the following:

(1) The adoption of a revolutionary scientific ideology (the ideology of the proletariat) which is anti-imperialist, anti-Zionist, anti-reactionary and anti-underdevelopment. The masses will be armed with this ideology, which will depend mainly on the more revolutionary and radical classes in society. Such classes do not have any interest in concluding a truce with imperialism, reaction and Zionism. They also do not have any interest in adopting a policy of retreat. The interests of these classes will be served by waging a bloody struggle by which they will lose nothing but will gain everything, i.e., nationhood, the homeland, and true political and economic independence.

The experience of our countries and that of the national liberation movements in Asia, Africa, and Latin America have proved the failure and incapacity of the feudalist ideology to lead the national liberation struggle. They have also proved the futility of the ideology of the bourgeoisie which leads its country to depend on and ally itself with colonialism and imperialism.

Furthermore, the ideology of the petit bourgeoisie has proved incapable of solving, and unprepared to solve, the dilemmas of national liberation or to adopt a policy of long term struggle against imperialism and the forces allied with it.

The national salvation course starts with arming the people with revolutionary ideas. These ideas are those of the revolutionary classes in any society, namely, the workers and poor peasants, whose sons are now taking part in armed resistance in the land of Palestine.

(2) The basic national political consciousness of the masses should be raised beyond the level of demagogic slogans. Our people are facing a modern enemy, supported by the strongest imperialistic country, the United States of America. A scientific national consciousness, depending on direct analysis of our situation and that of the enemy should be the main basis in the relationship of the resistance movement with the masses and the man in the street. National political consciousness starts by unfolding the reasons and causes for the failure of the Palestinian and Arab national resistance movements and then putting forward a program for national salvation and liberation.

(3) Defeatist proposals and the Security Council resolution of 22 November 1967 should be rejected. Furthermore, the resistance should insist on drawing up plans for a war of popular liberation by arming and organizing the people in popular militia troops. In this way the war will become that of the people as a whole and it will be waged against Israel and those who are behind Israel. (These include the interests and bases of imperialism plus Israel plus the Arab forces which are in alliance with imperialism and the protector of its interests in our homeland.)

A long-term war is the course of salvation and victory. For this way we must depend only upon ourselves. Everything must be mobilized for it—our economy and our lives—and to fight it we will be armed by the consciousness of the political ideology of the proletariat. It is also the only course to supersede the educational and technical superiority of Israel and imperialism, which depends on the strategy of a short-range war, the war of administering rapid blows and accomplishing swift victories.

The destruction of the counterrevolutionary forces and the breaking down of their morale and economy will not be accomplished unless a long-term war is waged.

(4) A program of national salvation will reject all forms of retreat and embark on operations on a wide front. Our aspiration to achieve such a program will not be accomplished unless the dialectical argument going on between members of the Arab national resistance movement is reinforced. For this reinforcement of the dialectical argument will distinguish the leadership of the vanguard of the movement, armed with a scientific revolutionary ideology—the ideology of the proletariat. This rejects the Security Council

resolution and will lead the organized masses in a long-term war, depending entirely upon themselves.

Without this dialectic, the resistance movement will remain captive of the wrong policies, which have been persistently followed and have made it a mere tactical pawn, to be used to apply pressure in the hands of the Arab regimes.

The road to national salvation requires strong wills from the members of the resistance movement. National salvation rejects whatever is existing and pushes forward on a new course—the course of transforming the resistance movement into an organized mass movement. It is armed with political, material, and radical national ideologies under the leadership of the vanguard fighting forces which are equipped with political consciousness and the ideology of the proletariat, hostile to Israel and imperialism and its allies throughout the Arab land.

The vanguard of the proletariat will bring about the national unity of all classes and political forces which are hostile to counterrevolution. These must be committed to a program of arming the people for a long-term war under the leadership of the revolutionary fighting forces in a wide national liberation front.

The spirit of resistance will spread among the Palestinian people; it needs the vanguard which will lead it on the road of national salvation. Such a vanguard, through analysis and criticism of the Palestinian liberation movement, has not yet been born.

The young elements among the members of the resistance movement and the Palestinian people who are armed with a consciousness of scientific ideology should lead the dialectical movement to bring forth such a vanguard, which will lead the people with all its classes and national political forces on the road of victory, the road of a long-term war.

THE ORGANIZATION OF COMMUNIST ACTION
IN LEBANON

A year after the announcement of the merger of the Organization of Lebanese Socialists and Socialist Lebanon, the unified organization—the Organization of Communist Action in Lebanon—held its founding conference (May 1971). Discussion was held concerning the organizations' activities as separate and as linked groups. A number of political and organizational documents were also discussed and the following statement was issued:

(A) Inauguration of the union: The conference noted that the union could come about as a result of the two organizations' arriving at unified positions arising from the national movement in Lebanon and the surrounding area and reaching out to include all the issues of the Lebanese, Arab, and world national and social liberation movement. This unity of views revealed itself in the joint struggle to support the Palestine resistance movement and the national movement in Lebanon—joint steps forward in the path of our struggle against the ruling alliance.

(B) The unified organization bears a new name, "The Organization of Communist Action in Lebanon." The organization regards this name as a frank declaration of its aims and definition of its position at this stage. The organization does not choose to form a party because the term "party" carries with it a class connotation which is not desirable, whereas the term "organization" is appropriate because it indicates that there are organizational bonds joining together the whole group. Since the organization is guided by the principles of Marxist-Leninist communism, and since the group that has borne that name in our country has adopted an opportunist, right-wing position which has no connection with the name's historical meaning and which no longer affirms the distinction between Leninism on the one hand and democratic socialism and the Third World traditions on the other hand, and since our commitment as an organization to the revolu-

Text of declaration published in *al-Hurriyah* (Beirut), No. 574, July 5, 1971, pp. 3–6 and 11, and *al-Nahar* (Beirut), August 6, 1971, pp. 9–10.

tionary classes of workers, farmers, and revolutionary intellectuals demands that we align ourselves with the great heritage of the workers' struggle and the struggle of the liberation movements under the banner of communism, our organization therefore chooses to call itself communist. And since the organization wishes to make its association with communism historically and intellectually clear, we fortify the name with "Action"—that is, with a further affirmation of the seriousness of our Marxist-Leninist beliefs. Finally, since the struggle of our people and of our organization to achieve freedom and socialism is a struggle that involves working closely together in this area, the name of the arganization defines its own geographical and historical position, in Lebanon, in its name also, without thereby intending to express any sense of exclusiveness.

(C) The organization issues a new constitution in order to set itself on the proper path toward the complete achievement of Marxist-Leninist democracy in its internal relations.

(D) The organization issues a number of recommendations for coming activities, for party relations, and for relations with sympathetic Arab organizations.

(E) The organization concludes its conference by drawing up a general plan of political action, dealing in the text which follows with subjects selected from this plan—with the whole plan to be made public in the near future. What follows is the statement issued by the conference:

I. IMPORTANT FEATURES OF THE WORLD SITUATION

Revolutionary nationalist and labor movements are now entering a new period in their history. A series of major events has taken place with sweeping effects on these movements. From the fission of the communist movement over the Vietnamese conflict, from the crisis of revolution in America to the reactivation of the labor movement in Western Europe since 1968, and from the liberalization in Eastern Europe to the Cultural Revolution in China—from all these events new issues have arisen for all the revolutionary powers of the world which cannot be dealt with according to the plan of action that was drawn up during the preceding third of a century (1928–1956) to direct the action of those revolutionary powers; nor can they be dealt with according to the theoretical and practical ramifications of that plan of action recently arrived at. The present effort to develop revolutionary positions is only an indication of the search for a plan that can unify a wide variety of attempts and efforts without covering over practical differences or overwhelming a point of view appropriate to the supervisory element at the cost of participant elements.

These events have brought many revolutionary principles into question, and have required a re-examination of the ability of these principles to act as a guide for revolutionary action and a motive of revolutionary leadership.

THE IMPERIALIST ASSAULT

(1) From the beginning of the 1960s the balance of power began to shift in favor of the imperialist interests on a worldwide scale. In the stronghold of captialism, in the United States and in Western Europe, governments remained in power which acted in accordance with the needs and results of capitalist growth. Kennedy's policies were aimed at gaining control over "liberal" interests within American society and at employing them in the service of an organized capitalism whose progressive industries were increasing its power. Likewise abroad Kennedy sought to make alliances with ruling elements, technocrats, and capitalists, rather than with a declining traditional leadership. The Italian right came out of retirement and began to participate in the government of the social democrats, with its bases among workers and educated petty bourgeoisie, under circumstances of rapidly widening industrialization. The government of de Gaulle set limits to internal political conflict, and undertook to eliminate the remaining element of colonialist imperialism while attempting to preserve an effective range of power for France's economic, political, and military bases, and at the same time providing relative protection for the industrial backwardness and economic stagnation from which French capitalism suffered. The government of the British Labour Party in England provided cover for the transformation of English capitalism into a new phase of international competition which required exact control of the consumption and salaries of labor of a sort to permit heavy profits and centralization. The growth of German capitalism continued, aided by the world distribution of labor and by the social democrats who in the end ceased to oppose the divided interests which opposed the capitalists in power.

In all these major nations the capitalists forced the workers' parties either to disperse themselves into the ranks of the social democrats in power or to belong to a false communist party that was no longer the political representative of the working class and its allies.

Contradictions Within Transitional Societies

(2) In the transitional societies the bureaucratic administrations adopted political positions of a retrogressive nature, seeking escape in liberal reforms. The crisis emerged clearly when the Soviet Union moved out of a stage of establishing a strong economic base compatible with a centralized and pyramidal social structure into a new stage of more diversified production requiring relations that spread out to meet expanding labor. Such relations represented a threat to long-established privileges of administration and party. The privileged preserved their positions at the expense of the inter-

ests of the socialist society and of the leadership of the working class. Production figures fell back, growth decreased, and agriculture floundered in a chronic state of crisis. The party leadership took on a repressive character within Soviet society and in relation to the other countries of the socialist bloc. In Hungary, Romania, Bulgaria, and Czechoslovakia the places of the decrepit Stalinist leadership were taken by a "liberal" leadership, which was able to lure a vast part of the working class and mobilize it in solving some basic production problems: how to make planning more flexible, how to increase incentives, and how to prevent consumer shortages. But in the process the working class was forced to ally itself with bureaucratic and technocratic elements which came to form a new bourgeoisie.

Local attempts were made to withdraw from stifling relationships, and the imperialists supported and encouraged these attempts. As a result the Soviet nation became the only country in the socialist bloc that could guarantee its security. This called for continual intervention by the Soviet Union —whether in the open or in secret, with a continual risk of the outbreak of international conflict always present unless there was a no-man's land maintained between the imperialists and the Soviets. The invasion of Czechoslovakia took place without a break in the disarmament talks between the two sides and without any lessening in the increasing good relations between West Germany and the countries of the socialist bloc.

(3) The imperialist assault upon the area was not restricted to capitalism or to relations with the socialist bloc but also entered into the countries belonging to the imperialists themselves and into the liberation movements. After the Soviet withdrawal in the Cuban missile crisis of 1962 and on the Berlin issue, and after the failure of the Laotian agreement and the initiation of the attack of the right with American support, the blows came hard and fast from an alliance of major landowners, industrialists connected with American property interests, and high-ranking army officers, all aiming at "national" governments. The government of Golar in Brazil fell; so did that of Sukarno in Indonesia; that of Nkrumah in Ghana. Fascists officers took over the government of Greece. The American CIA threatened Egypt's Nasserite government, and Israel, in its role as imperialism's reserve army in the Middle East, struck a severe blow against the progressive Arab governments in June 1967, shifting the balance of power—if on a limited scale— over to the interests of local reactionary forces linked with colonialism.

This assault was the result of the American imperialists' refusal to allow capitalist governments to transfer power from the hands of class elements no longer capable of leadership during the first stages of capitalist development, over into the hands of other class elements which undoubtedly, to secure control of capitalist interests, would oppose the large farm owners and major capitalists.

These governments could not defend themselves against the imperialists: they had made every effort to insure that the masses were not represented in any powerful organizations, in any independent organizations which might move independent class elements into positions of political leadership. The imperialists and their local allies, moreover, did not restrict themselves to binding these countries tightly to the imperialist market; they also undertook to cut off the few economic organizations which had a measure of independence from that market. The "new" governments which the new colonialism had set up were in some of the countries able to govern by parliamentary democracy—such was the case in Ghana and Mali. In other countries the army was able to deliver a stunning blow to the popular movement and cast its black shadow over the government.

The Latin American liberation movements went through difficult trials in Colombia, Venezuela, and Bolivia. It became absolutely clear that it would be impossible to repeat what had been attempted in Cuba, and that each separate Latin American people would have to find an answer suited to the conditions attending the local popular struggle. The imperialists made a great effort to extend the Vietnamese revolution into all of Indochina. They were able to protect hundreds of thousands of soldiers and to wage a war such as had not been seen before, directed through a government without any kind of support, and perpetrating daily the most heinous cirmes upon the struggling people.

What links these actions of withdrawal is the deceitful wing of the communist party throughout the world and found in each communist movement along with the "progressive democrats" of the imperialist countries. The transitional "socialist" societies have shown signs of coming dangerously close to returning to capitalism, especially in the places where working conditions are unequal and where a bourgeois production system prevails whereby a single social class has a monopolistic control over the right to deal with the means of production, and the actual producers have no means of intervention in the full economic process. As for the "nationalist democracies," their pattern of deceit is complete and has moved into all areas. These democracies have made alliances with the old capitalists in city and country and with the petty bourgeoisie which manipulate the country's centers of power through control of political power and never cut the bonds of dependency which link the country with the imperialist market and with all the other political groups connected to that market.

The Birth of the New Revolutionary Power

(4) However, this period has also witnessed the birth of a new power which has benefited from the tragedies of the revolutionary movement and has managed to overcome the tremendous difficulties which have grown out of those tragedies. Since 1960, the Vietnamese Revolution has been carving out its path in the face of American imperialism and spreading into all of Indochina in a vast popular war carried out by farmers and led by the

working class according to the working-class ideology, in a vast political front including every national element and not excluding the educated classes. Furthermore, it has become clear that the basic revolutionary force is popular and nationalistic in its roots, and that this popular and nationalistic force is the primary protection that the revolution has, not the official agreements, and not the various alliances, which cannot withstand narrow interests. Cuba was able to set the pattern by which it was possible to make the shift to socialism on the continent ruled over by the imperialists. Armed resistance in both cities and rural areas threatens the control of the imperialists on a continuing basis, encircling the government bases set up by a reactionary regime aided and abetted by the forces of colonialism.

The Cultural Revolution in China became a sharp criticism of the Soviet model for transitional societies, and made clear above all the significant role played by the revolutionizing of production relations and of ideology in building up a proletarian force. The Chinese Cultural Revolution also shown the richness of activity of the masses and their ability to develop a deep and cohesive strength.

Since 1968, and following after the relatively tranquil postwar period, Western Europe has witnessed an active labor movement that has included more than wide-scale strikes, impeding the power of capital in places of work, in schools and universities, and in political organizations. Through this movement it has become clear that a direct line linked the socialist revolution with the progressive demands of laborers, technicians, and minor professionals and students. Nor was the United States, the nerve center of imperialism, able to avoid the the spread of revolution: the black revolt, strengthened and redoubled by the anti-war movement, together created an explosion of dissent in the very heart of America.

In Eastern Europe, in Poland specifically, all labor activities were directed toward the formation of committees through which production would be administered and supervised.

THE INTERNATIONAL LINE INDICATED BY THESE VARIOUS ATTEMPTS CHIEFLY EMPHASIZES THE NEED TO GAIN CONTROL OF CENTERS OF POWER AND PREVENT IMPERIALIST DOMINATION THROUGH THE ESTABLISHMENT OF CONSTRUCTIVE SOCIALIST FORCES. IN ALL THE ACTIVITIES OF THE LABOR MOVEMENT, IN ALL THE WORKING CLASS'S IDEOLOGICAL AND ORGANIZATIONAL POLICIES, THIS NEED TO GAIN CONTROL OF IMPERIALIST CENTERS OF POWER EMERGES AS CENTRAL.

II. TOWARD THE WORKERS' LEADERSHIP OF THE ARAB LIBERATION MOVEMENT

June 1967 was a severe test for the capitalist interests of the Arab nation. For some time the forces of reaction in the Arab world had withdrawn from participation in the national movements and remained in their local strong-holds, having no power over government except through appealing for imperialist pressure. Now the capitalist interests were faced with progressive governments which were a link between the goals of foreign liberation and the goal of building a domestic production capacity which could be created only by wiping out the local centers of imperialist exploitation. These governments opened up a new phase in Arab history: they represented the development of an independent line of international power totally free of imperialist control, public utilities liberated from foreign control, active opposition to the remaining exploitative capitalists within, and increased productivity.

These accomplishments were achieved by the Arab liberation movement under the leadership of petty bourgeois elements which came to power. Into the melting pot of governmental power there was fused also a group of minor "national" capitalists and technocrats. Although these were opposed to the big landowners and carried out agricultural reforms, they thereby brought into their camp the smaller farmers and a part of the farmers of intermediate wealth, for they left the rural capitalist power centers untouched. Likewise they left untouched a relatively vast sector of small businessmen and industrialists, and they made no threatening gestures in the direction of property owners.

Failure to the National Bourgeoisie to Achieve Revolutionary Goals

(1) This national bourgeoisie of diverse composition and origin played a progressive role so long as its seizure and use of political power in production was carried out in accordance with revolutionary principles. After the withdrawal of British troops in 1954, the "Free Officers" took over the imperialist Suez Canal Company and seized the political structures that represented either large property owners or fascist elements of the petty bourgeoisie. Likewise the Ba'athist government in Syria seized the right-wing "feudalist" parties in the country, which were closely allied with colonialist powers in the area. The Ba'ath party in Syria took over the local petroleum interests, nationalized industrial capital, and limited agricultural land ownership—a stronghold of political reaction. Similarly the Algerian government took control of the local petroleum and gas interests and removed the Frech monopolies. The Libyan officers threw the Americans off their land and refused to allow the companies to charge higher prices than they had charged before. The Sudanese officers were victorious over the right-wing religious organizations in their country.

(2) These various steps, certainly, removed all traces of French and English colonialism from the Arab East and led to the departure of anti-colonialist alliances, opened the way to pressures from other areas, and dealt

a severe blow to their own former political principles. But these steps led primarily to the new leadership's acquiring autocratic power and having widespread control over the economic and material resources of the country, and to the opposition's being completely cut off from the center of government. In order to insure its continuation in power and to preserve its ability to represent the interests it had gathered around it, the new leadership had to seek to increase the national production capacity and broaden the base of production, and this led to a clash with the defeated colonialist interests and to an orientation in the direction of sources of aid and acquisition opposed to colonialism.

(3) The seizure of the various centers of power gave, and still continues to give, a progressive appearance to the country's capitalistic activities. But this is an appearance that should not be separated from the totality of the political views that brought the bourgeoisie to power, and the fact is that this bourgeoisie took the place formerly occupied by the old social classes in the exploitation process and kept the important features of the former production relationships. The new ruling bourgeoisie prevented the activities of the masses from having any direct connection with the processes of change, and so the interests of laborers, farmers, and revolutionary intellectuals were kept out of the picture. The masses do not seek and are not permitted to act except when their actions can be turned into a pledge of allegiance to the government or to some element in clashes between various wings of government, under either normal conditions or conditions of stress. But direct conflicts between the interests of the new bourgeoisie and those of the farmers and workers become increasingly severe with the formation of ruling interest blocs, and with the realization that the aim of these interests is to establish an internal capitalistic system suited to their own needs.

When a break develops in the alliance that has been formed between the national bourgeoisie and various wings of the masses—an alliance in which the bourgeoisie has had the ruling position—the rulers look around for new allies, which they find among the scattered survivors of the old social classes and among groups which have grown up on the periphery of the public sector. This is what happened in Syria when Hafiz al-Assad became the head of the government; this is what is happening in Egypt in the conflict which has led to the withdrawal of the Sabri-Jum'ah faction.

(4) Whenever the national bourgeoisie has come to power by revolutionizing the capitalist structure, taking power away from the large-scale rural property owners and ending their hegemony, shifting this power to the urban petty bourgeoisie and to the poor and middle-income rural property owners, the government must act in accordance with the primary interests of these groups, which grew up under the protection of the imperialist power structure. The result of this is that the primary effort goes into meeting the needs of domestic and foreign consumption instead of into fundamental growth and development, just as was true in the past, and there is a disparity in growth between the backward sectors and the progressive, imported ones;

between balanced prices and excessive ones; and between areas in which social needs are successfully met and areas in which mass poverty exists.

IN OTHER WORDS, INSTEAD OF THE FIRM AND BALANCED DEVELOPMENT OF PRODUCTION, THE REVOLUTIONIZING OF THE CAPITALIST STRUCTURE LEADS TO A GREAT INCREASE IN THE PRESENCE OF VARIOUS FEATURES OF MARGINAL CAPITAL-ISM INHERITED FROM THE PERIOD OF COLONIAL DOMINATION.

The Arab national bourgeoisie has failed to achieve the goals of the national revolution. Because of its class basis it has not been able to form a historically significant bloc that is independent and cohesive and has re-mained merely another power bloc exercising its power directly. Thus the Arab bourgeoisie has failed to establish parties that represent the masses and are effective in the lives of the masses, that are not mere tokens and formulas, that further the inetrests of the masses by permitting them to exercise con-trol over administration, prevent waste, show initiative, and discipline them-selves. Because of this failure the ruling Arab bourgeoisie failed in its battle against the Israeli enemy and in its effort to eliminate the colonialist parti-tioning of Arab territory. In both situations what emerged was the deep di-vision between "leadership" and "masses" in societies that are ruled by na-tional capitalism. In the attempt to face the Israeli enemy there emerged a professional military "vanguard" which was a product of the dominant bour-geoisie and which left the public scattered about "behind the lines." In the effort to end the division created by colonialism, "Arab unity" conferences were set up by groups coming from the national bourgeoisie. These groups followed their own principles and looked after their own regional interests—without which, in fact, they would not exist. Thus the movement for Arab unity split up into regional competitive moments, each of which took hold of a part of the control of government in their own region.

THE OPPOSITION OF THE ARAB NATIONAL BOURGEOISIE TO THE HISTORICAL BLOC LED BY AND FOR THE INTERESTS AND IDEOLOGY OF THE WORKING CLASS RESULTED IN INCREASED POWER FOR THE REMAINING TRACES OF COLONIALISM AND IN A BETRAYAL OF THE ARAB LIBERATION AND ARAB UNITY MOVE-MENTS, AND A BETRAYAL OF THE HISTORIC STRUGGLE OF THE ARAB MASSES EVERYWHERE.

The Resistance Movement and the Growth of New Revolutionary Forces

(5) The aims of the Palestinian resistance movement created a force op-posed to national capitalism. Facing the enemy lying at the crossroads of the Arab lands, preparing for the battle, the Palestinian resistance move-

ment gave a new sense of urgency to the Arab opposition to colonialism and to the principles of colonialism; facing the prevailing governments, the Palestinian resistance movement created relationships which were revolutionary and were those of a people's struggle. Instead of the isolation of the masses from governmental power struggles, there was the brotherhood of the camps, the brotherhood of battle and blood. And yet the leaders of the Palestinian resistance movement, working as they did under conditions of extreme peril, were not able to break the pattern already set by the capitalists of the national bourgeoisie and by the governments which were the agents of capitalism. The resistance itself was faced now with too many pressing questions: its relations with the Jordanian front, the need for unity within the resistance itself, and its relations with the rest of the Arab world. The resistance's preoccupation with these problems left the door open to pressure from the various Arab governments, and it was they that got control over weapons supply lines, the sources of manpower, and the media of publicity and communications. In fact the resistance was so preoccupied with these problems that it was not able to solve crucial issues concerning its internal composition: its political and military leadership, its organizational structure and relations with the public, and its ideology.

The way in which all these problems worked against each other and prevented the resistance from finding solutions to any one of them gave a tremendous opportunity to the agent governments to exercise their power in the Arab world and to make ever-repeated efforts to gain control over the Palestinian resistance itself. Likewise the way in which all these problems worked against each other to block the actions of the resistance caused the resistance to miss the opportunity of building up a wall of popular support that would act as armor to protect it from political pressure from outside, a wall of Palestinian and of Arab support against the capitalist agent governments and the connivance of international capitalism.

During the past four years the Palestinian resistance movement has been an immense crucible into which thousands of freedom fighters have poured their lives in the service of our people, and innumerable political experiments have come to fruitition in the process. The cumulative experience of these crucial years in our history has greatly enriched the Arab liberation movement, has renewed and enlarged its ideology, its structure, and its motivating power. One thing that is certain is that the Palestinian resistance movement is now at the heart of the Arab liberation struggle and is one of the sources of that struggle's energy and conviction.

(6) The cause of the Arab masses has won its independence and grown strong in many places, particularly in the Arab Gulf region. There, the area of Dhufar has witnessed the growth of an armed popular resistance of great force which has fought against imperialism and its local agents under the leadership of the Popular Front for the Liberation of the Occupied Arab Gulf. Into the atmosphere of reaction surrounding Saudi Arabia and its cata-

log of insane hostilities, into the atmosphere of neglect, and yes, into the atmosphere of hostility from the progressive Arab governments too, the revolutionaries of Dhufar have entered and won a victory for themselves, depending for rear support upon the national government of the People's Democratic Republic of Yemen and seeking to carry the torch of revolution forward against imperialism and all its local agents among the sultans and sheiks and princes everywhere in the Gulf, for they have created a national revolutionary struggle of significant proportion, with as its most notable elements the popular revolutionary movements in 'Uman and the Gulf and the National Democratic Front for the Liberation of 'Uman and the Gulf.

Whatever else may be said, the cause of the Arab masses is far from having fallen into an alliance with the governments that are opposed to its own interests. In spite of all the pressures upon it, the Palestinian resistance movement has been and still remains the vanguard action of the Palestinian people and has had and still has wide popular support. Governmental ineptitude has not caused the Egyptian people to stagnate: throughout 1968 they agitated for a government that could accept the burdens and responsibilities of the liberation movement. In the Sudan, there is a communist party led by a revolutionary majority that refuses to accept the national capitalists' growth plan and is working to lead the Sudanese masses to total national liberation and socialism. In Iraq, following a rash effort to establish an armed revolutionary center in the south, forces led by the Iraqi Communist Party (its central leadership) are re-examining the nationalist democratic movement and are leading a rigorous ideological struggle aimed at wiping out exploitation and deceit from the right-wing elements of the country and at uniting the scattered elements of the masses against the ruling fascist Ba'ath party, whose government is attempting to create an alliance of the army, the oil companies, and the major landowners, all controlled by a cluster of leading families.

In Morocco the farmers' movement is still scattered and divided, but since 1968 the strength of its opposition has grown enough to show that it is a movement of real vitality and that it will be a genuine threat to the puppet king whenever it chooses to become allied with the urban labor and student organizations of the country.

THOUGH ALL THESE FORCES MAY BE IN VARIOUS STAGES OF EVOLUTION, EACH OF THEM WILL RELY FOR ITS SUCCESS ON A PARTICULAR DEVELOPMENT THAT SHOULD COME ABOUT DURING THE NEXT STAGE OF OUR POLITICAL HISTORY: THAT IS, A GROWING CONFLICT BETWEEN THE FORCES UNITED AROUND THE NATIONAL BOURGEOISIE AND THE REACTIONARY ARAB GOVERNMENTS, AND THOSE OTHER FORCES WHICH ARE ABLE TO LEAD THE BATTLE FOR INTERNAL RECONSTRUCTION AND THE RESTRUCTURING OF SOCIAL RELATIONS, AND AGAINST THE IMPERIALISTS AND THE FACTIONALISTS. . . .

III. THE CRISIS OF THE LEBANESE CAPITALIST SYSTEM

Lebanon had not since 1958 entered into the heat of Arab conflicts as it has done since 1966–67. Lebanon is faced by the possibility of Israeli occupation; and, under this threat, Lebanon was persuaded by the Palestinian resistance to stand up against this enemy supported by the imperialists. Under these circumstances the nature of the government's alliance with the Arab national struggle was strikingly revealed, and so were the bases upon which local feudalist and factionalist elements maintain their control. The present government can in fact survive with these feudalist and factionalist bases by which it operates to maintain the division it has created between the local popular movement and mass movements of the Arab world as a whole. The role that the Lebanese government plays is that of a major local link between the forces of imperialist exploitation on a worldwide scale and the ruling blocs within the Arab region. The necessary precondition for the continuance and flowering of this role played by Lebanon is the maintenance of those blocs and their little sub-empires on the one hand, and the preservation of the ruling Lebanese alliance as a political buffer (of a factionalist and local nature) to prevent limited minor class conflicts from turning into major battles that would threaten the whole power structure. In accordance with these principles the Lebanese government has maintained uninterrupted good relations with the imperialist powers located in the Arabian Peninsula, the Arab Gulf, and Jordan. For this reason, the Lebanese government tried to prevent the outbreak of the national movement in Lebanon, where a bold attempt was being made to bring it by the forces of the Palestinian resistance movement—a disturbing development for the traditional states to which the Lebanese government is so firmly allied.

However, the Palestinian resistance movement broke through that barrier, aided by the Lebanese public which risked death in April and November of 1969 and set up bases for the resistance on the borders. Between the end of 1968 and May of 1970 the resistance played a major role in the discovery of how totally unprepared the country of Lebanon was to mount any kind of defense against the threat of attack from Israel. But the impulse that began to flow on 23 April 1969 was not powerful enough to generate lasting and effective power, or power effective enough to expand the horizons of the battle and bring the masses into contact with national democratic needs. It was not long before the impulse grew weak and became dispersed in alliances with feudalistic political leaders or their local strong-arm men, and in the numerous small political organizations set up by capitalistic interests in the Arab world. What did clearly emerge, though, was that the "special" situation of Lebanon, which encouraged isolationists, was not enough to cut off the link between the Arab liberation movement and that Lebanese impulse which, if only for a moment, could break the structure of local factionalism and join up with that liberation movement.

The Tightening of the Links with the Imperialist Market

Beginning in 1966–67, the Lebanese economy's commercial and exchange operations went into a period of stagnation which no governmental efforts were able to put to an end. The participation of Lebanese capitalists in the imperialist market had led to the creation of economic, social, and political structures which had come to be in opposition to the very needs of capitalist growth. Unquestionably the situation grew out of the flow of Arab capital into Lebanon, and the development of Lebanon's role as a middleman between Western capital and the sources of power in the region, which had created a vast bourgeoisie or middle class. But specifically this growth came from the tremendous growth of elements that played the role of connecting links locally: trade, exchange, certain industries. Whenever the local capitalists directed their attention to seizing the opportunity for quick profits in specific areas, they came to move closer and closer to the imperialist market. The linking up of the exchange system of Lebanon with the market of foreign capital led to the absorption of a vast quantity of exchange deposits in Lebanon. Likewise, protection of speculators in the European monetary market led to restrictions on borrowing in industry, and even in trade.

The result of the involvement of the powerful capitalists in the imperialist market was that growth was restricted to those local fields whose growth served this involvement. Once the Lebanese capitalists had set up a structure to serve their interests in this way, demand increased beyond the ability to meet it; for commercial and exchange operators had allowed industry only a very small area in which to operate, not a large enough area in which to operate, not a large enough area to fill the market's requirements, and not on a large enough scale to compete with the operations of the speculators in foreign money. Agriculture was allowed to develop only on a scale that was easily exploitable, so as not to interfere with the feudalist and factionalist interests in the area. For all these reasons the country was suddenly thrown into an inflationary crisis, which in fact was the crisis of the domination of inflated foreign prices over the market of a backward country, made really dangerous by the control of this market by commercial monopolies and by protecting small, crippled industries from having to produce low-cost goods. Here followed the crisis in the labor market or, rather, the crisis of breakdown in production, which there was no way of meeting locally and which led to the importation of labor from all over the Arab region, while a narrowness of political views kept the capitalists from realizing what was going on.

When this situation became evident, the country was plunged into a political and social crisis which is only now beginning the course which it is destined to run. On the one hand it began to become clear how incapable the political organizations were of meeting the urgent needs generated by the capitalist growth in commerce and exchange which control the Lebanese economy. On the other hand the base of these political organizations began to grow narrower, for they had begun to lose their complete control over the petty bourgeois groups that had been under their wing.

It is this general political and social crisis that explains the protest movements that began toward the end of 1970 and became acute and serious with the battle over health insurance. These are still going on today. This same crisis also explains why student unrest has been so great both on the secondary school and the university levels. In the face of all this, the groups whose interests were tied up in the former situation gathered together into a comprehensive alliance to oppose the demands of the working class, the farm workers, and groups from among the petty bourgeoisie: they refused to import medicines, they refused to abolish the two-year apprenticeship in the practice of law, they refused to extend the labor law to include farm workers, and they refused to set limits on independent money-changing.

The Political Crisis and the New Leadership

If the political leadership of the ruling alliance suffers from a fragmentation into parliamentary blocs and the inability to establish a national leadership through the parliamentary basis, the democratic movement also has a weakness in its political leadership's failure to enter into direct conflict with organized government through the protest movements, thus making good use of the current crisis. The leadership of the national democratic movement also suffers from the lack of the kind of strong organizational basis that would make it possible for the movement to stand firm in confrontations with the ruling powers gathered together with their associated pressure groups. Neither do they give the masses a way of gaining control of the course of the struggle. With aid and guidance from the government and the labor unions, an alliance of opportunist reactionary forces plays about with the national democratic movement in a way that markedly weakens it and slows down its operation.

WHILE THERE EXIST FORCES WHICH THE CURRENT LEBANESE POLITICAL SYSTEM CANNOT ABSORB, SOME OF THE REPRESENTATIVES OF THESE FORCES ARE SEEKING A SOLUTION IN THE DAYDREAMS OF LIBERALISM OR IN CRYPTO-FASCISM OR OPPORTUNIST REVISIONISM, BELIEVING THAT THE LEBANESE CAPITALISTS' CRISIS IS ONE OF ECONOMIC STAGNATION AND IMPROPER POLITICAL STRUCTURE. BUT THE ORIGIN OF THE WHOLE DISTURBING CRISIS IS THE INVOLVEMENT OF RULING ELEMENTS IN THE COUNTRY WITH IMPERIALISM. AND SINCE THE ROLE OF LEBANON CANNOT BE ISOLATED FROM THE SITUATION OF THE ARAB WORLD AS A WHOLE, THE BIRTH OF THE NATIONAL LIBERATION MOVEMENT IN LEBANON, THOUGH

MARKEDLY DIFFERENT IN FORM AND STYLE, IS DIRECTLY RE-
LATED TO THE BIRTH OF THE TOTAL ARAB REVOLUTIONARY
MOVEMENT.

IV. AGAINST RIGHT-WING OPPORTUNISM

In the mid-1960s there developed on the margin of the "National Progressive Front of Parties, Organizations and Individuals" numerous right-wing
groups which made clear their opposition to the nationalist parties and the
Lebanese "communist" party. These groups were one of the symptoms in
Lebanon of the crisis of the Nasserites and of the world communist movement. They also represented a limited reply to the crisis in commerce and
exchange capitalism in the world of the petty bourgeoisie and minor intellectuals. Faced with the relative stagnation of that time, and the fact that
the Arab liberation movement was inactive until 1967, the Progressive Front
and its right-wing opportunist wing especially gave material aid and political support to the groups we have mentioned. The front became involved in
a policy of close cooperation with Shihab's supporters in the government.
This was enough to make the front keep silent about the importance of the
"Intra" crisis, and its leaders canceled a popular conference which had been
scheduled to be held at that time. They refused to take the least responsibility for defending the interests of the working class; when the strikes of
electrical workers occurred in the summer of 1966 they charged the strikers
with instigating riots because Kamal Jumblat was in the government [and
they did not want to disturb the status quo]. The energy drain which these
forces represented led to the complete ineptitude of Lebanon's organized
governmental response to the events of June 1967. The alliance broke up
on the eve of the spring elections of 1968 due to the fear of the losing side,
Kamal Jumblat, that his electorate would suspect a link with the "communists." Since 1967 this wing of the national movement has held to a reactionary position that is based upon the Soviet position and that of the nationalist capitalists with regard to the Security Council resolution and with
regard to the Palestinian resistance movement.

It has been through their system of alliances that the right-wing opportunists have revealed their total disregard for the interests of the masses,
just as another system of alliances has revealed the determination of the
leadership of the working class to participate in national liberation. But these
systems of alliances are merely a natural outcome of the ideological and
class identities of the parties involved. As a result of the betrayals of interest we have already described, the "communist" party of Lebanon turned
into the party of the interests of petty bourgeois and intellectual elements
connected with the government and of inherited groups of laborers and
petty employees overwhelmed and dominated by their status as small-time

producers and hirelings of business. This group, which had its status imposed upon it from above rather than defining its status for itself, was held together by a "popular" ideology which was a mixture of diverse ideologies: that of the technocrats, which threw the party into the embraces of the Shihab supporters and included a touch of anti-imperialism; and the philosophy of a "labor economy," which the party carried along as an inheritance from the days of its labor origins and which from the beginning had been contaminated by a willingness to bargain with the traditional local and Islamic Lebanese leaders.

The political style that marked the "National Progressive Front" from the time of the outbreak of the Arab liberation movement, the crisis of the national capitalists, and the crisis of stagnation in the Lebanese economy had to a dangerous degree shown the front to be retreating from the issues to which these events had given rise. The front also showed a right-wing opportunism which was disabling to the working class and to the other democratic national elements. And this they augmented with a whole chain of corrupt practices.

On the other hand, the groups which refused to follow this opportunist line acquired for a period of years a degree of political and fighting experience sufficient to prepare them for the difficult task of bringing the national democratic movement to maturity and spreading it to its present wide extent. They participated in this development both through the labor protest movement and through the national liberation struggle, and their participation was of significance in strengthening the movements with which they were connected and making them movements of a popular, democratic majority.

This participation came to an end finally only as a result of sharp criticism received concerning organizational ties inherited from two groups, Socialist Lebanon and the Organization of Lebanese Socialists. These organizational ties were disparaged as having weakened the role of their members and of having robbed them of what independence they should have had. This resulted in destroying the innovative role of these organizations. Thus, the organizations were overwhelmed by events imposed by the struggle for political power. In this the interests of the working class and the poor farmers and their day-to-day role were neglected. The work of these organizations instead became chiefly a matter of creating propaganda among petty bourgeois intellectual circles. However, this situation changed. Study of the national liberation movement and of the latest developments in the protest movement, which had progressed so much in recent days, set the organization back on the road toward a fuller participation in the progress of the democratic national movement and toward establishing the working class in a firm position within that movement. The first conference, which was held in the spring of 1971, set forth plans for such activity after a detailed discussion had been conducted in each organization. Chief among these plans was to organize the dedicated, fighting communists through an ideological and practical alliance that would bring the working class, the farmers, and all the struggling masses together on a daily basis to learn from them and permit them to learn from each other.

The path to be followed by these organizations of revolutionary forces in the world is a clear and firm one, and the ties linking them are not local class ties and matters of general belief alone. The leaders of the revolution have taught us that the little associations are also an inspiration to the people in their hard, exacting, and many-faceted activities.

Now the enemy still occupies a large and vital part of our Arab lands, and the imperialists are still plundering the wealth of our lands and controlling its vital destiny. The heritage of domination is still strongly evident in those countries where the colonialists exercised direct control. There are still borders behind which protected blocs exploit the masses. It is in these places above all that our leaders must seek to win the support of the working class and guide it politically and ideologically in the struggle to achieve full liberation and socialism.

❅   ❅   ❅   ❅   ❅   ❅   ❅   ❅   ❅   ❅

The Communist Action Organization of Lebanon is a revolutionary political organization guided in its activities by the basic principles of Marxism-Leninism, which the organization regards as the proper guide for the struggle of the working class and the toiling masses gathered under their leadership in opposition to their national and class enemies. The organization applies Marxist-Leninist principles in order to understand the true nature of the existing situation and take action to alter this situation both through the development of theory and through practical steps. And in doing this the organization seeks to benefit from the experience gained in revolutionary movements throughout the modern world. The organization follows all struggles against the enemies of Marxism-Leninism and against all those who would corrupt Marxist-Leninist doctrine to serve bourgeois interests, and the organization fights to further the interests of Marxism-Leninism in every practical way.

The goal of the organization is to represent within Lebanon one of the revolutionary elements which are struggling to achieve the liberation of the Arab world from imperialist domination; to achieve Arab unification without favoritism or partisanship; to achieve victory for the socialist revolution throughout the Arab land; all of this in order to create the dictatorship of the great alliance between workers, farmers, revolutionary intellectuals, and all the struggling masses who strive under the leadership of the working classes for the final victory of their people, which is to stop the exploitation of man by man in their country and is the establishment there of true communism.

The organization is totally committed to the principle of international solidarity and considers itself as one unit among the units of the worldwide national liberation movement and as one organization among the organizations working to achieve communism. And it believes that international solidarity receives its most fundamental expression in the serious struggle in which each of its elements fights against class domination and imperialist exploitation.

The organization also seeks, in this its present transitional period, to prepare itself to play the role of the revolutionary party of the Lebanese working class, and to do this through striving within the ranks of the struggling Lebanese masses to achieve their democratic national goals and through winning a place among its own ranks for the revolutionary vanguard of making every effort to build its membership in accordance with the ideology labor, leading the masses in the battles upon which they have embarked and of the working class and the point of view of the revolutionary masses.

INDEX

Abu-Iyad, 108
Adeeb, Albert, 54
Aflaq, Michel: on Arab unity, 32–34; on communism, 44; Dean of Ba'ath Party, 22–23; sentencing of, 28–31; National Leadership member, 28; and New Left, 102; on Palestine, 37–38, 42
Akhdar, al-Afif al-, 104–106
Al-Fateh, x, 94, 108, 170
Algeria: liberal nationalism in, 11; New Left in, 107; and Palestine, 41–42; revolution in, 94
Al-Hadaf (The Goal), 99, 110
Al-Hizb al-dimuqrati al-thawri al-Yamani. See Yemeni Democratic Revolutionary Party
Al-Hurriyah, 68–69, 97
Allayli, Abdullah al-, 54
Al-Muharrir, 69
Al-Nahar, 82, 83
Al-Raay, 63
Al-Shararah, 99, 110
Al-Tali'ah, 110
Al-Tariq, 110
Al-Thawra, 21, 40, 49
Al-Thawral Al-'Arabiyah (The Arab Revolution), 84
American University of Beirut (AUB): Arab Nationalist Movement in, 63–64; Ba'ath Party in, 23
Amman, Jordan, 63
ANM. See Arab Nationalist Movement
Arab Ba'ath Socialist Party. See Ba'ath Party

Arab Gulf Sheikdom, 100
Arab-Israeli War, June, 1967: and Ba'ath strategy, 36, 40–41; and Israeli expansion, 87; influence on New Left, 101, 106; lessons from, 160–167; peace resolution, 158–59
Arab Liberation Front, 38–39, 42
Arab Nationalist Movement: Arab Socialist Union, 65, 67; in Egypt, 67, 72; historical background, 62–70; influence of Marxism-Leninism on, 68–70; influence of Nasserism on, 64–68, 71, 75; influence on New Left, 96–100; in Iraq, 64, 67; in Jordan, 64; in Kuwait, 77; in Lebanon, 64, 67, 77; in Libya, 72; 1962 conference of, 65–66; in Palestine, 64, 72–74; petty bourgeoisie, 64–68; policy on Arab unity, 63, 70–72; policy on communism, 63; policy on socialism, 75–77; rightest orientation of, 63–64; and Southern Yemen, 67, 77; splinters of, 99–100; in Sudan, 72; in Syria, 64, 67, 72; and UAR, 64–65; 68, 96–97; Western influence on, 63, 65
Arab Socialist Action Party: 62, ally of Communists, 70; in Iraq, 98–99; and New Left, 98–99, 109; policy on socialism, 75; policy on unity, 71–72
Arab Socialist Party, 23; *see also* Ba'ath Party
Arab Socialist Union (ASU): emergence in Egypt: 65, 81–82; as official party, 97–98; in Syria, 82, 84

THE ARAB LEFT

was composed in 10-point Linotype Caledonia, leaded two points, with
display type handset in Ludlow Bodoni Bold by Joe Mann Associates, Inc.;
printed letterpress on 55-pound P & S Special Book
by York Composition Company, Inc.
Smyth-sewn and bound over boards in Columbia Bayside Linen and also
adhesive bound with Corvon Linen covers by Vail-Ballou Press, Inc.;
and published by

SYRACUSE UNIVERSITY PRESS
Syracuse, New York